PRINCE OF
AESTHETES

Also by Philippe Jullian

Edward and the Edwardians

PRINCE OF AESTHETES:

Count Robert de Montesquiou,
1855-1921

PHILIPPE JULLIAN

Translated from the French by
John Haylock and Francis King

New York
THE VIKING PRESS

To Marie-Laure de Noailles

Published in 1968 by The Viking Press, Inc.
625 Madison Avenue, New York, N.Y. 10022

Library of Congress catalog card number: 68-11419

Printed in U.S.A.

First published in France as *Un Prince 1900: Robert de
Montesquiou* and in England as *Robert de Montesquiou:
Fin-de-Siècle Prince*

Contents

Illustrations

Acknowledgments

I SHOULD not have undertaken this work if Countess Corisande de Gramont, the god-daughter of Robert de Montesquiou, had not generously put at my disposal her library containing the complete works of the poet, some of which are not to be found anywhere else, her photograph albums and several pictures from her collection and a long unpublished letter of Proust.

Among those who knew Robert de Montesquiou and were very willing to speak of him at length, I must place first his only niece, the late Countess François de Pange, who described for me the family life and country visits of her uncle. The prodigious memory of Princess Bibesco brought back to life for me the person who was one of her first admirers; Countess Gabriel de la Rochefoucauld spoke to me of her husband's cousin, Madame Paul Morand of meetings at St Moritz. Miss Natalie Barney has also remained faithful to the memory of this difficult friend.

Of the other people who met Montesquiou in their extreme youth and who communicated to me their dazzled recollections of him, I shall mention Madame Lise Deharme, Mrs Howard-Johnson (daughter of Helleu), Count Gautier-Vignal, Monsieur Bouvet de Thèze and Monsieur Lachat-Berlioz.

Among those who were very willing to seek out recollections of Robert de Montesquiou, whether in family tradition or family papers, I express my gratitude to the Duke de Montesquiou-Fezensac and to those of his cousins who kindly encouraged me, to the Marquise de Casa-Fuerte, to Mademoiselle Antonia de la Gandara, to Madame Schnerb (née Pierre Lièvre), and to Monsieur Alain Ollivier, the great-nephew of the Princess Edmond de Polignac. Monsieur Baignères told me about the unhappy meeting of Proust and Wilde, as recounted to him by his grandmother.

Mademoiselle de Saussine was very willing to make researches into Montesquiou's musical tastes and activities; Madame Charpentier and Monsieur André Ostier acquainted me with letters to Madame Scalini and to Madame Straus; Mr Michael

Dugdale provided me with some entertaining information about his great-aunt Lady Archibald Campbell. Monsieur André David authorised me to reproduce a letter which he received from the poet; Count Jacques de Ricaumont, the letters addressed to Prince Sevastos, published in the *Revue de Paris*; and the University of Glasgow, the correspondence with Whistler.

Monsieur Thomas, the curator of manuscripts at the *Bibliothèque Nationale,* generously put at my disposal some 500 files compiled by Montesquiou's secretary, and recently acquired by the *Bibliothèque.* Madame Callu prepared a summary of these with an indefatigable kindness.

I was very much helped in my researches by Monsieur Chapon, Director of the *Bibliothèque Doucet,* who patiently allowed me to draw on his erudition as much as on the collections in his keeping. Mademoiselle Roselyne Bacou was my guide to Odilon Redon and Madame Monnier to the Gustave Moreau Museum. I often put to the test the memory and the library of Monsieur Jean Vergnet-Ruiz.

Monsieur Guy Tosi kindly showed me some extracts from the work he is preparing on d'Annunzio, and Monsieur Yves Clogenson the unpublished pages of his life of Huysmans. Mr George Painter let me use the sources of his admirable *Life of Proust.* Monsieur Olivier de Magny was very willing to study Montesquiou's poetic works for me, and Madame Gallé elucidated for me the spiritual experiences of the poet. Monsieur Roger de Candolle enquired into the poet's supposed Genevan origins. The heirs of Jean Cocteau, of Colette, of Bernard Berenson, of Sarah Bernhardt, of Gallé, and of Marcel Proust, together with M. J. J. Pauvert, proprietor of the rights of Raymond Roussel, graciously authorised me to publish extracts from letters. Messrs. Chatto & Windus gave their kind permission to quote various passages from the translations of Marcel Proust's *A La Recherche du Temps Perdu* by C. K. Scott Moncrieff.

Finally, Monsieur Guy Dubeau looked at my manuscript and made numerous suggestions.

PRINCE OF
AESTHETES

Introduction

THREE GENERATIONS, two wars and an economic crisis separate us from 1900; from that so-called 'Belle Époque', which fashion is now discovering with so much enthusiasm thirty years after Paul Morand jeered at it. But whether in yellowing snapshots, in the paintings of Sickert and Vuillard, or in caricatures in *Rire* or *Punch*, our grandparents or our great-grandparents appear as our familiars. Their names may be Cottard or Bergeret, we may surprise them in a Feydeau dressing-room or a library of Gide. They may perhaps be a little more lecherous or a little more pompous than ourselves, a little more anxious about politics, a little less worried about cancer. But essentially these middle-class people are near to us. Apart from changes in women's fashions and the hastening rhythm of life, the difference between them and us is small.

There is, however, another 1900—artistic and worldly, snobbish and equivocal, vibrant and febrile—the heroes of which belong to a Fable doomed to extinction at the outbreak of the 1914 War. Its portraits, now exhumed from our attics, seem as bizarre as those from Fayum or Knossos; Boldinis staggering under d'Annunzio's lash; opulent Sargents; Helleus stretched out by fashion on Louis XVI furniture; Mucha posters shrouding Europe in a web of Byzantine-Viennese lianas. These women are moths, dragonflies, praying mantises, created by perverse fashion and a chimerical heart.

Fin-de-siècle insects, gorged on a diet of exaggerated compliments and rapturous articles, they speak with the tongues of Péladan or

Rostand, their malice perhaps frightening if one judges them by the venom of their friends or their enemies; Bloy, Léon Daudet and above all, the redoubtable, the scandalous Jean Lorrain.

Among these extravagant creatures the Count Robert de Montesquiou-Fezensac resembles a shining, buzzing, virulent scarab. This man, who gave Whistler and Boldini the subject for two masterpieces, on whom Huysmans modelled des Esseintes and Proust the Baron de Charlus, seems to have left his substance on those canvases and between those pages, to become himself no more than the dry carapace, light and golden, of a beetle among the dust of out-of-date, forgotten butterflies: butterflies which, in the vulgarity of the Belle Époque, massed around him for thirty years their ravishing colours and their mad ideas.

Stir this dust and one finds Gustave Moreau and Gallé, the drawings of Beardsley, the fabrics of William Morris, the flowers of Klingsor blooming again at Bayreuth, Klimt at Vienna, Horta at Brussels: a fantastic and fragile art which, coming from the north, perhaps charms us precisely because it seems to derive from another world. The belated but final success of the Impressionists and the vagaries of fashion have allowed unimaginative people to condemn Art Nouveau as severely as the Empire condemned Louis XV. Only the surrealists in the 'twenties and 'thirties remained faithful to the sources that had enchanted their youth, even if they often adulterated them. One sees that the revolution of Cézanne and Monet ended in the tedious desert of abstractionism. One looks for canvases expressive of more than just an apple or a spot. Moreau takes his place among the greatest.

In spite of rediscoveries and rehabilitations, Montesquiou himself, who did so much for this art, remains a subject of mockery. Mention is made of his jewel-encrusted tortoise; one or two malicious witticisms, perhaps by Forain, are recalled; an account is given of how at a charity bazaar (which, in fact, he never attended) he knocked over women in his panic to escape from a fire; and finally, after all his charming and agreeable absurdities have been attributed to Huysmans, all the vices encountered in the work of Proust are unloaded on to him. The time has now come to show that his wit could be more incisive than that of Forain; his panache more impressive than that of Rostand; his follies gayer than those of *À Rebours*; and his only vice a passion for Beauty.

This passion won for the poet the derided title of 'aesthete'. It led him to discover Gallé, encourage Moreau and Debussy, and read deeply in Gautier and the Goncourt brothers. But being a man impatient when confronted with stupidity, insolent to pretension and cruel to success, Montesquiou wounded too many people to avoid creating around himself a conspiracy of silence. His poetic work, heavily burdened with symbolist preciosities, is buried in oblivion. Of it, one title remains: 'The Commander of Delicate Odours', to excite laughter in those who do not know that it was first invented by Flaubert. But from this shipwreck it is possible to rescue some noble poems and some singular lines. (Apollinaire made good use of these in *La Chanson du Mal Aimé*.) A greater misfortune is the engulfment of Montesquiou's critical work. A sharp eye which is always quick to single out the beauty of the new; a vocabulary which conveys every nuance, every detail; a taste which owes more to experience than to theory: all these qualities make him deserve Proust's title 'The Professor of Beauty'.

The hawthorns and the cattleyas, the symbolic book-bindings, the magnificent portraits: the novelist picked all these up in Montesquiou's various houses, but none the less saw only the baron's malignancies and follies. There is another, graver injustice: Charlus is a very great personage, but only in society, whereas his model was a faithful and generous friend to such creative artists as Mallarmé, Verlaine, Whistler, Gallé and Fauré. Proust also touches on Montesquiou the spiritualist. Son and grandson of excellent mediums, the poet constantly believed himself to be in touch with the Beyond. Both this faith and the vocabulary associated with it sixty years ago, again serve to set a distance between him and us.

Montesquiou's idealism in a century that was too affluent, in a society that was too conventional, explains the contradictions within him: his dreams and his cruelty, his chastity and his entourage of young men. His humour, his acts of malice, his elegance and his magnificent entertaining all derived equally from a desire to shine in a world that he despised. His birth and his great personal beauty sustained him in the belief that he was Parsifal or Ludwig II; but it was in the world of Bourget that he lived. None the less, with another figure from Wagnerian legend, his cousin the Countess Greffulhe, he waged a positive crusade for Beauty. Since their weapons were worldly, they were often confused with those they wished to convert. It must be said that some of the knight's arrows were poison-tipped, and that he was obliged to give up the idea of publishing comments and poems calculated to wound old men still held in honour and probably honourable families. These fragments, collected by a secretary, will be as cardinal to the history of the end of the nineteenth century as the Little Histories of Tallemant des Réaux. But in contrast to the other annalists of his period, Montesquiou's hate was never political: he was never anti-semitic or revengeful, preferring to keep his weapons for the Philistines.

The marvellous and formidable scarab dried up when denied that rare air the composition of which includes both esotericism and worldliness and which allows both aristocratic pride and humility before creative artists to exist side by side. His parties and pronouncements (the crepitation of his elytrons) today would seem equally improbable in a Paris in which the rich see no one but each other and wits must weigh their words. Montesquiou died ruined: exhausted by this long struggle to unite Fashion and Beauty and to serve an art the deep springs of which never irrigated the countryside of the Impressionists—those painters whom Redon characterised as 'low-pitched'. No one was less 'low-pitched' than the man of whom Proust wrote: 'The subject is inexhaustible. Injustices have their day. And, at least in spirit and in truth, he will be reborn.'

CHAPTER 1

The Upper Crust

<hr>

Of my grandfather Clovis memories abound:
Than in one's family what happier place is found?

A glance at the Faubourg Saint-Germain

LE GRATIN, the Upper Crust... People first began to talk about it during the Second Empire, when the ruling classes ceased to be good company, money gained the ascendancy over birth, and the clubs and the races were enough to occupy gentlemen whose grandparents had been field-marshals or ambassadors. Its territory, bounded by the Quai d'Orsay, the Rue Bonaparte, the Rue du Cherche-Midi and the Esplanade des Invalides, was a grid of silent streets bordered by mansions, the blinds of which were often drawn, gardens and high gateways: streets where there were no omnibuses and which were ploughed less by ordinary four-wheelers than by impeccable carriages. In this quarter servants made up the majority of the population. One saw them from early morning scurrying from mansion to mansion in order to distribute express letters or invitations; and in the evening there they were, in full livery, standing guard in the courtyard of any house in which a reception was being held. There were also many priests and many old ladies, whom only an insolent aigrette distinguished from the women who hired out chairs at Saint-Clothilde. Elderly gentlemen, wearing decorations, took off their hats to young girls escorted by their maids. The regular itineraries of this population wove from St Francis Xavier to St Thomas Aquinas: zigzagging between four or five drawing-rooms, between the Senate and the Institute, between the Convent of the Sacré-Coeur and the dancing class. The men would cross the Seine every day to go to the Bois and then to their clubs: to the Jockey in the Boulevard des Capucines, to the Épatant in the Rue Royale. Only the more fortunate of the women went to the Bois in an open carriage and in the evening to the Opera in a brougham.

Marriages and funerals had an immense importance, for the families were both large and united by a tribal instinct. All those who had a Montmorency for a grandmother or could claim the Gontauds as cousins adopted the stance of confronting God-alone-knows-what dangers threatening the virtues or the benefits inherited with such blood. The titles 'uncle' and 'cousin' were used to the fifth degree, and heredity fixed a man's reputation from the cradle. The tradesmen who had supplied the same families for sixty years attracted their customers neither by advertisement nor by dazzling shop-windows. There were more bookshops, but fewer theatres than on the right bank. The ducal families—Luynes, Rohan, Bauffremont, La Rochefoucauld—whose smallest movement was the object of notice, often confined their whole lives to their enormous mansions.

In this tribe the men were more elegant than the women and the women often more cultured than the men; in fact, horseracing and exile from power had considerably lowered the intellectual level of the aristocracy. Excellent French was spoken, rapidly and in a high voice; laughter was approved; and the general tone of conversation was far freer than among the bourgeoisie, provided that religion was not mentioned—the Faubourg Saint-Germain could be Rabelaisian, but could never simulate Voltaire. These emigrants kept admirable tables to console themselves for having to miss balls, and they were attended by generations of servants. Charitable and miserly, pious and libertine, worldly and retiring, the Upper Crust, though they occupied a very unimportant part in the society of the nineteenth century, none the less fascinated novelists from Balzac to Barbey d'Aurevilly. Yet they themselves relished only history and memoirs which recalled their past.

The aristocracy was the only class in France to produce eccentrics who gave full rein to their fancies without a care for what others thought of them. People seldom moved house in the Faubourg Saint-Germain; they kept the furniture they had inherited from their forefathers. Fringes and tassels seemed to them vulgar, comfort immoral. 'Bathrooms!' humphed the Duke of

Doudeauville when reconstructing Bonnetable. 'Just like in a hotel!'

Having become a dead arm of society after 1830, this group had lost contact with modern life. But in an age of steam and industrialisation that fact was fortunate rather than otherwise. More serious was its horror of innovation of any kind. To continue a life that would have been completely delightful if its members had not regretted the past so much, the aristocracy was obliged to make rich marriages.

The greatness and wealth of the Montesquiou family

Of these families one of the most illustrious is that of Montesquiou-Fezensac; and it is also probably—the line wavers at the turn of the tenth century—the one whose genealogy goes back the furthest: to the Merovingians by way of the dukes of Aquitaine. Voltaire did not take these claims seriously: 'The history of the little sovereigns of Fezensac would only be good for their heirs—if they had any', he wrote—without due consideration, since they did have heirs. In fact, the genealogists of Louis XVI vindicated all the titles of the Montesquious.

It is a warlike and harsh, yet also brave and good-humoured family: as is fitting since its estates cover a part of the Armagnac country and stretch as far as Béarn. Its greatest men are not called Montesquiou. There is, for example, Blaise de Montluc, the defender of Siena, the Huguenots' hangman and the author of those Commentaries which were, according to Henry IV, 'The Soldier's Bible'. There is another uncle by marriage, the Maréchal de Gassion, who was a close intimate of Henry IV; and there is, above all, d'Artagnan, son of a female Montesquiou who gave him the name of one of her estates (he was called Charles de Batz de Castelmore, and would have had a considerable fortune if he had not died at Maestricht). The debt of Dumas to his apocryphal Memoirs is well known. D'Artagnan, cousin of Captain Fracasse and uncle of Cyrano de Bergerac, often set the pattern of conduct of his distant nephew Robert and passed on to this fin-de-siècle Aramis both his panache and his sword. Saint-Simon also glorified the Maréchal de Montesquiou. After the marshal there was an academician, the Marquis de Montesquiou who was the author of light comedies. During the Restoration the great man of the family was an abbot, who had joined the Louis XVIII exiles; returning to France as Prime Minister and author of the Charter, he was rewarded with the Order of the Holy Spirit and with the title of Duke, which he left to his nephew, a general.

These are the glories of a senior branch of the family, called Marsan, separated in the reign of Charles VII from the branch which is our concern. No matter: all successes are claimed and divided by both branches. The only descendant of d'Artagnan whose name is remembered today is the great-grandmother of Count Robert, 'Maman Quiou' of the King of Rome, about whom Napoleon wrote in his *Mémorial*: 'She is a woman of rare merit . . . She was perfect in Vienna with my son.' Apart from all her virtues, this governess had an immense fortune, being a descendant of Louvois. It was she who brought the Château de Courtanvaux in Maine into the family. Her son, Count Anatole, collected all the honours made available to him by the governments under which he lived. Aide-de-camp to Napoleon, Spanish grandee of the first class, Lord in Waiting to Marie-Amélie, field-marshal, knight of Saint-Louis, and grand officer of the Légion d'Honneur, he had ready this retort, often repeated by his descendants, whenever anyone reproached him for having served the Empire: 'What do you mean, for us the Capétiens were already usurpers!' Only the Academy refused to honour this gallant man, who accepted all distinctions as his due without ever seeking them. When quite young he wanted to follow Napoleon after Fontainebleau, rather than present himself to the king and his powerful cousin, the abbot-duke. He improved on the good luck of being born a Montesquiou by marrying his first cousin. No one was less pompous than this dignitary. A prolific and regular poet, Count Anatole was, above all, a conversationalist, who enraptured the blue-stockings of the Faubourg Saint-Germain, such as Madame de Boigne and Madame de Bloqueville, and a connoisseur whose distinguished silhouette, crowned with white hair, was familiar to the art dealers. He was also a man with one foot in another world, a devotee of occultism, a frequenter of clairvoyants and himself an excellent medium. In his latter years the lord of Courtanvaux turned his back on a century which had, none the less, offered him a multitude of honours and grew old in the tradition of a society which, in respecting the hierarchy, did not upset his idle fancies.

After so much glory, the next generation of Montesquious, born under Charles X, became fossilised, ceased to question the future and drew its rules of conduct from the pompous portraits of Largillière or the elegances of Vigée-Lebrun. Dowagers and clubmen scaled genealogies with the dexterity of mathematicians unravelling square roots.

The Anatole de Montesquious realised after the reign of Louis Philippe that the future lay with money and negotiated opulent marriages for their three sons. The eldest, Napoléon, discreetly called Léon, married Mlle Quiller-Perron, daughter of a general who had brought an immense fortune back from India; the second son, Wlodimir (yes, Wlodimir! A Montesquiou could not be called Wladimir like anyone else) married Mlle Sauvage, whose brothers became de Brantes; and the third, Thierry, married Mlle Pauline Duroux in 1841.

Thierry tried his hand at diplomacy for several years, but the parsimony of his parents and his own lack of ambition impeded his progress. With his wife's dowry he bought Charnizay, built a mansion in Paris and was elected Vice-President of the Jockey Club; his perfect manners hid any regret he might have felt about not becoming an ambassador or about being the husband of such an ugly wife. Not only was Pauline ugly but she was also a Protestant. In contrast with so many marshals, she could only offer a father who had been a general of the National Guard; but the important thing was that he had also been a stockbroker, who had left her hundreds of acres in Brie, several blocks of flats and a skilfully assembled portfolio of shares.

Pauline, an orphan, was married from her mansion, 80, Rue de l'Université, with the blessing of Lamartine, tenant of the first floor. Her marriage invitation presents an amusing instance of social parthenogenesis: DuRoux is still written as a single word but with a capital R, to indicate the birth of the *particule*.

The young married couple were introduced to their cousins in order of importance: first of all to the pompous and abominably rich Duc de Doudeauville; then to the Chimay sister in the mansion on Quai Malaquais, today a School of Fine Arts; and then to several branches of the Montesquiou family. The young wife's modesty caused her to be thought assimilable, and it is quite possible that her mother-in-law used the same phrase ascribed today to a contemporary duchess in circumstances not

much different: 'After all . . . everything rights itself in the end'.
It is said that Countess Thierry was happy and that she even
eventually became a Catholic in order to please the husband she
so much loved. However, in photographs she seems a severe
woman, her forehead lined by some private obsession and her
gaze slightly mad. She divided her time between creating hideous
tapestries and doing good works. In Count Robert, magnificent
and insolent aesthete though he was, one finds two traces of this
Protestant heredity: first, a disgust for debauchery when the upper
crust went to extremes and secondly, an intellectual integrity, an
unshakeable faith in some higher truth (in his case Beauty, not
religion). It is also probable that if his mother had been born a
Noailles or a Mortemart, he would have cared less about recalling
the grandeur of the Montesquious. Mme de Montesquiou had a
sister who made an equally brilliant marriage, with Count
Hippolyte de la Rochefoucauld, the lord of Verteuil. Although
beautiful and elegant, she was so little remembered that when
anyone talked about her to her son Aimery, he would comment:
'A very distant mother.'

A sweet child

The upper crust was a clan that entertained among itself: by
family rather than by household, under the aegis of the family-
heads or of the dowagers, and with the support of poor cousins,
of abbots, of governesses and of old friends who always found a
place laid for them at table. The young married Montesquious
lived with Count Anatole at the Béthune mansion, 60, Rue de
Varenne, which remains intact today thanks to the descendants of
Comte d'Hinnisdäl, the owner. One can still almost catch a
whiff of horses in the courtyard; the windows still look out on the
Bauffremont mansion; and the famous salon, the tapestry of
which, designed to match the woodwork, excited the curiosity
of Proust, is still in its place. In the simply panelled, mirrored
apartments of the second floor, chestnut trees before the window,
Count Robert, last of the children of Count Thierry, was born on
the 7th of March, 1855. Did the father in fact speak those words
which he often had occasion to ponder later: 'Children—those
strangers we introduce so imprudently into our lives'? After the

christening, there was an omen: the godfather gave to the god-mother a porcelain vase from Japan. The child was frail; but his grandmother speedily reassured her husband, absent in England with Queen Marie-Amélie: 'The child is alive, a wet-nurse has been found for it.' Robert, like all 'Maman Quiou's' descendants, was dressed from the King of Rome's layette, his governess drawing from it bonnets, lace dresses and even diapers of the finest cambric. His eyes first looked on to a garden; his first steps were made in the courtyard, swept clean by a groom in striped waistcoat and breeches of leather, to an ecstatic audience of chamber-maids and kitchen-maids and under the eyes of the beribboned nurse who had been brought from Courtanvaux.

Countess Thierry was too weak to trouble herself with this last-born child, and it was therefore the grandmother who assumed the task of bringing him up. She amused him with the fans, secret boxes and dolls of her own childhood, now recovered from the attics. She would take Count Robert on visits; and in the brougham, like a favourite pug, the child would nestle against the sables that always had about them a musty smell of naphthaline and would then trace with his fingers the folds of a cashmere shawl. They would make excursions to see some cousins who lived in a villa in the middle of a great park in Avenue Montaigne. This eccentric couple divided their time between a farmyard, the inhabitants of which got mixed up with the visitors, and auction-sales, their acquisitions from which had begun to overflow out of their house into the garden. Dressed with an opulent indifference Aunt Alfred travelled in the company of a stuffed eagle. Her mother was Indian and she would show the child jewel-encrusted daggers and stuffs embroidered with gold, which she would then fold up again before returning them to their sandalwood caskets. This lovable woman would cut out of tissue-paper friezes of dancers, flowers and lanterns.

The child and his grandmother would also visit a stout aunt whose conversation delighted the family. On meeting an engaged couple, both of whom were short, this lady commented: 'Their children will knock down – strawberries'. There was the Princess of Chimay, who was very beautiful; and there were other Montesquious, who were mocked for showing off their wealth. The child's eyes opened on salons, his ears opened to worldly chatter; so it was not surprising that he was less pleased when, a little older, he was obliged to play with a tribe of male and female cousins, to chase a balloon, to trundle a hoop, to skip. Such exercise seemed pointless to him, and he would feign fatigue to return once more to the drawing-room. It was in recalling these childhood associations imposed on him by his family that he later quoted a dictum of Mérimée: 'I don't like relations. You are obliged to be on familiar terms with people you have never seen merely because they happen to be the children of the same father as your mother.'

The grown-ups chattered away, without concerning themselves about the child crouched near their crinolines. He remembered everything, so that fifty years later he could triumph on the boulevard with remarks that had amused the upper crust during the Second Empire: such as the 'I am well' which seemed to the Duc de Doudeauville an engaging formula with which to end a letter, or the reply which Proust attributes to the Duc de Guermantes, but which in fact was spoken by Aimery de Rochefoucauld to a female cousin who had just informed him of the death of a close relative as he was getting ready to go to a ball disguised as a bee: 'These things get exaggerated . . .' At times the child did not understand why the grown-ups laughed. He asked his nurse-maid: 'Why did Aunt Léonie say that now that men no longer wear breeches at balls, one can't tell what they are thinking?' and was chided 'Sh, Master Robert!'

However the same maid, in the hot weather, had no compunction about pulling up her petticoat and opening wide her thighs in order to cool herself. When his first curiosity had been satisfied, the child nursed an invincible horror for this woman, a fool who threatened him with stories of how a wolf would eat him. In such households the servants are much closer to the children than their parents, to whom they are presented at fixed times, carefully dressed, silent and smiling if possible.

'My maid! My maid!' called Count Robert from the bottom of his bed or on the Esplanade des Invalides; for all the world like one of those heroes of the Comtesse de Ségur, whose adventures had begun to appear within the red and gold covers of the *Bibliothèque Rose*. This 'Comédie Humaine of Childhood' established the little boy's social values forever. The bad do not have prefixes to their names and are too rich; they end up ashamed after having lived ridiculed. The good poor go to mass and work.

The lazy get penal servitude. He would look with the benevolence of Mme de Fleurville on the little Proust or the little Reynaldo Hahn, who put themselves to so much agony to arrive in society. He thought that 'the people' was composed of servants and of the crowds jammed together at the Invalides fair.

His two brothers and his sister, being much older, were not interested in Robert. Élise was like her mother, quiet and ugly; Gontran and Aymery grew too fast and so were often ill. Count Robert wrote under a photograph of the three boys together: 'Ipse, ille, iste'. It was from the servants that the child learned what was going on outside the Faubourg Saint-Germain and outside the family. One day the valet raised him on his shoulders so that he could glimpse the Empress opening an exhibition in the Champs-de-Mars, and he saw, through the windows of her carriage, an idol daubed with paint and covered with jewels.

If Comtesse de Ségur provided an explanation of society for him, Toepfer's caricatures showed him its absurdities, so that in later years Count Robert would often see his scapegoats in the guises of Vieuxbois and Cryptogame. On the other hand, Grandville's illustrations—Animated Flowers, Animals Painted by Themselves, Another World—unlocked for him a universe of fantasy. These poetical metamorphoses, these marvellous non-sensicalities were his real fairy-stories.

Thus Count Robert's first years passed either among the old or among picture books. His eyes gazed out on a world that was ancient, imposing and polite, but from which fantasy was not excluded. The months he spent in the country, in the châteaux, recreated for him a closed world in which it was possible for him to think that he was the Dauphin and so made him as much used to solitude as to the feeling that he was important. He was far less the child of his parents than of his grandparents; and in consequence the ties of blood were never to be very important for him.

CHAPTER 2

The Child of His Grandmothers

When I dream of my grandmothers—Pictavine,
Claude, Auriane, Alpais, Blanchefleur, Belgart,
Miraumonde, Jacquette, Aude . . . long, divine
Crown of beauties, of whom these are the merest part . . .

From château to château

THE MIGRATIONS of the Thierry de Montesquious to this or
that château were even longer than was the custom among the
upper crust. Indeed, Mme de Montesquiou had such delicate
health and her children were so sickly that it was necessary to
leave Paris for whole seasons on end. On one occasion a villa
was taken at Enghien, but that was extremely bourgeois; all
of a sudden Pau was preferred because of the fox-hunting. Then
it was decided that it was pointless to rent houses when there
were already so many châteaux at the family's disposal, of which
one, at Vicq-de-Bigorre, was not far from Pau. The small manor,
which had once given its name to d'Artagnan, stood among pop-
lars, chestnut forests and maize fields, in a valley freshened by the
river Adour, one tributary of which resembled a canal. It was
a simple and ancient dwelling, with a square tower, mullion
windows and mansard windows put in during the reign of Louis
XV. Orange trees in white boxes relieved the brown of the stones
which made up the courtyard. The interior was almost rustic—
huge beams, paved floors: only the chimney-pieces, fashioned
from the same Sarrancolin marble used at Versailles, were
suitably manorial. The woodwork, painted in bright colours;
the curtains, made of toile de Jouy; the engravings of ancestors
in the corridors; in the drawing-room the pastels and the furniture covered in *petit-point* by a patient grandmother: all these

might have been at Les Charmettes. The dining-room walls were covered in canvases painted in imitation of foliage; under flowered bed-canopies of printed cotton straw mattresses were piled. Old papers grew mouldy in the ancient private chapel.

Yes, all this was very simple. But what a multitude of coats-of-arms were painted at the bases of the beams in the great hall: those of all the houses allied to the Montesquiou family— Xaintrailles, Foix, Durfort, Castelbajac, Castellane, Lautrec . . . At the same time that Robert learned the alphabet, he also learned to decipher the poetic language of heraldry, with its sinople and vair, sable and gules. These colours were more familiar to him than the multiplication table. He knew that a Montesquiou wore: gold, with two crabs of pale gules, surmounted by the crown of the dukes of Aquitaine with its red bonnet and dangling tassel.

The Béarnais good humour survived in M. de Montesquiou. At Artagnan he was less preoccupied by the serious problems of the Jockey Club elections. Decorum and marriage restrained his fancy, which at times was pretty lively, and limited his attachments. As a rule the neighbours and the hunt were sufficient to amuse him. Perhaps because he was in the country of Henry IV, he had himself photographed playing horses with his children: whiskered, with a pointed nose and a sour mouth, Count Thierry lacked vitality as much as his frail, etiolated off-spring.

Towards the end of August the family went north, where the hunting was better. The first stop, near Angoulême, was at a house imposing in a different way from Artagnan. Verteuil, the towers of which dominated an immense park, was the residence of the Hippolyte de la Rochefoucauld family. The lady of the manor, an imposing and extremely artificial beauty, was not very like her Montesquiou sister. Since her husband had once been ambassador at Florence, she always put herself on show, her ample crinolines sweeping the galleries in which hung, among a hundred ancestors and collaterals, portraits of Francis I and of Charles V, who had met each other there. However, the greatest artistic treasure at Verteuil was 'The Hunt for the Unicorn', now in the Cloisters Museum in New York. Robert would wander from tapestry to tapestry, following the pursuit of this white animal which only a virgin could capture, until he reached the last one, in which the peasants are shown bringing the unicorn back on a hurdle, its horn sweeping the flowers.

These cousins lived, surrounded by servants and tutors, as though they were princes; among the children there was more consideration than affection. Life was more amusing at the home of another Montesquiou family, owners of an estate near Versailles. Robert evoked the atmosphere of this house as follows:

> Mothers fanned themselves in the sombre dwelling,
> In the obscurity of the closed rooms . . .
> The summons to the fresh repast of cakes and fruit.

Sometimes a villa was rented at Houlgate or at Dieppe, where the bourgeois families watched the pale and begloved little Montesquious walking on the front with a retinue of maids. In 1873, during an excursion to Guernsey, family and friends were photographed in a group worthy of Boudin; to its composition Robert's suit adds an elegant white streak.

As soon as he became a widower, Count Thierry set about introducing the children to the world of fashion: at Baden-Baden, where they met a number of highnesses; at the residence of the Prince de Chimay, quasi-sovereign of the Ardennes—an amusing château this, almost a town, with Madame Tallien's theatre in it.

Count Thierry's favourite home was Charnizay, a castle in bogus gothic style 'at the only spot in the Touraine that is not beautiful'. Conventional and gloomy, within its setting of miniature firs and geranium plots, this house always seemed to Robert to rival his father in disagreeableness. Poisoned as it was by his memories on the one hand of his doleful mother and of the obsequious nuns who surrounded the new convert and on the other hand of his father's pompous and reactionary pronouncements, he was never to feel at home there. However, there existed even among the most morose members of this family a certain artistic sense, a taste for the odd. Thus Count Thierry conceived a mania for photography, making his wife, the neighbours, the parish-priest and even the kitchen maids sit for him in remarkable compositions. As for the odd, the Count indulged, like his father, in supernatural experiments, with much table-turning at the Tuileries and in Guernsey.* More gifted, it seems, in this direction than he really wished to be, M. de Montesquiou attracted to the house phenomena so disturb-

* A reference to the Spiritualistic experiments of the Imperial Court and in Victor Hugo's exiled household. Trans.

ing that it had to be exorcised; having once smelled brimstone, he no longer strayed from his wordly routine. The family went to Charnizay as often as possible, for it was there that the Count was lord of his own domain. But it was the September visit that Robert looked forward to: for then his grandfather brought all the family together at the Château de Courtanvaux in the Maine.

First encounters with the Supernatural

The family left the train at Saint-Calais station and seated themselves in the brake, while the servants and the baggage were stacked on the roof; after several miles of journeying through woodland, they arrived at a Renaissance postern on which the arms of the Louvois and the Souvrés were carved. Beyond, built on the side of a hill and dominating the pepper-pots of immense oaks all around it, the château stood out like a Victor Hugo drawing. The apartments opened on to successive terraces, on each of which the busts of emperors alternated with orange-trees. Lanceolate dormer windows and chimneys painted with coats-of-arms pierced the high slate roof.

The carriage would enter the park at dusk: the first bats would be fluttering hither and thither and the peacocks would be uttering their final squawks. The servants would appear at the little doors at the foot of the towers. They came racing down all the staircases: both those covered with carpets that led to the drawing-rooms and those that spiralled inside the thick walls. There were twenty-eight staircases in all at Courtanvaux. Some gave on to the terraces, others wound upwards to linen-rooms and lofts; some were carpeted, some were of stone and were polished by the servants' brooms and the running feet of children.

What an adventure it was for Robert to embark on a voyage of discovery along one of these stairways; on and on to the shut rooms or to the end of a passage, until, all at once, his heart would miss a beat at the sounds of a pole-cat scrabbling in the loft above him or the blundering of a moth against a window pane! In the galleries below, the pendulums of the great clocks seemed both to impose order and to extend protection. The child knocked on the door of the old female cousins who skulked in the depths of their apartment, repeating to each other, over and over

again, remarks long since out of date; he followed the valet in his
task of lighting up the drawing-room where everyone assembled
after dinner, watching him as he now illuminated the tall Chinese
vases and the crystal chandeliers and now brought to life the
shepherdesses on the Aubusson sofas, and the allegories on the
clocks. Robert followed the ceremonies of a whole Chinese
population on Coromandel screens, on embroidered panels, on a
Vernis Martin desk. Sometimes he stole into his grandmother's
apartment. She would select one of the keys dangling from her
chatelaine to open a cupboard for him, and he would sniff in the
aroma of pot-pourri, furniture polish and pepper that would be
wafted from the bundles of paper, before beginning to rummage
in earnest among the old ribbons, the note-books covered in
mother-of-pearl or ivory and the remains of old dresses in heavily
figured silk hoarded up as materials for covering chairs. His
grandmother allowed him to open a fan or a snuff-box from the
bottom of which a charming face looked up at him; then she shut
the cupboard once again. To console the child she would begin to
tell him the names of the figures—bewigged, holding marshals'
batons and with the Order of the Holy Spirit draped across their
waistcoats—hanging on the walls in gold frames. Magnificence
and mystery, fragile things and things forbidden, formed the
child's taste: a taste both exquisite and susceptible, which was
to fear the impulses of the heart as much as the nonchalance of
pleasure, but was none the less destined to foster the imagination
with a thousand impressions accumulated at this château. The
mind awakened by these portraits was destined to return ceaselessly to those who had posed for them, to those who had loved
all these knick-knacks, and so to death. Robert de Montesquiou
was to see the world as a place of vanities, in which, under a heap
of roses, ivories and carved goblets, one discovered a skull of
exquisite proportions. Even during his most frivolous moments
it was always possible to apply to him these lines of Platen,
written in the solitude of a Prussian castle after having loved
so many beautiful faces:

> He who looks Beauty full in the face
> Is already dedicated to death.

Death was, indeed, a familiar presence at Courtanvaux. Tired of
having served so many governments Count Anatole maintained

a continuous relationship with the Beyond, filled notebooks with automatic writing and entertained the children with thought-transference. This elegant and vague old man was something of a sorcerer. The servants claimed to have seen him pass down the gallery at a distance of two metres from the floor; and the story is told of how, when one of his daughters-in-law told him that she had a craving for exotic fruit, he merely said 'Open the door' and there, outside it, was a basket of pineapples. Thus it was that the child apprehended that under the trivial stories, the trivial teasings that made up the conversation of the adult world, another world lay hidden: a world which he tried to glimpse at the end of the galleries or in the empty rooms and with which he even perhaps attempted to get in touch through all those dead, delightful objects so pleasing to his fancy.

The grandfather guessed that Robert was the only one of his grandchildren who would one day be able himself to penetrate the world which had now become his chief preoccupation. Assuredly he read to the child his insipid alexandrines, thus visibly boring him; but he also took him out for walks in the park, where he could see the game-keepers lift the bow-nets from the fishponds or watch the white peacocks roosting in a catalpa-tree. The old man and the child understood one another; mystery and tradition were thus to survive. In the evening they would all sit round a large table, on which the albums lay thick, while the women, lit only by a single lamp which threw vague glimmers on to the tapestries at the other end of the room, busied themselves with their needle-work. As in all the châteaux, there were humble relatives and old women friends who had acquired the characteristics of furniture, so fixed were they in their memories and eccentricities. There was also a priest, the Abbé Charpentier, to whom Robert gave the nickname 'The Butterfly': a personage from the previous century, a little like Voltaire, frivolous, malicious, two-faced, yet possessed of a nimble mind and quite devoted to the family. This black Butterfly introduced the child to odd practices, retailing to him the gossip of the servants' hall and viewing the staff through the loop-holes as they whiled away their time on the many-holed privies by telling each other scabrous stories. No doubt it was from this cleric that Robert got his taste for scatological jokes.

The Butterfly was an excellent pianist and a collector of curios.

Frank to the point of insolence, he amused the child, but never won his affection: this man who had such a sense of the ridiculous was its first victim. He had some young protégés, among whom were a pianist and a pale artist with a cynical manner who sometimes met Robert: Jean-Louis Forain.* Too frivolous to be alarming or to commit himself completely, the chaplain amused himself by confusing people's minds; and in this task his young disciple supported him, even at the risk of being disowned by him if the family protested. At Courtanvaux birthdays were a pretext for charades and recitations. Once, as a pretended compliment, Robert made his male and female cousins learn a fragment from Hugo's *Travailleurs de la Mer*. 'The sword-fish has a sword,' said a little boy. 'The octopus has no sword,' replied a little girl. 'The numb-fish has its electric ray.' 'The octopus has no effluvia.' From the depths of a cardboard grotto Robert then intoned into a shell: 'This single opening—is it the anus or is it the mouth?... It is both. The same aperture fulfils the two functions.' The abbé, having glanced at the old lady, put a stop to the recitations and the children were packed off to bed.

The abbé was the inventor of the game of Inevitable Epithets. (At this same period Flaubert was composing his Dictionary of Accepted Ideas.) 'Work?' asked the Butterfly. 'Arduous,' Robert replied. 'Kindness?' 'Unfailing'.

Years later Robert was to rediscover and embellish some absurd questionnaires which had embarrassed both parents and children: What is the tribe among whom the women conceive at the age of five and die at the age of eight? What is the tribe whose smell puts crocodiles to flight? Is it true that the ibis can be regarded as the inventor of the enema? Which is the bird that goes bald in the turnip season? What connection exists between the lobes of the liver of the mouse and the phases of the moon? What is the name of the King of Epirus whose big toe cured diseases of the spleen? The name of the woman of ancient Rome who never spat? The name of the historian who paid 21,000 of our francs for a plate of speaking birds' tongues? Of the poet whose mistress received the favours of an elephant? Is it true that female quails are so lascivious that it is enough for them to hear the voice of the male in order to conceive? That a serpent barked when the Tarquins were

* Brilliant painter and draughtsman; an anti-semite famous for the cruelty of his wit.

expelled? That Aristomenes of Messena, who killed three hundred Spartans, had a heart made of hair?

A young poet's sufferings

Alas, he had to return to Paris to reply to gloomier questions; serious teachers took the place of the Butterfly. After two not very brilliant years at the Lycée Bonaparte (Condorcet today) M. de Montesquiou placed his son as a boarder with the Jesuits at Vaugirard. Thus Robert had to leave his grandparents, the beautiful house, the kindly servants.

The hideousness of the college distressed the child more than the exile from home or—since he easily learned everything that interested him—his scholastic tasks. The ugly chapel and the stupid hymns·gave him a long-enduring disgust for religion. His friends thought him a snob; when they reproached him for addressing them in the plural, he replied, 'But I don't wish to be your intimates.' He was astonished that the other boarders should be so much concerned whether a ball went to one side of a field or another. Perhaps he had a number of romantic friendships, but he only mentions one. One day he was watching the opening of a rose in the Superior's garden. 'One of my fellow-prisoners, who happened to be walking by and to whom I had never spoken, caught my gaze, felt something of its rapture, and—probably knowing enough to aspire to work a miracle, whatever the condemnation that might follow it—picked the flower and, without saying a single word, presented it to me. I at once realised that this was Friendship on Earth.'

One talent saved Robert from being unpopular: he was very amusing. He gave cruel imitations of the teachers, saddled them with ridiculous nicknames and drew caricatures of them. He also showed courage in replying to them with an irony so suave that he gave them no opportunity to punish him. In any case, he was one of the most brilliant pupils in the college, and the Jesuits, though often exasperated by his preciosities and his insolence, were none the less anxious to keep him.

Robert would always finish his preparation quickly, learning Latin verses or the names of provinces in no time at all; then, behind a wall of dictionaries, he would set about discovering

Hugo, Lamartine, Gautier, Michelet. He copied out *La Fête chez Thérèse* and some lines of Gérard de Nerval which reminded him of Courtanvaux.

He began to scribble poems, which he then read to the boy who seemed to be the most perceptive of all his friends. Alas, one day when he was leaving the refectory, he thought that he would faint at the sound of one of the superintendents derisively murmuring some of his lines from a poem to the moon: 'This glimmer dreamy and pallid . . .' This indiscretion made him retire within himself, and thenceforward he cheered up only on visiting days. The mothers and sisters doted on this pupil, who was so engaging, and so well dressed and who knew everybody. In the chapel the sensitive boy sought for no vision more spiritual than that of the elegant and perfumed women who for an hour transformed the parlour into a drawing-room. Otherwise he lived with his books, in the hope of returning to Courtanvaux.

Long letters from his grandmother helped Robert, while at Vaugirard, to be patient and gave him courage.

The war of 1870 and the Siege of Paris caused him to spend an entire year in the country. Although repelled by compulsory games at the college, he willingly learned to ride and fence; he wished to be a dandy, in emulation of Balzac's heroes, whom he had begun to discover. Balzac was for the generation born during the Second Empire what Proust was for those born between the two wars: but the *Human Comedy* is a better guide for a young man than *Remembrance of Things Past,* being at once more generous and more complete and affording astonishing glimpses into occultism, religion and politics.

First steps in the fashionable World

Robert's head was full of Balzac when, at his cousin's house, he met a charming man with a red beard and green eyes, whom the women adored and the men admired for his bravery in the war and his knowledge of art. Charles Haas took an interest in this little Montesquiou, so passionate and so lively under his dreamy manner. A famous conversationalist and a great authority on Balzac, he repeated to the young man his remark about Vautrin in front of the château de Rastignac: 'The Olympio-like sadness of pæderasty.'* Proust, who created Swann out of Haas, was to quote this phrase. Haas knew almost as much about painting as about society and a great deal about antiques. At dinner parties he aroused interest without offending convictions; scandal he would not endure unless it was extremely funny, and he knew how to be discreet. So many qualities are often possessed at the cost of naturalness. 'This Haas, how contrived he is . . .' Degas remarked. None the less, a young man of society, passionately fond of literature, could not have found a wiser counsellor—perhaps one a little too wise. This Mentor, who was also to be met at Dieppe, introduced Robert to some of the beauties who had shone at the Tuileries: for example to Mme de Pourtalès and to the Princesse de Sagan, both as ostentatious, as adorned and as impeccable as circus horses. However, young Montesquiou's first social events were débutante balls.

Robert did not dance; the mere idea of pressing to his heart girls overheated by a dozen polkas, brought him to the verge of nausea. His irony—a true *noli me tangere*—repulsed anything that might disarrange his appearance and at the same time redeemed whatever factitious elements such perfection must inevitably have in one so young. The chief butts of this irony were mothers eager to marry off their daughters and all the match-makers of the Faubourg. In this Robert was more adept than another young man of his class—Astolphe de Custine,† whom he resembled in many respects—had proved himself under the Restoration. On the one hand Robert's great name and a handsome fortune further increased by the death of a brother, and on the other hand delicate health and a personality which might discreetly be termed eccentric, were in society the pros and cons for this youth who, each evening, descended the staircase of the Quai d'Orsay mansion in a tail coat. His father and his uncle Wlodimir had just finished building this pompously banal house. Thin and pale, with a light moustache and crinkly chestnut hair parted in the middle, the ill-nourished and solitary schoolboy gave place to the fop. He had been bored at college and had wanted distraction; but at the balls he found only respectability, cupidity and boredom.

* A reference to Victor Hugo's poem 'La Tristesse d'Olympio'. Trans.

† Discredited by a homosexual scandal, this man of distinguished intellect devoted himself to letters. A friend of Balzac and Heinrich Heine, he has put us in his debt for an admirable 'Travels in Russia'.

A tiresome father

This man-about-town was lonely at home. His grandfather hardly
ever left Courtanvaux and died in 1876. His father, whom he met
at meals, exasperated him by his habit of deciding what was good
or bad in ethics or in literature with the assurance of someone
infallible on worldly questions. There is no doubt that the views
of Count Thierry were thoroughly bourgeois: he chuckled on
seeing how Cham (his friend Count de Noë) had caricatured a
picture sent by Manet to the Salon with the inscription 'On
becoming mad, Hamlet sits for Manet'; and he waxed indignant
on the same ground as *Le National*, which denounced 'a criminal
plot between Manet and Mallarmé'. To have caused so much
exasperation to the Philistines these artists must be marvellous,
Robert decided; and he at once bought all Baudelaire and the
Parnasse Contemporain in which Leconte de Lisle's *Cain* appeared alongside Mallarmé's *Herodiade*. Thus the poetry which he
liked on his emergence from college resembled the works of Hugo
he had read at college in also being forbidden fruit. His father grew
anxious: horses and women played no part in Count Robert's life;
his irony might presage some catastrophe; his days of gloom
might perhaps precipitate scandal. (The same situation in a similar
but provincial environment can be found in the Toulouse-Lautrec
family.) His sister, always in the background, had just married
the Duke of Padua, formerly the husband of the dead Princess
Mathilde Bonaparte, and was soon to become a model widow. His
brother chose from the most severe section of the upper crust a
delightful wife: Pauline de Sénety.

A tall, elegant and cultured woman, with a sad expression,
whom ill-health often kept out of society, Pauline immediately
became attached to her brother-in-law. When the doctors ordered
the young wife to live in the Midi, Robert would join her there as
often as was possible. He himself was not too robust, his chest
was a source of anxiety and he had just been undergoing treatment.

'I should have passed my infancy among a protective swirl of
skirts,' confided the young brother-in-law, 'instead of being
surrounded by dirty cassocks.' Indeed, as though to compensate
him for his motherless youth, women were to assume a far
greater role in the life of this man who did not like them, than in
that of a Don Juan. He was to be surrounded and sometimes even

submerged by women. Unfortunately, the doctors discovered that mountain air was best for Count Robert and he was despatched to Switzerland for a treatment of 'Engadine-isation'. He was only to return to Menton to attend the last days of his sister-in-law's life.

To the Saint-Germain observer Robert seemed to belong to the serious side of the upper crust: that which would end in the Academy; which devoured without wincing the works of Toc-queville and Barante; which was imbued with the 'enlightened' ideas of the Broglie family and the principles of Montalembert. It read 'Le Gaulois' for society news, and the 'Débats' for the leading articles; it wrote for the 'Revue de Deux Mondes'. Respectability deadened this section of good society, which was not the victim of frivolity.

Only those dowagers who had led fast lives during the Restoration maintained a certain sprightliness in this bastion of right-thinking people. Mme de Beaulaincourt, née Castellane, and Mme de Bloqueville, née d'Eckmuhl, gave Count Robert an agreeable welcome. These old friends of his grandmother had none of those hidden matrimonial motives which froze the young man whenever he crossed the immense drawing-rooms of the Crillon mansion to greet the Duchesse de Polignac, possessor of so many grand-daughters, or whenever he bowed at Maintenon to the imposing Duchesse de Noailles, whose husband was both an Ambassador and an Academician. This was the period of the Republic of Dukes, with Mac-Mahon at the Elysée, Broglie as Prime Minister, and Decazes and Audiffret-Pasquier among the ministers. After Sedan there was something like a new Restoration, and a Montesquiou who was cousin of so many ministers and senators could enjoy a fine career in politics, in the diplomatic corps or in official literature. But towards such a convenient destiny, which would require a great resistance to boredom, ambition did not lead this youth of twenty. He had already been bored too much, first at college and then at the balls, to be able to tolerate idle talk and approved ideas. He became bored quickly, very quickly; that was evident, even though it was taken for a pose. As for morals, the foundation of this reactionary society, Robert concerned himself so little with them that he did not even defy them. During receptions, behind a mask both attractive and timid, there would in fact be building up an immense store of invective, an inexhaustible reservoir of comical observations and of worldly erudition, which he would put much later at the disposal of ungrateful disciples.

CHAPTER 3

A Much Admired Young Man

You whom a rarity has exiled from your species.

About beautiful women friends . . .

MUCH SOUGHT after in the World of Boredom, Robert was less often a guest in the World of Pleasure, at the houses of the young couples who still continued the festivities of the Second Empire. However, he did meet in that world some charming women, connoisseurs of antiques, like the Marquise de Brigode and the Comtesse de Courval. There was also the Comtesse de Beauvoir, who dressed in ancient silks in order to look like a painting by La Tour; and the Marquise d'Aoust, always accompanied by a monkey—so eighteenth century! Cabinet-makers and milliners ransacked collections of engravings for these women of taste. There were also the two nightingales, Mme de Tredern and Mme de Mailly, at the dazzling height of their beauty and vocal powers; they entertained as much at the Opera as in their houses. All these would later come frequently to entertain the little Montesquiou; some doted on him already. But their circle of club-men did not like him: he was interested neither in hunting nor in politics, and from time to time a curt insolence would rear up among his politenesses like a viper on a well-cut lawn.

Thus, from his twentieth year, Robert's life and above all his judgments were to receive a continuous commentary from a chorus of ladies: a commentary which, adequate or inadequate and with many false notes, was to accompany him until his death. Dowagers and women of artistic talent would retort to the young man's detractors: 'But he has so much taste! It was he who advised me to have a dress made like my grandmother's in the Vigée-Lebrun portrait. . . . He presented me with a Japanese

vase overflowing with chrysanthemums. . . . And what originality!
He fastened a bowl of gold-fish to his hanging-lamp . . . And
then'—the chorus would melt in tenderness—'he is so wonderful
to his sister-in-law.' The men said nothing, but they had relented
not a whit. None the less, they allowed Robert to accompany their
wives or their beautiful mistresses on outings in the Bois, to
antique-dealers or to exhibitions; 'He is not dangerous', they
would declare.

At the Salon Count Robert jibbed when he had to admire
portraits of Mme de Pourtalès by Carolus Duran or of the
Princesses d'Orléans by Chaplin: he preferred the elegant Stevens
to the sulphurous Henner; that anglicised Degas, Tissot, to the
syrupy Bouguereau. In gallery after gallery in the Champs-
Elysées Palace, the young man made ironical comments about the
masters of the day; then he proceeded to contemplate the picture
exhibited by Gustave Moreau, too moved before it to utter a
word. At the Salon of the Water-colourists he was stirred by the
pictures of old Eugène Lami, which reminded him of the elegant
days of his grandmothers. On these visits he would meet with
Charles Haas, who would applaud the young man's preferences,
and another, slightly younger and less charming Jew, called
Charles Éphrussi, who would extol Manet as well as Roll and
Gervex. Director of the Gazette des Beaux Arts, he too in some
small part suggested the character of Swan to his creator. However, the young Montesquiou also had several friends among the
eccentrics of the Faubourg Saint-Germain. The two sons of the
Duke de la Roche-Guyon were interesting: the elder, Hubert de
Rochefoucauld, was both a wonderful horseman, who gave
exhibitions of his skill at Mollier's circus in aid of charity, and the
possessor of such personal beauty that Count Robert hung in his
bathroom a life-size photograph of him in running-clothes; the
younger, Antoine, was, in contrast, a dreamer, who was to
become one of the first disciples of Péladan, the Rosicrucian.

The only cousins who understood Montesquiou were the
Chimays. The Princess, born a Montesquiou, was a woman of
poetical beauty, with a real talent for painting on enamel; she
entertained artists in her colonnaded mansion on the Quai
Malaquais. The Prince remained in Brussels, since he was the
Belgian foreign minister. They had inherited the house from a rich
grandmother called Pellaprat, who may also perhaps have

bequeathed to them some Napoleonic blood. Was it from this
heredity that the black eyes and the regal manner of Princess
Elisabeth, the eldest of the Caraman-Chimay daughters, derived
their origin? She was five years younger than Count Robert,
but when she was barely old enough to go out, her 'uncle'—
as she sometimes called him, though he was in fact her mother's
first cousin—took her in hand, choosing her dresses and escorting
her to concerts. This Elisabeth, he thought, deserved the destiny
of her namesake, the Empress of Austria. But wisely the young
princess, who had no dowry other than her beauty, wed Count
Greffulhe, a handsome, red-bearded man, possessed of immense
wealth. This Jupiter, a descendant of Louis XV and one of the
Mailly sisters, and heir of Dutch bankers, owned both a vast
mansion in the Rue d'Astorg and a very ugly château, Boisboudran, in the middle of thousands of acres of hunting country
in the district of Brie. A friend of the Prince of Wales, he possessed
the most beautiful horses and the most beautiful women in Paris.
Robert did not greatly like him, but they got on with one another
in the company of the young wife like the director of an opera
with his stage-manager. Count Robert chose the sumptuous and
often extravagant clothes for which the husband paid and helped
to organise the superb parties which the husband gave for a wife
of whom he was so proud and whom he yet deceived so publicly.
Right at the end of his life Count Robert could recall that his
cousin wore on the day of her betrothal 'a hat of rice-straw, the
vast brim of which sagged in front under the weight of a rose'.
Through the Princesse de Chimay, who was a close intimate of
Mme Ratisbone, a collector, Count Robert saw for the first time a
picture which was covered with flowers and gold and yet communicated a feeling of mystery and profound melancholy. Later
his cousin took him to the studio in which Gustave Moreau
elaborated these morbid fancies, about which the young man was
destined to dream at length.

Introductions to great men

But where could he meet the poets who, he guessed, were close
to this painting: Mallarmé and Villiers de l'Isle-Adam, and so many
other writers whom he admired? (His god, the aged Victor Hugo,

had become a republican pope, and Verlaine's reputation frightened him.) Houses in which the guests were not Academicians must exist. Montesquiou met some of these great men at a fancy-dress ball given by the Baronne de Pouilly in the winter of 1875.

This former beauty of the Tuileries—'a majestic corvette laden with riches, aromatics and keepsakes'—often gave receptions in a mansion, situated on the corner of the Rue de Colisée and the Avenue Montaigne, which was furnished in exuberant taste. The Renaissance dining-room gave on to an aviary full of cockatoos; vine-branches in crystal hung from the pillars in the salon; and bear-skins covered the steps down to a marble pool. The guests were as incongruous as these details of the décor. Side by side could be found the cousins Gramont and Harcourt, two such reminders of the Second Empire as Mme de Pourtalès and General de Galliffet, and a whole group of writers: an old admirer of the Baronne, Barbey d'Aurevilly, who had brought with him François Coppée, trailing clouds of glory from his *Passant*; Judith Gautier and her husband Catulle Mendès; the charming doctor, Armand Rodin; Heredia, 'hirsute to the eyes'—as Léon Daudet put it. All of them noticed a young man who, alone of them, appeared not to be 'dressed up', in his white Louis XV costume braided with gold; he held his powdered head proudly, his profile was perfect, his eyes bright. Beautiful hands emerged from the lace of his sleeves to mime a conversation, the shrill tone of which caused men to frown and women to rave.

'It's the little Montesquiou, so artistic, you will dote on him . . .' And the kindly baronne pushed Count Robert in the direction of literature. The excessive deference of society people, so gratifying to writers, was for once sincere.

Already very famous, José-Maria de Heredia became infatuated with this curious boy who recited to him his first poems. He treated him as an equal and confided in him the following: 'I have composed twenty stanzas of terza rima—very beautiful—on the Cid. But I fear that they would not please you. It's a metre barbarous in its simplicity.' This heroic writer used the language of Achilles in express letters (later, Proust's Bloch was to adopt the same tone): 'I have tamed the Chimera, and cut off the head of the Medusa; the conquered Harpies have brought me back this inelegant fal-lal, which I send to you by the horrible Hydra of the post.'

From a greater and less worldly master, Mallarmé, Robert

received many elegantly composed visiting cards, inviting him to attend an exhibition or to hear a lecture in his apartment.

In return for many gifts Mallarmé presented Count Robert with rare editions. 'Don't await the translation of Poe's "Raven" with too much impatience. It crosses "the lordly domain of Night". That means that I am following a confused, even a bizarre, course of negotiation, which may enable me to have a number of copies and to give you one.'

Only Barbey d'Aurevilly remained distant, constricted by his moth-eaten dandyism. He did not then guess that Montesquiou would adopt both his swagger with more brilliance and his pen with less force, or that he would indulge in insolences of which Barbey himself would only dream. Much later the poet was to recall an incident at an evening party which served to break the ice and so enabled the over-reserved young man to express his admiration: 'Misjudging him, blockhead that she was, by the rig which it pleased him to put on, a woman guest assailed him, from one end of the room to the other, on a subject entirely improper when addressed to a man of his standing. "I say, great man, don't you hear what people call you?" Draped in his invisible purple and his visible majesty, he ignored her. The insolent woman repeated her remark. Then, turning back, he crushed her with a dignity the like of which I had never seen before. "Madame, such a vulgar question came to my ears that I could not believe that it was addressed to me."'

Paul Bourget, who would like to have been the new Barbey, seemed, on the other hand, very interested in the young nobleman. Montesquiou once spent a day with him at Versailles, after which the author of 'Disciple' sent him some verses of a surprising tenderness. They met in the drawing-rooms of beautiful Jewesses, whom the novelist was later to turn into duchesses; drawing-rooms 'in which he walked as though on eggs, wearing a monocle and lisping in the English manner'.

As for Coppée, to understand his success one must look at the most frequently reproduced pictures in the Salons. The little grocer from Montrouge is worthy of the brush of Chocarne-Moreau; his patriotic flights evoke Detaille. Thanks to *Passant* he had been able to qualify as a true poet and had kept his friends in the highest places.

Later we will examine Count Robert's success in the world of

letters at greater length; but let us now continue to follow him
merely in society or, rather, in the society of the Right Bank.

He had only to cross the Seine to make the transition
from country to capital. The paintings of two young Italians, de
Nittis and Boldini, the early works of Béraud and the sketch-
books of Caran d'Ache, give us an idea of the elegant side of
Paris in the years 1875–1885. There was even greater luxury then
than during the Second Empire. After the defeat of the leading
families and of the Republic of Dukes, the business world
assumed power and began to construct palaces for itself from the
Plaine Monceau to the Champs-Elysées. The more recent dynas-
ties—Cahen d'Anvers, Porgès, Bamberger, Ephrussi, Deutsch de
la Meurthe—rivalled the three branches of the Rothschild family
already settled in Paris. Their carriages rolled down avenues
bordered by houses heavy with caryatids and bank-like mansions
in a style calculated to appeal to Ludwig of Bavaria. Driven by
English coachmen, baronesses muffled in sables left their cards at
the houses of Rumanian princesses, Spanish highnesses and
American commoners (these last, it was beginning to be said,
perhaps even richer than themselves). The financiers, making
their way from the Stock Exchange to the mistresses they kept
in some little establishment near the Rue de Prony, would visit
the auction-rooms and the picture-dealers.

In the morning the world of business and the Faubourg Saint-
Germain greeted each other in the Avenue du Bois. The
hard-up members of the upper crust founded the Dead Beats
Club near to the Étoile, to pass severe judgment on every carriage
and disseminate the ukases of the Prince de Sagan. In the evening
the financial world gave interminable dinners, served by male-
volent footmen, in order to entertain a heavy mixture of
ambassadors, academicians and bankers, who were cheered by the
professional wit of people like Haas, Scholl or the Marquis de
Modène, and revived by the sight of the splendid wives. A society
of young girls blossomed on these money-bags. Passionately fond
of painting, music and, above all, anything new, the 'Jewesses of
Art' (as Forain called them) included the Warshawski sisters,
Julia Cahen d'Anvers, Marie Kann, Baroness Gustave de Rothschild and Ernesta Stern. Count Robert was introduced into this
society by Mme de Poilly and Charles Haas. He liked its hot-house
atmosphere, in which works of art opened into bloom. Not only

was he paid far more attention than in the Faubourg Saint-Germain but there was limitless scope both for artistic conversations and for indulging in insolence. Bullied in his own world, he was for thirty years to present a brilliant and absurd image of it on the Right Bank. Bankers' wives, however, have sturdy appetites and it requires a Maupassant or a Bourget to satisfy them. Count Robert avoided too close an intimacy with them.

A frigid temperament allied with a concern for perfection made Count Robert one of the few dandies France has ever produced. There were, of course, men of great elegance, like the Prince de Sagan and Boni de Castellane when they made their debuts; but being ladies' men and even business men, they lacked the detachment which true dandyism exacts. Poetry was a lesser disadvantage in this quest for which Barbey had just established the rules in his book on Brummell: 'The dandy is a bold man, but one with tact, who stops himself in time and so finds between originality and eccentricity Pascal's famous point of intersection.' Barbey himself should have pondered this rule; and later we shall see that Count Robert was to ignore this advice of Brummell: 'In society, stay for just as long as it takes to make an impression. After that—go!'

The dandy is a Narcissus. He wants to see himself reflected in admiring eyes and looks to find again in portraits of himself the compliments already paid him by his mirror. Did he have a new outfit? If he decided to go to the seaside or to the mountains, Count Robert went at once to Otto, a photographer in the Place de la Madeleine, to pose in suitable clothes. In 1879 he commissioned a society painter, Doucet, to execute the first of a long series of portraits, which, because of the way in which his slender profile emerges from a sumptuous fur coat, he entitled 'Greyhound in an overcoat'.

The rarest sort of taste

Such a personage required a setting worthy of his personal beauty and his reputation as a connoisseur. In a few years Count Robert had arranged at the top of his father's mansion an apartment that was to become famous and was to enable him to experiment in a whole philosophy of furnishing. If we follow him into this apartment, we can soon discern the debt owed to its decoration by two fictional characters who, at an interval of thirty years from each other, made Montesquiou both celebrated and misunderstood.

I decided to procure a quantity of old tapestries of so-called forest foliage and to decorate the climbing and twisting passage with them. The addition of a faintly spotted, moss-coloured carpet then succeeded in making it look like a leafy lane. Some earthenware and bronze animals were added to complete the illusion of being out of doors . . . Some old musical instruments remained suspended from the branches of my greenery, like the harps hung by the waters of Babylon. These were the bag-pipes in shot silk, the flutes, the viols d'amore, the guiternes and the rebecks so gallantly attached to the branches of the tapestry, in a false impression of disorder. . . . A string of bronze monkeys linked to each other by their outstretched arms served as a bell-rope to set off a monastery or cattle bell, in harmony with the rustic staircase. Cleverly contrived between the bars of the grilles set into the front door was a perspective of the interior of the hall which, with honeysuckle clambering up its wall, sustained the garden effect. The same effect could also be found in the little dining-room, which, thanks to one of those English cretonnes of the great designer William Morris, the friend of Burne-Jones, also gave the appearance of being out of doors. To this design, called 'Honeysuckle', I brought a little stratagem. As its motifs were reproduced in a number of different shades, I chose four of them, one for each of the walls; this disparity seemed to bring the walls into play, with the result that they almost seemed to be moving . . . I also thought of a pleasant fantasy in front of one of the windows—one not for ventilation but only for illumination. Rather than obscuring it with a real glass window, so often far too sombre, I had placed in front of it, on a rack, a collection of flagons and goblets in coloured glass, which merged together to make a sort of stained glass window, inebriating not merely the eyes but even the throat . . . In a library above, the walls were covered with green and gold leather, stamped with peacock feathers in obvious representation of the hundred eyes of knowledge. In a photograph I have kept of this library I see my first and as yet unpublished manuscripts lying out on top of a beautiful green leather chest, which Greffulhe had constructed especially to contain them. The adjoining room . . . I exploited the oddness of its shape by decorating it with another leather, which reproduced in gold on a red background the network of a spider's web repeated a thousand times. Knickknacks and pieces of furniture, reduced to the exiguous proportions of the place, were imprisoned in this mesh in the same way as my reveries—gold flies awaited by the invisible Arachne who menaces dreams.

It was of this same shade of gold that the diaphanous English glass leaves were coloured, so that they truly did not allow the outside gloom to penetrate into the drawing-room. The effect it gave was that of feeling one had been shut up in one of those lacquer boxes of different shades of gold . . . To get this result the three walls that were most brightly illumina-ted were each covered in gilded leather, of varying intensity and each with a different pattern, so that the walls seemed iridescent and the room itself larger than in fact. This illusion was extended by the fourth wall which was made to seem deeper by being covered with a claret cloth. To produce a similar illusion about its medium height, the ceiling was covered with the same amaranth-coloured cloth on the side of the windows, thus extending the room, and the floor itself was hidden under a coraline flood of Khorassan rugs. . . . The furniture, so many skiffs and wherries afloat on this roseate tide, consisted of cane or lacquer chairs, preferably rather low, banquettes, stools, chests from Old China, aventurine cabinets, winged occasional tables, and vases in deep pink cloisonné con-taining hyacinths of the same colour. . . . Two screens in gold leaf by turns absorbed and allowed to run over their smooth surfaces the purple shades which made this room so joyful.

Let us pause for a moment. It was here that Count Robert received Paul Bourget, whom he dazzled: and who was to ask him: 'Shall the rite, Prince Charming, of a renewal of life and of friendship be celebrated by an appearance at your palace on the Quai d'Orsay?' Here too he received such men of his own milieu as Charles Haas and the delightful Prince Edmond de Polignac, ten years his senior. By means of notes written in coloured pencil and stuffed with English proverbs and Latin quotations, the latter, a patron of the musical world, would invite Count Robert to accompany him to concerts. He also lent him scores of Wagner, so that Parsifal became a model; together they went to Bayreuth, where they renewed their friendship with Judith Gautier. Women who had achieved fame as much by the fullness of their figures and the opulence of their busts as by their position in society would make their way up the stairs to Montesquiou's apartment. There was the Princesse de Sagan and her friend, Mrs Standish, who looked like the Princess of Wales and dressed like her; there was the beautiful Comtesse Edmond de Pourtalès. Robert would make them tell stories to him about the Tuileries and describe the clothes of Mme Castiglione. If his friend Paul Bourget was there he would make his lady visitors speak about the Prince of Wales, whom they knew well. Tea was served by the master of the house himself, in the English manner. A lady visitor asked to see more of the apartment. This is how her guide described it:

The next room was dedicated to the moon—like the terrace from which Hamilcar's daughter hurled poetic incantations in the direction of her lover Astoreth. The same witchcraft that was used in the other rooms to summon and keep Apollo's rays was here practised in tones of azure and silver in order to evoke and fix the moonlight. The wall by the window was midnight blue and made a shady corner into which a seat covered with the same material was set; the wall facing it was covered with a grey material, on which were little *camaïeu* drawings sprinkled with pale gold; the wall by the fireplace was in silver leather, brushed with bluish twigs; and the fourth wall was covered with velvet in that charming shade which I call 'Stevens grey' though I believe that the right term for it should be 'mouse-grey'. The carpet, also in two shades of grey, resembled the soil of paths on which the leaves above cause the shadows to tremble. . . . A piece of transparent gauze, stretching all along the largest wall, and painted with fish that might have been real, let the silver reflection of the tapestry I have mentioned shine through its light material, and so almost exactly reproduced the illusion of water. *Kakemonos* and Japanese embroideries, selected with care, took on the shape of castles, not in Spain, but on the disc of that star dear to those suffering from nyctaolopia. A crystal box contained pieces of stuff that made it look, when it was full, like a block of marble with the softest veins. A conical flower-vase, made of glass and as tall as a young slave, lifted on high a purple iris or a bunch of musk; while an ivory mandoline, hung on the wall, seemed to suspend, within its smooth curve, antennae extended to honour the milky star. The room that followed this confusion, at once so ordered and so crowded with a wealth of symbols, was more a passage than a room and seemed to have as its special function the representation of mysticism through mystery. A cloth the colour of stone screened the walls to which were attached *quite literally* (I underline these words with fixed intent), a very attractive ecclesiastical chair in carved oak of the period of Louis XV, three or four choir-stalls, the seats of which could be lifted, a fragment of a perforated balustrade, a bell with a religious tone. . . . Behind this cathedral corner were two small rooms, one a rest-room and the other a bath-room. The first of these was ordinary; the second striking, with its walls of turquoise blue tiles providing the setting for an enamel basin of the same colour. Glass of a similar shade enveloped everything in a similar turquoise light. Set back a little, an elephant—of course very small for an actual proboscidian but huge for an animal made from ceramics—expelled from his lapis lazuli blue trunk, which held a pair of the finest sponges, two harmonious and fresh jets of water. . . . Two curved doors, with gold-inlaid posts and inset into them windows of old glass on which I had had some mottoes engraved, allowed one, before one had entered, to see to the right and the left my bedroom and my dressing room. For the first I had imagined a satin wall-paper in plain mauve, the colour of which would also assume a variety of gradations according to the waning of the light. On the walls, in a frame lacquered in lilac, were a *kakemono,* entirely occupied by a long swathe of wisteria, and a many-coloured Ch'ien-lung plate. On the deep violet carpet a low bed, which I had had constructed from pieces of wood carved in China, took the form of a chimera. Surrounded by antique cupboards, carved and with glass doors, in which could be glimpsed gorgeous waistcoats, the dressing-room abjured all symbols and, in consequence, had only realities to express and embellish. Smaller glass cases contained socks as well as ties, folded and arranged like Elzevirs in the most luxurious of libraries.

One of the dazzled visitors was a young Englishman, first met at St Moritz, Graham Robertson, who described the apartment as follows: 'It was curious to leave the stately, almost austere rooms of the old count and to climb up a dark stairway through tunnels of tapestries to the eyrie which Robert had elected to inhabit and to come into the exotic atmosphere of his rooms like a vague dream of Arabian nights translated into Japanese: the room of all shades of red, one wall deep crimson, the next rose-colour, and the last the faintest almond pink; the grey room where all was grey and for which he used to ransack Paris to find grey flowers; the bath-room where one gazed through filmy gauzes painted with fish into a great gloom that might have been under the waves. It was all queer, disturbing, baroque, yet individual and even beautiful, and as a transmutation of a set of unpromising attics into a tiny fairy palace, little short of a conjuring trick.'

These experiments seem to have been directed by the wish of Baudelaire: 'In an apartment decorated with cleverly-contrived pieces of furniture and seductive colours, one feels one's spirit brighten and one's being prepare itself for fortunate events. . . .' Perhaps certain recollections of Poe's 'The Domain of Arnheim' had also polarised this taste. Poe, in turn, was familiar with descriptions of Beckford's Fonthill Abbey and between Montesquiou and Beckford there were many points of resemblance: both were men of brilliant talents and difficult dispositions, both great collectors and bibliophiles. Count Robert's apartment owes no less a debt to the houses dreamed about by Gautier, to the pieces of furniture described by Hugo, and above all to the example of the Goncourt brothers. One can also quote a more mundane source for this mode of aesthetic decoration. *La Vie Parisienne* of July 1875 suggests various pieces of furniture for an apartment in which there must reign 'a perfect understanding between colours and things and where one is more delighted than astonished by the unheard-of amassing of bizarre and curious objects. . . . Thus Monsieur's bedroom is Chinese, the ceiling represents a vast aquarium, a huge silver moon illuminates the curtains, the pieces of furniture are only monsters and bats, and there are also gold fish in the hanging lamp.'

What then were Count Robert's contributions to this apartment at 41 Quai d'Orsay? Chiefly, the ability magnificently to realise the dreams of the poets in the works he amassed around him; the energy and flair of the collector; the need to leave his stamp on the outside world; and also perhaps the craving to meet someone

more or less star-born whose personality would open out amid
so much refinement. From the moment when the last picture had
been hung up in this apartment, furniture, which from Balzac
to Zola had played in novels a social role, began to play a psych-
ological one. There was to follow, in *Le Crépuscule des Dieux*, the
poisonous chamber which shrouded the incest of Hans-Ulric and
Christine; the drawing-rooms of Dorian Gray; and so many other
'troubling exquisitenesses' in the works of fin-de-siècle authors.

These aesthetes' apartments were to become pretentious night-
mares. Lorrain was to hang on his wall a plaster head daubed
with blood and with golden lilies in its hair. Loti was to mix
Louis XI and Suleyman the Magnificent, Oscar Wilde Greece
and Japan. It must be confessed that, if one looks at photographs
of the apartment on the Quai d'Orsay, one sees on the yellowing
bromide paper no more than an accumulation of incompatible
objects, the good with the bad, a bazaar piece beside a museum
one. Drapery made the eye mistake packing-cases for pieces of
furniture. Kimonos, Louis XV dresses and Spanish chasubles
were either artistically thrown over a piano or around an easel,
or concealed some useful but inartistic object. Count Robert had
yet to learn that taste is, above all, selection by suppression. But
the colours of the interior of his apartment must have been
delightful and novel at this period of red plush and mustard
damask. They are the same colours with which a young artisan
in Nancy, Émile Gallé, was then making experiments in his studio.
Gallé was to feel warmly grateful to Montesquiou, as though this
apartment were a hothouse bringing to their full development
objects which he was to describe as follows to the poet: 'A crystal
lamp, aubergine-violet in colour clouded with blood-red flashes
of rubies; purplish and livid plants, carved in vague relief and with
their edges tinted with a flame-red, both sombre and opaque.'

This extraordinary interior in fact attracted to Count Robert
writers who did not normally frequent society. Antique dealers,
upholsterers and bookbinders spread the news of his experiments
and his exacting demands. Had he any talent except as an interior
decorator? It was rumoured that he wrote poems on rare paper
for mysterious women. A magnificent and scandalous novel
would be the fruit of this curiosity, and long before Montesquiou
had published a single poem, was to make him one of the most
conspicuous figures of his day.

CHAPTER 4

Des Esseintes

Watcher, who prays unwonted nicotine
And magic Kummel may produce some vision,
A glimpse of mysteries but rarely seen,
A mirage of precision.

Prince of the aesthetes

A Rebours appeared in 1884 and was at once an immense success. The author, Joris-Karl Huysmans, had detached himself brilliantly from the naturalists. This delicate spirit had had enough of novels like *Pot-Bouille* and *L'Assommoir*; interested in every oddity and erudite in the manner of Flaubert, he wished also to be a 'modern' novelist—that is to say, perverse like Edmond de Goncourt in *La Faustin*. When Huysmans decided to abandon the suburbs for Byzantium, he knew nothing, insignificant civil servant that he was, of the life of Paris and was obliged conscientiously to swot up vice and elegance. Mallarmé was the first to speak to him about Montesquiou and his apartment. At once his curiosity and his aspirations took on a definite shape around this young aristocrat whom he glimpsed at the Goncourts'; fascinated, he asked a hundred questions of those who were close to him. Thus Count Robert de Montesquiou-Fezensac became the Duke Jean Floressas des Esseintes. The hero of *A Rebours,* incarnation of the Baudelairian ideal and of the decadent preoccupations of that period, was for a whole generation pre-eminently the fin-de-siècle man. Was he not perhaps the last of the romantic heroes?

Let us consider first of all the resemblances and the differences between the model and hero. Both have in common a great lineage, but so far from there being any fragile prettiness among the Montesquious, we have on the contrary Montluc and

d'Artagnan. Count Robert suffered from delicate health but that
came from his bourgeois mother. In actual garments worn they
resemble each other, but not in their kinds of elegance. Count
Robert could easily have dressed in white velvet suits or gold-
embroidered waist-coats; but would he have put 'a bouquet of
Parma violets at the opening of his shirt as a substitute for a tie'?
It is true that he summoned his tailor and his shirt-maker to
Quai d'Orsay and added to his commands detailed pronounce-
ments on the aesthetics of clothes; but that touch is from
Brummell.

When we get to furniture, Huysmans' debt is very great:
'Once the panelling was ready, he had the beading and the tall
plinths painted a deep indigo, a lacquered indigo like that used
by coach-builders for the panels of coaches. The ceiling, slightly
rounded, and also covered with morocco leather, opened, like a
huge oval window in its setting of orange skin, a circle of the
firmament in royal blue silk, in the middle of which swiftly rose
up silver seraphs, embroidered by the guild of Cologne weavers
for an ancient cope'; and later: 'He limited himself [sic] to scattering the floor with skins of wild animals and blue fox furs and to
installing near a massive 15th century money-changer's table
deep arm-chairs with side-pieces and an old pulpit from a chapel
in wrought iron—one of those antique lecterns on which the
deacon formerly put the antiphonary and which now supported
one of the heavy folios of the *Glossarium mediae et infimae latinitatis*
of du Gange.' In the place of this folio Count Robert in fact had
one of Baudelaire's poems in manuscript. The whole Quai
d'Orsay apartment is found again in the *Pavillon* of des Esseintes,
not excluding even the windows: 'The cracked, bluish panes of
the windows, interspersed with faulty pieces of glass, the protuberances of which were dotted with gold, cut off the view . . .
and only allowed the faintest of light to penetrate. The windows
themselves were, in turn, decorated with curtains cut from old
stoles, the darkened and as it were smoky gold of which was
extinguished in a thread of an almost dead russet colour.' There is
even a bejewelled tortoise—in fact the invention of Judith
Gautier. The death of this wretched creature under the weight of
rare stones has a symbolic meaning. In his description of this piece
of walking jewellery, Huysmans identifies himself so well with
his hero that he writes as Montesquiou might have written: 'The

sapphirine that lights up bluish phosphorus fires on a chocolate background, a dead brown; the aquamarine, glaucous green; the balas-ruby, vinegary-pink; the Sudermanie ruby, a pale slate. Their feeble flames were enough to light up the shadows of the shell but not to eclipse the glimmers of the stones which they circled with a fine garland of vague fires.'

In the library were all the books in sumptuous bindings which, fifty years later, were to appear at the sale of Montesquiou's effects: Petronius next to Ernest Hello, Ruysbroek the Admirable next to Swedenborg. On the walls were the paintings of the artists that Count Robert passionately admired: Moreau, represented by his Salomé, the famous description of which would serve as a breviary for fin-de-siècle eroticism: 'The deity symbolic of indestructible Luxury, the goddess of immortal hysteria, cursed Beauty, elect among all goddesses for the catalepsy that stiffened her flesh and hardened her muscles. The Beast—monstrous, indifferent, irresponsible, callous'; Odilon Redon, 'in a frame of rough pear-wood piped with gold'; even Bresdin, whom so few people knew and one of whose engravings Robert would describe as follows: 'All creatures hairy and feathered, veined like marble with an enigmatic light that picked out the surface like the corroding pallor of moonlight.' The bouquets for which des Esseintes pillaged tropical hot-houses are even more weird than those with which our Narcissus paid honour to his own beauty. As for the acrobat who troubled des Esseintes—is this not an indiscreet allusion to that La Rochefoucauld horseman whose photograph Count Robert had enlarged? In the transposition made by Huysmans there is even more intuition than indiscretion. Des Esseintes and Montesquiou, with whom Huysmans had never exchanged two words, have the same admirations: Mallarmé, whom this book made famous; the *Isis* of Villiers de l'Isle Adam; Gaspard de la Nuit; and even Judith Gautier.

None the less, what a host of differences there are for those who know the model! Count Robert was, above all, a sociable person, who brought an immense talent for improvisation to the service of being amusing. Certainly he had melancholic periods, but fundamentally he liked to laugh and to make others laugh—at family dinners the footmen could hardly keep straight faces on the occasions when he deigned to amuse his relations. Montesquiou was only a misanthrope at the end of his life: he was never enough of one, one might think, seeing him sparkle at some absurd *salon*. His motto would be the sufficiently elastic one of 'To the happy few, rather than des Esseintes' one of 'Anywhere out of this world'.* Montesquiou was pugnacious: after having broken his first lances against the Philistines of his family, he became the champion of Mallarmé and the supporter of Verlaine. Unlike the duke, whom syphilis had reduced to a state of neurasthenia, Robert had a will of iron, and if he could be cruel in his inter-course with society and impatient of stupidity or pretension, there was nothing sadistic about him; the idea of corrupting a poor young man or of throwing cakes to children for the pleasure of watching them fight over them would have horrified him. Huysmans is nearer the truth when he suggests that des Esseintes had two temptations: paederasty and diabolism; these were also Montesquiou's two temptations. To give the lie to the novelist, the poet on the one hand became more worldly and more brilliant and resolved to show that he was capable of more than just designing an apartment; and on the other hand he repressed the deepest needs of his nature, and avoided scandal and black magic.

Count Robert's reputation had reached Huysmans when the latter was taking his very first steps in the literary world towards the end of the seventies. Coppée, Dr Robin and Bourget often spoke of the remarkable young man.

Even more interesting, really affectionate, was Judith Gautier. Because of her imposing beauty and her milky complexion, Mme de Poilly called her 'My white elephant'. For Wagner she was 'my living excess' and to her husband Catulle Mendès 'my brother of the Holy Grail'. Curiously, this fervent Wagnerian wrote delightful works on oriental themes, and for the Baroness's theatre composed some pieces drawn from Japanese legends. Count Robert quickly became an assiduous visitor to the apart-ment in the Rue du Berri, with its clutter of bronze buddhas, pottery elephants and paper lanterns. A marionette theatre stood behind the grand piano; a snake curled round an incense-burner before being made to serve as a bracelet for Judith; and a tortoise sparkling with rhinestones crawled about between ornamental vases containing flower-pots. Low divans and silk cushions are propitious for confidences. Gautier's daughter spoke of Wagner; of Hugo, who had also loved her; of Flaubert, who had amazed

* Both phrases are in English in the original. Trans.

her by going off one day to take lessons in magic; and of the Goncourts, to whom she boasted that she had revealed Japan as early as 1865. Perhaps among his women friends Count Robert had a more tender affection for the Marquise de Casa-Fuerte; perhaps Countess Potocka amused him more; certainly Countess Greffulhe was more beautiful. But none was as interesting as Judith; interesting and also useful, for it is said that she knew everyone in the literary world. Not only did she introduce Count Robert to things Japanese, but she was a link between him and two people who played leading roles in the mythology of the century that was closing: Ludwig II of Bavaria and Sarah Bernhardt.

Fin-de-Siècle Valhalla

The king and the actress brought to the last third of the nineteenth century, invaded by machines, divided by socialism and led by capitalism, a folly which went beyond taste, whether good or bad, a grandeur sometimes pasteboard but which inspired deep enthusiasms, and a passion for Beauty which enabled poets to exist in their epoch—in much the same way as saints helped the righteous to live in the Dark Ages. Ludwig was to decadent romanticism what Byron had been to triumphant romanticism. Wagner's friend told Count Robert about performances in the grotto and the King's caprices; described the castles which reared up on some mountain peak or in the middle of a lake; and spoke of the golden sleighs which, driven by handsome coachmen, travelled at night.

He collected photographs of the king, had framed an envelope addressed in his hand, and kept the written recollections of an actor invited to the castle of Linderhof, which in their fantastic naïveté seemed taken from Jules Verne. He copied out a letter addressed to Wagner in 1863, which ended as follows: 'until death, until the beyond, in the empire of the worlds of night, I remain always your very faithful . . .'

The character of Ludwig II grew in the young man's imagination exactly as it did in those of Verlaine, of Elémir Bourges and of Laforgue. For that generation castles in Spain were castles in Bavaria. Montesquiou thought that he was much nearer the king than these writers; after all, he was also handsome and from a quasi-royal family. Often he justified his passions and his extravagances by reference to this gloomy example.

During the years in which Ludwig II lost his looks and his reason to become a legend, the other myth of the century was building up her own legend with an infallible sense of publicity. The Byzantine or Florentine palaces in which the world was to see her blossom provided a setting like those of the king—but in cardboard. What Ludwig was to the poets, Sarah Bernhardt was for the public at large; and, extravagant creature of beauty that she was, always rushing to extremes, she too had poets of her own. Count Robert came to know her when she was quite young, through Judith Gautier and above all through François Coppée, that sentimental and revengeful little bourgeois, whose Le Passant foretold the triumphs of Rostand. In a tight-fitting page's costume, slender and crowned with a mass of curly blonde hair, this twenty-five-year-old woman was already a legend. As Dona Sol she had Hugo, an old man, at her feet; as la Dame aux Camélias she won the Prince of Wales as an admirer. Her tantrums terrified the Théâtre-Français, her follies delighted the journalists. She was a sculptress, she hunted wild animals, she slept in a padded coffin, she dressed in men's clothes. Above all she had a remarkable voice, which gave to poetry a magic that had been lost since the death of Rachel.

For thirty years Sarah was to represent the modern woman or, rather, the hermaphrodite who haunted the end of the century. In turns she was Le Passant, Lorenzaccio, Hamlet and finally L'Aiglon. At first thin, with hollow cheeks and arched nose, her body seemed to bend as though in obedience to the canons of Art Nouveau; her hair was like the helmet of a Medusa, her gestures evocative of creepers or snakes. Every picture-gallery had at least one portrait of Sarah. Carolus Duran painted her sunk in a tomb of cushions, Dagnan-Bouveret as a Pierrot. Then Louise Abbema drew her profile and Clairin did a three-quarter length portrait of her under palms. Narcissism and publicity went hand in hand. Dumas wrote L'Étrangère for her and Sardou Fédora. Later she was to devote herself entirely to history with her Gismondas and her Theodoras, Tosca and even Saint Theresa.

Moreau and Mallarmé, the demi-gods

Ludwig II and Sarah did not appear in *A Rebours*, but this book revealed to the public two arcane artists whom Robert had known while still in his youth: Gustave Moreau and Stéphane Mallarmé. The gems, the brocades, the transparent veils, the garlands of flowers mixed with pearls, Byzantine or barbarian decoration: all the things that Sarah had discovered through her friend Count Robert and was now going to vulgarise, Gustave Moreau had already been lavishing on his canvases for the last twenty years. Count Robert turned the interpreter of Dumas away from dresses by Worth and fusty upholstery towards this treasure looted from some greco-Buddhist tetralogy and now displayed on the persons of ravishingly handsome archers or criminal queens. Art Nouveau owes as much to the sinuous lines of Salomé as to the fantastic entwinings of Sarah. One drawing kept with the hundreds in the Moreau museum shows this art at its inception. It is a drawing representing a strelitzia well set on its rigid stem. One might mistake the long black train of the pistil darting under the thick corolla for a cobra. The painter inscribed in a corner 'A flower given by Count Robert de Montesquiou 2 February 1887'.

As early as 1885 the friendship had begun, 'Monsieur', wrote Moreau to Montesquiou, 'I have often heard you talked about; I knew your delicate and exquisite taste for artistic and spiritual things; I even knew that you had honoured me with a little benevolent artistic sympathy.'

Princess Chimay had taken her very young cousin to the studio in the Rue de la Rochefoucauld; 'Since when have you not had the advantage over me', wrote Count Robert in 1887, 'luminously, mysteriously, almost mystically? I remember—am I not right?—Oedipus at the Salon, at any rate some Jasons, some Medeas and his strange suggestion for a child . . . unforgettable.' Moreau was courteous and gentle and lived in a simple house (the huge studios were built only just before his death to protect his legacy of paintings). In front of walls covered with rough sketches of massacres or equivocal visions, Moreau and the young Montesquiou talked about their mutual love of certain master-pieces such as Mantegna's *Saint Sebastian* and Delacroix's *Sardanapalus*. 'Moreau remained obdurate in his conviction that the reproduction of ugliness could not make a beautiful work of art; he could forgive neither Manet nor Degas for the use to which they put their gifts—for him all the more sacrilegeous because he recognised that those gifts were very real—and when pressed to explain his judgments, one sensed that he was nearer to lavishing affectionate abuse on those two painters than to discussing art with an esteemed friend and eminent colleague like Bouguereau.' (Montesquiou's Preface to the catalogue of an exhibition of the works of Moreau.)

Later Mme Howland, friend of Degas, who lived next door to Moreau, took the painter to the Rue Franklin.

In a poem Count Robert conjured up Moreau's heroines:

> Salomé, whom a stupor of the blood holds still
> And Helen, standing in the evening that descends
> Upon the infinite sorrows that her beauty reaped . . .

Moreau felt that he was well understood when Montesquiou underlined the irresponsibility of the painter's creations, writing to his friend Rupp: 'This bored, fantastic woman with the nature of an animal finds delight—a rare thing for her, so much is she disgusted with all ways of satisfying her desires—in seeing her enemy in the dust.' Painter and poet were as profoundly misogynic as each other, and this woman, always cruel and always protected by a carapace of jewels, obsessed them both. Just before meeting Whistler, Robert thought that Moreau was like a Socrates, begetting inspiration, a wizard initiator: 'Dear master and dear priest', he wrote to him. 'You constitute and you create the integral part of my intellectual and esoteric breathing. I evoke, in order to dream about them, many sacred subjects touched on that certain evening at your house in the uncertain and august twilight . . .' Following the painter's example, Count Robert reburnished the poems that Salomé had inspired him to write when very young: 'You said that on even the most thoughtful of artists a great and striking epoch unconsciously imprints the stamp of its claw: the stamp of serene impersonality in the beautiful.' Count Robert described the work of Moreau with the extremely 1900 epithet 'unfading'.

Mallarmé, being too intellectual for a visual person like Montesquiou, played a far less important role in the Count's thinking than Moreau and had little influence on his poetry, unless to excuse, by his own example, affectations and obscurities. However, there was a keen sympathy between the two men. Certainly they were very dissimilar, the one being discreet and the other ostentatious, but they had in common the excellence of their manners. They could have become acquainted through Judith Gautier, but it was in fact in the studio where Charles Cros carried out his experiments in colour photography for the Duc de Chaulnes that Montesquiou was introduced to the poet whom he admired more because of his taste for quality and the difficult, than because of any real poetical affinity between them. Mallarmé, too, was at once charmed by Montesquiou's elegance: he liked the luxurious and the unusual. Perhaps he saw a similarity between this young Maecenas and William Beckford, for whose oriental story *Vathek* he had composed a preface. There was in both men the same taste for curios, the same knowledge of painting, the same passion to create around themselves a setting that matched their dreams. Certainly the top rooms of the mansion on the Quai d'Orsay had none of the immensity of Fonthill Abbey; but in them also one found the same contradictory mixture: a fervent quest for the past and a passion for whatever was new.

Two or three times Mallarmé was invited to admire some new discovery, some new book-binding. In spite of his exquisite politeness, the poet was, for once, indiscreet, and he briefed Huysmans both about the marvels of the apartment and about the peculiarities of his host. Thus it came about that his admiration of Mallarmé caused Montesquiou to be confused with the sinister des Esseintes. Count Robert was to suffer for his friendship with a writer deemed to be scandalous. 'Young Montesquiou'—the words are Juliette Adam's—'is a modern in the extreme and a fanatical admirer of a hypercritical poet who, according to him, is the chief ornament of contemporary literature. Few initiates know his worth, and his glory is limited to the bosom of an élite who are worthy of appreciating him.' The irony of the journalist echoes, at an interval of twelve years, the sneering of the Jesuit at Count Robert's first literary steps; she goes on in her work on Parisian society (published under the pseudonym of Count Vassili), to provide this portrait of Count Robert: 'Monsieur de Montesquiou also himself writes pretty little poems, of which copies inscribed in gothic letters on vellum circulate in the most select coteries. He cleverly introduces into them adjectives invented by the master. They have caught, it would seem, to the life the sharpness of a sentiment and from it they produce an excitement in senses brought to the degree of refinement that is needed if one is to savour the adorable linguistic mannerisms of the Deliquescents.'

With the appearance of Mme Adam's* article the Count heard, for the first time, the hiss of slander. In future he was to cultivate an insolence that was scathing enough to scatter the vipers from his path; but none the less he had to be careful not to parade his relationships with writers of the too conspicuous kind. He would come to prefer painters. Still, he never withdrew, like des Esseintes, from a world which disgusted him; his aesthetic experiments were to remain public. At home in the fin-de-siècle Valhalla of Sarah, of Moreau, of Mallarmé, Count Robert was to sustain, for nearly two decades in the life of Paris, the same role which Klingsor played in the Wagnerian universe: keeper of a garden in which the flowers he extolled were women of the world as well as poets, ballerinas as well as great painters.

---

* A journalist who, in the 'eighties, published three works entitled *The Society of Paris*, *The Society of London*, and *The Society of St Petersburg*.

CHAPTER 5

Seraphitus

A lady whom I loved
Dropped from her delicate fingers
On to a piece of exotic wood
Violet-coloured flowers.
(Passiflora)

Spiritual embraces

THE GROSS luxury of bankers and courtesans—this Second
Empire prolonged into the 'eighties, of which the weekly *La Vie
Parisienne* was the arbiter—caused des Esseintes to flee to his
laboratory and nauseated delicate sensibilities. Thus Prince
Edmond de Polignac wrote to Count Robert about the Jockey
Club: 'Blinded by the thick, smoky atmosphere and bewildered by
the still thicker atmosphere of the talk.' Count Robert had a real
horror of the men of his class, whose only preoccupations were
women and hunting. Happily he found in his sister-in-law a
confidante to whom he sent amusing reports of life in Paris,
interspersed with mystic reflections. He chose dresses for her to
wear and books for her to read. At Charnizay, in order to have
something to do during a boring exile to the country, he photographed the thin young woman in the style of Fantin-Latour.
Together they made bouquets of flowers, which were also photographed and then reproduced on blue paper. On the Riviera
Robert and Passiflora ('Passion Flower' as he nicknamed her)
escaped in a barouche from the frightful ornate villas and from the
promenades on which Grand Dukes and fast women rubbed
shoulders with each other, to walk together on deserted beaches.
They read philosophy, the Christian spiritualism of Hello re-
assuring his sister-in-law who felt she was so near to death, and

studied Michelet and Hugo. The young woman listened to Robert's first poems and inspired him to write several that are quite as good as those of Sully Prudhomme. In the company of the invalid the poet developed a macabre frivolity, which was one of his favourite sources of inspiration. In this vein he wrote one of his most famous poems, *Le Coucher de la Morte*.

But in Paris, while he was still quite young, in 1876, Montesquiou charmed the most brilliant, the most eccentric and above all the most modern woman of the time, Sarah Bernhardt, and received from the actress a mass of notes hastily scribbled on grey-bordered visiting-cards. He was addressed as 'little brother', 'friend of my heart', 'my soul', 'my forever'. Sometimes anxiety was expressed: 'Yesterday you seemed less fond of me. I deeply love you always . . .'

Sarah lived surrounded by aged admirers such as Marshal Canrobert and Émile de Girardin. In turn she loved Dr Robin, Dr Pozzi and even the tedious Schlumberger;* it is possible that she also had a child by Prince de Ligne and an affair with Louise Abbema.† Count Robert was handsome, he recited poetry well, very well: she was infatuated with him for a season. He confessed to her that he had loved her ever since he had seen her in a fairy play to which he had been taken at the age of twelve. As much in love with each other's voices as with each other's faces, they recited together Hugo and Gautier, the latter's poem *Contralto* exactly suiting their emotions:

> Is this a young man? Is this a woman?
> A goddess or a god?
> Love, fearing to commit an infamy,
> Hesitates and delays its avowal.

They were the same height and had similar profiles and hair. Both put on the tight costumes of *Le Passant,* so that the photographer Nadar might perpetuate the disturbing resemblance; they improvised some bizarre comedy, which finished in their rolling about on the cushions. This Narcissistic embrace was not a happy one. It is said that after it Robert went home and vomited for twenty-four hours.

* A Byzantinologist, less famous for his works than for the size of his feet, and a great enemy of Proust.

† A woman painter who used to dress as a man and smoke cigars.

The affair continued on a more ethereal plane: 'I love you with a tenderness both sweet and infinite, I love you with a love both material and divine. I am certain that my life hangs on yours', wrote *Doña Sol*.

Sarah had forgotten the unhappy episode and, intelligent woman that she was, was always to remain friendly to this man who had left his mark on her. Was not his advice about the choice of an intonation, a gown or a stage-set precious to her? Sometimes Count Robert attempted to check the actress's rampantly bad taste: thus he took her to antique-dealers to choose chasubles out of which to make tea-gowns or lamp-shades, or to Bing's, where old Goncourt glimpsed her, disguised in a long rain coat, choosing some piece of Japanese lacquer. The poet showed the actress Moreau's pictures and at once she was tottering about under the weight of the precious stones and the flowers that lay about in the blood of Salomé and Helen. When she acted the role of Izeyl, he gave her a pink coral necklace that had belonged to the empress of Brazil.

The press noticed this influence. When Sarah returned from a tour and the whole of Paris crowded round the Saint Lazare Station, one report said: 'Deliciously blonde in a dress of pale sea-green, a colour as dear to M. de Montesquiou as to Mlle Abbema, she bowed to the right and to the left.' One notes that the influence was attributed not merely to Montesquiou but to another as well.

Montesquiou offered to his young English friend, Graham Robertson, a picture of Sarah Bernhardt in her coffin, and later presented him to the actress, with whom he struck up a lasting friendship.

Count Robert was the lover of the soul, the master of spiritual embraces—as it might have been phrased at a time when a whole seraphic vocabulary, a complete way of immaterial existence, had emerged in reaction against the vulgar sensuality of Parisian life and the coarseness of the naturalists. The best examples of this style were produced by a friend and contemporary of Montesquiou's. To us now Paul Bourget's phrases seem highly equivocal; perhaps in their day they were no more than fashionable. At all events we have already seen how this future academician and pillar of the Church was intoxicated by the elegance of the Count. Was Montesquiou for him Rubempré or the Duchesse de Langeais?

One hardly knows. One can only wonder how far such a friendship went when the novelist's numerous letters seem, even when
one accounts for the manners of the period, passionate. However,
whether these compliments were due to snobbery or to love, it
seems that Robert's response to them was no more than a sentimental affection in the German style.

These two men, both about twenty-five, often returned together
from the Baronne de Poilly's house: 'Prince of returns on foot to
the deserted abode, will you come to my phalanstery of solitude
this evening?' They talked of Barbey. Count Robert quoted these
words of the master, after a short affair with Mme Rattazzi de
Rute, an ageing beauty: 'She is less hard of skin than of hearing'.
And his friend replied with this distich of Mallarmé:

> What topaz-coloured or dry chignon
> Has now subdued Champsaur?

Robert made up a thousand similar pieces of nonsense. His
friend, who had a respect for society, was shocked. But on the day
following he wrote to him: 'Yesterday I ran to the Bois with this
green-eyed she-wolf, nostalgic for your elegance and your
virginity.' Robert, who for a long time had been bullied by his
family, suddenly realised the power of his charm. He became
mocking and capricious. The companion of the 'returns on foot'
wrote him this beautiful letter: 'Strange friend, Do you always
knit your brow as at the end of that evening party when I displeased you? If I explained myself to you, not as I am but as I see
myself to be, you would pity a person who, nearly twelve hours
out of twelve, does the complete opposite of what he would like
to do. Believe me, there is little elegance of which I have not
dreamed without at the same time craving artlessness. Unhappily
life—this sting-ray, which is not *Esther Heureuse*—deadens my
nerves. I would like to have savage blood so as not to feel a lump
in my throat when I see the sunset at the corner of the Bois de
Boulogne swarming with broughams and victorias. It is a purely
plebeian point of view and I reproach myself firmly. But what can
be done?

> While thinking of me, sniff one of those extravagantly delicate
> handkerchiefs permeated with an aphrodisiac scent that Sarah
> must like. If only fate were different and it were possible to
> have feelings of this kind. . . .

The love of literature was perhaps the only tie between the two writers; it was in any case a pretext for a meeting:

Seraphitus . . . If tomorrow, Sunday, you are at the corner of the Rue Cassini and the Avenue de l'Observatoire, you will find me there paying my devotions to that street where the great Balzac wrote *La Peau de Chagrin*. From there we will go and visit the desolate tomb of Albert's friend. Yours.*

A mystic Narcissus

Seraphitus . . . Let us re-read Balzac's mystic novel. Does not the description of the ambiguous angel who descends on the Norwegian fjord correspond to the twin image of Sarah and Montesquiou?

His body, thin and delicate like a woman's, affirms that his is one of those natures which, though feeble in appearance, are possessed of a force matching their desires and are strong at the time for strength. Of ordinary height, Seraphitus grew taller when he faced anyone, as though he wished to bound forward. His hair, curled by a fairy hand and looking as if a puff of wind had raised it, added to the illusion that his ethereal attitude produced; but this effortless bearing came more from a spiritual phenomenon than from any corporeal trick. The head looked down disdainfully like a sublime bird of prey, whose cries disturb the air; it submitted like the turtle-dove whose voice pours tenderness to the depths of silent woods.

The young men read together the chapter in which Balzac gives an exposition of the theories of Swedenborg. Robert found his credo in these exalted pages. Until his death he was to believe in another world with which certain rare people, a sort of spiritualistic aristocracy, could communicate: a poetic order of the Beyond, the expression of which he was to find in the archangels of William Blake and the translucent apparitions on the sides of Gallé vases. The following phrase of the Swedish visionary, quoted by Balzac, was constantly in his mind: 'To some death is a victory, to others it is a defeat.' This man, who was so hard to

* This last word is in English in the original. Trans.

living people, so capricious, was to maintain with the dead whom he loved a tender and constant intercourse, either by thought or, in moments of depression, through the offices of mediums. Montesquiou always thought that he possessed a part of the Revelation, and this conviction expressed itself in a sovereign scorn for any ridicule he aroused. Handsome and virgin, he considered himself to be a magician. Did he not ask his friend Georges Hugo if he might wear for a whole day, as a poetic sacrament, a ring of Victor Hugo? On leaving college he talked with his cousin Antoine de la Rochefoucauld of the mysteries that would be studied and consequently debased in the magazine *Le Coeur*. Perhaps Montesquiou was, after the Duc de Fréneuse, the model for the Marquis de Tournesol in a novel that mocked the Rosicrusians; but he was never counted as being one of Péladan's disciples. Wagner, Swedenborg, Huysmans himself: all the spirituality of the 'eighties derived from the north. Confronted with realism, people felt a desire for dematerialisation: a trend which Burne-Jones and the first lithographs of Odilon Redon were already expressing.

Burne-Jones might have used as a model a pale and blond Englishman of twenty, Graham Robertson, whom Montesquiou first met at St Moritz, and who already knew 'everybody' in London. The two men became the closest friends and went on long mountain walks together, the languid French aesthete becoming a creature of the woods, whimsical, faun-like, a tireless walker, responsive to all the moods of nature.

Precious ideals

It seems extremely difficult to reconcile esotericism with worldliness; but Robert managed to do so wonderfully well. He was aided in this *tour de force* by a woman friend of his sister-in-law who was to dominate his thought and inspire his poems for several years.

This exquisite young man found the *odor di femmina* which was indispensable to him, tenderness without ulterior motive and delightful wit in the Marquise de Casa-Fuerte, née Flavie de Balserano, half-Italian and half-French, young widow of a member of the illustrious family of Alvarez de Toledo. Entering society at a time when the fashion was for curves, she arranged her ash-blonde hair in the same style as the Empress Eugénie, who liked her very much and with whom she was distantly related. Greta Garbo in *Anna Karenina* gave us an idea of what she was like: a pale beauty with almost sharp features and an intangible grace. Mme de Casa-Fuerte always dressed in black and white and lived in a simple apartment in the Rue de Bassano; one was always certain to find her in at the end of the afternoon. Too serious to be surrounded by a multitude of friends, she kept round her all those who demand of a woman not so much pleasure as elegance; a very exalted and very respectable court of admirers, the doyen of which was Prince Edmond de Polignac and the youngest member Pierre Loti, now back in France between two voyages. Mme de Casa-Fuerte succeeded Passiflora in Count Robert's heart. Together they shared an enthusiasm for Flaubert. Pale and distant, the Marquise was a 'sidereal person', a sacred priestess of the moon, a star whom Count Robert had adored since the nights at Courtanvaux.

He spent hours at this charming woman's house and asked nothing of her except that she let him draw her. He imagined there were bats and orchids entangled in her hair; he outlined her profile against backgrounds of violet ink sprinkled with gold; he buried her elongated silhouette in undergrowth reminiscent of the grottoes of the Rhine Maidens. Robert de Montesquiou's letters to the Marquise de Casa-Fuerte are models for those soulfully precious women who go each summer to Bayreuth and each spring to Florence. They felt that they were bound to each other by the memory of his sister-in-law, Passiflora, who had died in 1887. 'The person whom you loved and who loved you is nothing more than a dream.' Count Robert placed this friendship on a plane sufficiently exalted to prevent himself from again being found in an embarrassing situation. This was easier with the Marquise than with the actress: 'Not at all is the flesh corrupted in the transitory and deliquescent world.' He became a real director of conscience, but the extravagance of his ideas was still apparent under his mysticism. 'We must hope that our disappointments and despairs, amassed, hoarded and garnered into the domain of the heavenly creditor, will be given in exchange for our endurances and patiences, in an unconscious barter that will redeem us from our frailties.' Perhaps Donna Flavia had temptations, perhaps she had grown a little tired of soaring; there followed a coldness between them.

But the clouds quickly dispersed and the post brought on exquisite silvered or nacreous paper all the flowers of the new rhetoric:

Dear Eurythmie, No one, not even I, would know how to go deep enough into the mystery that lies palpitating and at the same time foreclosed in this heart of hearts that has been pierced a thousand times.

It was only a matter of 'foreclosed souls' and 'prestigious idealities'.

The divine countess and the little baroness

But with the years the fervour abated. Aesthetes are in fact faithful to one kind of face, to one style of life. Once the perfection that seduced them has passed, they begin to seek for it again in others. The over-sensual Frenchman is as rarely an aesthete as he is a dandy. Robert de Montesquiou, who was both, was to join with two or three women whom he found to be his equals, in representing for a dazzled but more often bewildered Paris and to the extreme misfortune of creatures of all the sexes who were excited about literature and fashion, the myth of Seraphitus and Seraphita.

The first of these chosen souls and the one who remained so until the poet's death was the Comtesse de Greffulhe, who assumed her position when the Marquise de Casa-Fuerte began to fade out of the picture. She was to follow her cousin in his enthusiasms, help his crusades and write to him many years later: 'I have never been understood except by you and the sun.' This beautiful woman reflected about things and committed her thoughts to paper. 'I returned from the opera and was astonished with the transfiguration that the crowd made me undergo. I don't believe that there has ever been in the world a pleasure comparable to that of a woman who feels that she is being looked at by everybody and has joy and energy transmitted to her.'

Countess Greffulhe always had the calm assurance of perfection. One day Count Robert read to a few intimate friends a eulogy of this beauty in dithyrambics, which ended with the line: 'Beautiful lily, whose black pistils are your eyes.' The subject of the poem turned to her sister and said simply, 'Absolutely right, isn't it, Ghislaine?'

There were many other candidates for the role of Seraphita: among them the Princesse de Léon (the future Duchesse de Rohan), who was good, rich and enthusiastic, but not beautiful enough and a little too much of a blue-stocking; and Comtesse Jean de Montebello, very beautiful but not rich enough—the angels must not be troubled by material circumstances. There was also a new arrival on the Parisian scene who, because of her English friends, interested Montesquiou for a while. This was Baroness Deslandes. Born an Oppenheim, this little person who had first been Comtesse Fleury and was subsequently to become Princesse Robert de Broglie, was the ambassadress of the aesthetic movement in Paris. 'She had languid eyes, a mouth with a tenderly sad expression, an outthrust bosom, and arms that gestured widely like wings heavy with rain.' She would receive her guests lying on a precious carpet beneath her portrait by Burne-Jones, in the company of a bronze toad which she fed each evening with her jewels. In 1885 no one could be more modern than Mme Deslandes. The 'Jewesses of Art' and La Potocka were either too healthy or liked official society too much to be the ancestors of the surrealist ladies or even to be the leading ladies of 1900. England herself never produced anyone more ethereal or more sophisticated than this little German who, a myopic Lorelei, peered at people through a monocle rimmed with opals. Draped in vaporous tea-gowns, she seemed to have no other occupation than posing for painters while listening to poets. Wilde brought her armfuls of lilies. The very young Henri Bataille hardly dared shake hands with her; but she very much wanted to teach some refinements to this little provincial sent to her by Maurice Barrès: 'But, caro, it is too frightful,' she confided to Robert. 'He wears grey underpants!' Yes, the baroness was a soul; she who said to her last husband, 'You would be the perfection of beauty if it weren't for that little thing you have there. . . .'

CHAPTER 6

The Japanese of Passy

Fish, crane, eagle, flower that a bird bends,
Tortoise, iris, peony, anemone and sparrow;
All the beautiful Japanese pictures embroidered in gold and in silk . . .
All the kakemonos! . . .

The chased daggers of slander

THE SUCCESS of *A Rebours* brought fame not only to Huysmans but also to Mallarmé, Moreau and Redon, the artists dear to des Esseintes. To Montesquiou, however, it brought a renown bordering on scandal. At twenty-eight he was a personality in Paris. The chorus of ladies who accompanied his first steps in society had now been swelled by the wives of bankers and a hundred other women as mad about modernity as about the nobility: Bourget used Darwinian jargon for these women and called them 'the struggle-for-high-lifers'.* We now enter upon a period of triumphant snobbery, for many had rapidly acquired the means but not the education to reach a superior stratum in society. For a third of a century our des Esseintes was to be the guide, alternately inspired and sarcastic, of this society. Let him appear at a five o'clock tea and at once he was surrounded by a swarm of corseted, heavily adorned and garrulous women. One notices, for its sartorial interest, the harmony between the iron-grey of the tail-coat and the mouse-grey of the gaiters, the boldness of the mauve-grey gloves which call attention to the pearl-grey waistcoat embroidered with chrysanthemums and the stone with a rare name that is pinned into the dove-grey tie.

'All this grey! Are you in mourning, Count?' asked a foolish woman.

* In French 'struggle for highlifeuses'. Trans.

'Yes! For the dead leaves.'

'How divine! The dead leaves!' The answer reached the modest ladies and the caustic dowagers at the farthest end of the drawing-room; that same evening it would be repeated at a dozen dinners. Each lady wanted to quote some witticism she had heard: 'When the baroness became a convert, he declared, "She has forgotten all her sins and only remembers mine"'; and 'When a very malicious woman friend in Switzerland passed away, the Count sighed, "The air of St Moritz has become much less *biting* since she breathed her last".' If he was accused of slander or snobbery (this last word was gaining currency at that time) there was always a lady ready with the assurance: 'But no, he has so much heart. I was made to read some really touching poems.' 'What, he writes?' 'For a few friends,' the initiate would retort, putting on airs. It was, in any case, well known that the Count, when animated by compliments, would compose couplets about the guests of the week before, which made those of that week wonder what would eventually be said about themselves. Was the conversation about 'Gégé'—Comte Primoli, who would sponge on his cousin Princesse Mathilde (Robert insisted on calling her Princesse de San Donato, ignoring her divorce)? At once Montesquiou tossed into the air:

> The greater softness Mathilde shows
> For Primoli it harder grows.

He did not even spare his own family—after all, Elisabeth's husband did not like him.

> This golden Count (with o or not)
> Greater than him I know not what.

On the other hand, for his beautiful cousin who arrived wearing a veil, he improvised:

> See her come, Countess Greffulhe!
> Two dark glances swathed in tulle.

'Enchanter! Divine!' rejoined the ladies, while the men hid their noses in their glasses. Certain people might protest if Montesquiou attacked the perfect Mme Gauthereau, great official beauty of the day and the Mme X of Sargent's famous picture:

> To keep her figure she is now obliged to force it
> Not to the mould of Canova but a corset.

But society could not contain itself from laughing when he taunted the imposing wife of the Ambassador Montebello, whose conversation was reminiscent of an editorial in *Le Temps*:

> Political and transcendental though she be,
> Aliette remains a busy-body, busy bee.

His train of bustle-wearing sirens drew Count Robert into grottoes covered in plush, where the furniture was too small and the ornaments were too big. In the really 'stylish' mansions, among the green plants, family furniture was swamped by junk; Gothic pieces were placed next to Moorish ones; tassels and fringes debased Louis XIV treasures. Never was taste so low as in this decade, which worsened the confusion of the Second Empire but which lacked its gaiety. In the year 1884 the ideal of elegance was, in the opinion of Montesquiou, the portrait of Mme Gauthereau; that masterpiece, the only one, of Sargent, prophetic of all the sophisticated chic of *Vogue* and of expensive *haute couture*.

While examining this picture, Montesquiou met a young, dark and bearded Breton: Helleu. This excellent disciple of the Impressionists abandoned their style to accommodate himself to the demands of the *salons* to which Count Robert introduced him. In pastel, in red chalk and above all in dry-point etching, taught to him by Tissot, Helleu sketched all the beautiful women friends of this connoisseur who, at their first encounter, had bought from him some engravings for 100 francs. Helleu was invited to Mme Greffulhe's at Boisboudran. Robert brought to his studio the immensely wealthy Princesse de Scey-Montbeliard* (soon to be Polignac) who in turn paid a visit with some very pretty women 'among whom was a captive with red hair'. At the Goncourts the young man studied Watteau and Hiroshige. Then his wife Alice became his best model, and the Helleus would tolerate only the white-and-grey walls of the Louis XVI period. With gloved finger Robert would decide at his friends' houses what could, in all strictness, be kept, and what must be burnt or, better still, given away to cousins.

---

* Born Wineretta Singer, heiress to a sewing-machine fortune and an ardent patroness of music. Died in London in 1942.

Long before Gide, in fact, Count Robert uttered the famous cry, 'Families, I detest you!' for the Montesquious did not in the least appreciate having des Esseintes for a cousin. They winced when these arrogant words were retailed to them: 'Our ancestors having exhausted the spirit of the family, my father inherited only a sense of grandeur. For my brother there was nothing; but he had the courtesy to disappear. As for me, I will have the glory of adding to the ducal bonnet of the Fezensacs the laurel crown of the poet.' The success due to his being confused with a personage who in fact exasperated him forced Count Robert to adopt an attitude very different from that of des Esseintes. He became hard, insolent and bellicose. If he was all simplicity and kindness to touching people like Mallarmé or his sister-in-law, he could be ferocious towards those whose furnishings, whose faces or whose guests did not have the luck to please him.

The Circes of the Plaine Monceau

Montesquiou guffawed in the face of old Mme Aubernon—was it not the 'greenish, pug-nosed face of a gargoyle'?—when she asked him, after Mme Arman de Caillavet had taken Dumas away from her, 'Help me to re-stock my *salon*'; but all the same he would go to dine in the little house in Messine Square. Here, as recollected by Renan and Caro, there was quite a circle of young women both up to date and satirical in the spirit that Forain was later to capture: for example, the two Baignères, one of whom, too witty for academic talk, Mme Aubernon once chided: 'Laure, don't snip the conversation up with your golden scissors'; or Mme de Pierrebourg; or Mme Howland, a friend of Haas whom Degas found 'a snob'. Count Robert also met there a very young novelist, Abel Hermant, who had a cat-like head with pointed whiskers and the quacking voice of a duck. Jacques-Émile Blanche, brilliant and sly, would talk to him about London and the aesthetes. There, too, he renewed acquaintances with Forain and encountered Hervieu, so sad because he believed that sadness, like the colour black, was distinguished.

On Sundays, in summer, the faithful would dine at the villa 'Le Coeur Volant' near Marly. Robert suffered the agony of first being seen at the station and then being perched on the promenade beside a cousin of Mme Aubernon, Baron Doazan, whose manner was appalling. A Polish violinist went everywhere with this character, who was said to be ruining himself for him. In this very Parisian but not at all upper-crust company, Count Robert praised the elegance of such waning beauties as Mme Standish—'whose rigidity has grace ... the only woman with her hair properly arranged'—or the Princesse de Sagan ('a Primaticcio* face') who, when she was being sprayed with scent, would turn round and round on her stool so that she would be equally perfumed all over.

Count Robert found the most brilliant elements of Mme Aubernon's salon at Mme Straus's. Born Geneviève Halévy, this widow of Georges Bizet had remarried a lawyer, an illegitimate son of one of the Rothschilds. Edmond de Goncourt went to see her in March 1887: 'Wrapped in a pure silk dressing-gown that was soft, puffed up and decorated from top to bottom with large flossy knots, she was idly ensconced in a deep armchair, with her soft black velvet eyes darting about feverishly and each ailing pose a coquettish invitation.... The decoration of the room was charming; around her, on a panel, was a splendid Nattier.... In the centre of the chimney-piece, against the marble of which the mistress of the house sometimes leaned her brow, there was an elegant statue in white marble attributed to Coysevox. She spoke about love with a kind of bitterness. . . .'

Count Robert and the young woman formed one of those friendships, faithful but lacking intimacy, which are typical of society. In Mme Straus's circular salon, situated at the corner of Avenue de Messine and Boulevard Haussmann, there came about, during the 'eighties, the formation of that 'Tout-Paris' which was to succeed the 'Boulevard'. Geneviève Straus mixed together high society, businessmen from the most obscure circles, journalists and the artists who had surrounded her before her second marriage. These last willingly abandoned the cafés for the *salons*. The Boulevard had been masculine, 'Tout-Paris' was feminine. In 'Tout-Paris' society could be found: the Robert de Bonnières, he a right-wing journalist who was an intimate of Hugo and Michelet and extolled Wagner, and she, madly up to date, knowing everything about the *salons* and exhibitions; the Ganderaxes; Mme de Broissia, who adored Haas and whose language startled

* Primaticcio (1505–70) painter, sculptor; decorated châteaux at Chambord, etc. Trans.

the upper crust; the British Ambassador, Lord Lytton; and some
such Highness as Alice, Princess of Monaco, née Heine, and ex-
Duchess of Richelieu, whose alliances inspired Robert to write
these verses worthy of a fan inscribed by Mallarmé:

A great banker—a great cardinal—gold and red—
Roulette—the red and black—where chance has led.

Robert took Countess Greffulhe to Mme Straus's; but she
could not accompany him to another house where he spent a lot
of time, even though the mistress was Countess Nicolas Potocka,
née Emmanuela Pignatelli, niece of Chopin's and Delacroix's
great woman friend, herself a pupil of Liszt and passionately fond
of music. Robert saw her for the first time at Mass at Saint-
Sulpice, where she was turning the pages for Widor the organist.
He was dazzled; was Seraphitus going to burn his wings for this
demon? He met her again at dress rehearsals and at concerts; he
could also have seen her at academic parties and in the Chamber of
Deputies on an open-sitting day, if he had not shunned these
sanctuaries of the common herd. Always late, she used to glide as
far as the first row and then would emerge from her famous
sables, to show her slender figure in that black velvet dress made
famous by Bonnat. Her scent, 'Show Caprice', invented especially
for her by Guerlain, unsettled the famous old men before her.
Manuela, with 'Aphrodite's wide and low brow' framed with
black ribbons, made people uneasy with her 'Muse's smile that
succeeded her Maenad's laugh'. This laugh resounded through the
immense mansion in the Avenue Friedland—christened by those
who cadged off her 'the Polish Bank'—to which her husband
rarely came to disturb her parties. Every day for tea and almost
every day for supper, Manuela summoned her admirers, who
formed a kind of club, the Maccabees. Maupassant was its Don
Juan, Bourget its confidant, the Byzantologist Schlumberger its
scapegoat. Manuela's flirtatious manner infatuated the philosopher Caro and little Jacques-Émile Blanche. She forced the latter
to paint a portrait by threatening him with a revolver, and he in
turn threatened to kill himself. Manuela found that extremely
comic. How she laughed when the Marquise de Belbœuf* performed a trapeze act above a table laid for twelve. What applause

* Daughter of the Duc de Morny, she dressed like a man and, twenty
years later, lived with Colette.

when the Legrands invented a hoax. Odd people these Legrands:
in order to remind everyone that she had lost rank in marrying
the son of a rich industrialist, Clothilde Legrand repeatedly liked
to recall that she was 'born a Fournès'. Admirably drèssed, a
cynic and a gambler, Mme Legrand reigned over racing society,
shared Maupassant's favours with the countess and had a brief
affair with the Prince of Wales. It is certain that Count Robert
enjoyed himself at Manuela's. He was proud to arrive at the Opera
with such a beauty on his arm; but he was cautious of having
private conversations with her and he feared the Maccabees'
familiarity. What secret shortcoming was concealed by this *noli
me tangere,* which already at college must have repulsed more
intimate friendships? Delightful or mocking, he remained elusive.

In this hot-house Art Nouveau ripened

So as not to resemble the cheap aesthetes who had been multi-
plying rapidly since the success of *A Rebours,* Count Robert left
the Quai d'Orsay, having renounced his ecclesiastical furniture,
now imitated as far as the *Chat Noir* and redolent of black masses.
A devotee of the Japan being discovered since 1865, he frequented
the exhibitions at the Palais de l'Industrie, organised by Henri
Cernuschi, and the shop owned by Bing, and bought for himself
screens and boxes enamelled with:

> Peonies, irises between the files
> Of red Mikados and blue Samurais.

Thanks to Judith Gautier he learned, at the same time as
Goncourt, to talk about Japanese embroidery, netsuke and
kakemono. He fingered with a tenderness he certainly would not
have had for a woman's arm or even a boy's face:

> Sand-stone, jade, nacre, ivory, shells
> Cracked, singed and egg-shell coloured.

This conception of Japan, at once poetical and absurd and
knowing nothing of the austerities of Zen, so much sought after
today, was nearer to Chinese rococo. Japanese literature was
hardly known. Count Robert never read *The Tale of Genji* or
The Pillow Book of Lady Sei Shonagon, in both of which are recorded

brief moments of enchantment and poetic epigrams similar to those that he wanted to perpetuate in his verse. However, in 1885 Japan was the rage. Bing published *Le Japon Artistique* in three thick volumes, Loti, *Madame Chrysanthème*; Renoir painted Mme Charpentier under some *kakemonos*; Burty the critic and Haviland the potter argued at Goncourt's about the latest consignments at Sichel's or Bing's. These Japanese ornaments and fabrics met a need for novelty that our artisans, busy making imitations or mass-produced furniture, could not satisfy; only England, thanks to William Morris, was in process of creating a style truly new. Japan was a forerunner of Art Nouveau, so many elements of which it provided.

Count Robert abjured bishops' chairs and lecterns. Protected by a parasol he wrote the lines:

> Beneath the glaring dog-days heat
> Moves a procession of blue people . . .

Ten years later, in a study devoted to Robert de Montesquiou in his *Livre de Masques,* Rémy de Gourmont was to write: 'If he thinks, it is in the manner of a Japanese—in ideograms.'

This 'Japanese' thinking took place in the Rue Franklin, in a ground floor apartment which gave on to a large terraced garden overlooking the Boulevard Delessert (the site of the present Clemenceau Museum). In this garden Montesquiou installed neither a Mme Chrysanthème nor the mincing errand-boy who played a similar role for Loti, but a Japanese gardener, Hata: 'charming Monsieur Hata', whose axiom 'In Japan, nothing in mass' Robert would like to repeat while making up bouquets of peonies and irises. Hundred-year-old dwarf pines were put in blue porcelain pots; on dinner-party evenings a valet, who was also Japanese, would place lanterns in a rock-garden which Robert had had made. In February 1891 Montesquiou announced to Whistler: 'A little eccentric and resuscitated pensioner of a dwarf-tree extends to you its Japanese arms, sumptuously knotted and robustly rickety, from the depths of the Chelsea of Paris, or rather from its heart.' Whistler, by now infatuated with Japan, was to have a great influence on the young man who, in London, had been stirred to admiration by a 'Japonico-Hollando-Britannico blue and white' room in Tite Street.

In turn Countess Greffulhe wanted her Japanese Trianon at Boisboudran, with a red lacquer bridge, a pagoda and a lawn on which bronze cranes perched; the Kahn Gardens at Boulogne give us some idea of this sort of Japan. If it rained, tea was taken in a winter garden, where Robert had himself photographed in this or that costume of a surprising simplicity: that of a gymnast or gardener; or in a kimono, with an angora cat in his arms; or merely serving tea in gloved hands to his cousin Elisabeth and Charles Haas.

It was here that he recited the first *Chauve-souris* poems:

> Ah! Bats in the twilight
> Near blue fish in azure lakes.

or quoted the remark of the Emperor Ch'ien-lung referring to a certain blue colour as the 'blue of the sky after rain'. Robert compared Botticelli, with whom the English were infatuated, to Utamaro. This sort of Japan had already been discovered by another artist at the exhibition of 1878; or else at the exhibition of a painter whose invitations to his private view were phrased as follows: 'Monsieur Yamata requests the honour of being reflected by your eyes in his studio.' The artist was Émile Gallé, who engraved on glass the impressions Robert wanted to convey in the poem:

> Two fish in combat there below revolve,
> As though their self-effacement would dissolve . . .

'*Les Chauves-souris* had also inspired Gallé to create compositions —this time in glass—in which engravings now bizarrely volatile and now cloudy, the names of constellations and the tonality of fogs all mingled together.'

Montesquiou received hundreds of letters from Gallé, whom he inspired with a Wagnerian fervour. He was his Parsifal. 'My dear and immaculate guide', Gallé wrote to him. Robert sent the glass-maker to Bayreuth with a recommendation to his old friend Cosima Wagner: an expedition from which Gallé returned in a state of stunned excitement over the second act of *Parsifal*. Indeed, the girl-flowers of Klingsor's garden are the source of the art that he cultivated like so many precious orchids in his studio in Nancy. From 1887 Gallé sent Robert letters written on strips of veneer or on pieces of paper ocellated or striped with twilight colours; but beside these wavering forms he would draw very precise and very Japanese flowers. For the decorative section of the Salon of 1892 at the Champs-de-Mars, Montesquiou commissioned from Gallé a chest-of-drawers decorated with hydrangeas, and watched over the smallest detail of its execution. Gallé replied by sending him samples of marquetry: 'Thank you for sending from the other side of the Channel a real hydrangea with petals of a blue which reddens and leaves the sunflower hesitating. One ought to go back to the capture of this flower which I love through some mosaic of skin devoid of colour, since these petals are the flowers of the flower of the skin.' This sending of the flower earned Montesquiou the congratulations of Puvis de Chavannes. In 1894 Gallé and Montesquiou devised a cheval-glass, inlaid with wisteria, which enchanted Proust, and later a clock, decorated with pansies, to 'strike the mauve hour'.

The aesthete commissioned from the glass-maker a huge electuary: it was to be in crystal, the colour of night, a night colour of damson, on which stars scattered clusters of brilliance. In the Japanising atmosphere of the Rue Franklin Gallé devised for this exhibition of 1892 his platter for cooking-herbs, described to a friend in the following terms: 'In the centre of a vast polychrome mosaic there extends, on a phylactery that doubles up like the silk of a *kakemono*, a length of wood shaded with heliotrope, recalling the wall-paper of the apartment—this lilac colour shading off to a brownish violet, dotted with pale petals.' Montesquiou sent to the Gallé family mother-of-pearl ornaments and embroidered silks.

Montesquiou also gave work to the book-binders; but these, being more ordinary, could not produce marvels comparable to those of Gallé. Lortic covered *Les Chansons de Bilitis* in green and violet leather, with violets embroidered on the silk fly-leaves. Violet was Sappho's flower:

Whose smile of death attracted the doves.

Pierre Louÿs loved this line of Montesquiou's. Robert had acquired his passion for exquisite and always allusive detail from the golden lacquer boxes he had now been collecting for some years.

A Japanese des Esseintes—that would cause a lot of talk. But Montesquiou distrusted writers; what more might they report

of him? Edmond de Goncourt was the only one of his profession
deemed worthy of appreciating this house, giving an account of
it with some errors which Count Robert himself points out:
'Tuesday 7 July 1891. A ground-floor apartment in the Rue
Franklin, pierced with high windows with little 17th-Century
panes, that gave the house an odd look. A house crammed with
a jumble of incongruous objects:* old family portraits, Empire
furniture, Japanese *kakemonos*, etchings by Whistler. An original
room was the dressing room, its bath made of an immense
Persian tray and having by its side a most gigantic Oriental kettle
in beaten and repoussé copper. One room has hydrangeas—no
doubt as a pious token of remembrance for the family of Queen
Hortense†—represented on everything and used as the motif
for every style of painting and drawing. In the middle of this
dressing-room stood a little glass show-case, which displayed
the pastel shades of a hundred ties. . . .'

Often Countess Greffulhe accompanied Count Robert to Goncourt's house. The novelist's judgments on her vary from
'eccentric' to 'supreme aristocratic and artistic elegance'. The
beautiful young, dark-haired girl had become by this time the most
conspicuous woman in Paris, and so she was to remain until
after the 1914–1918 War. She stayed at Sandringham with the
Prince of Wales; she entertained all the grand dukes and the
archdukes. Her mansion in the Rue d'Astorg was not merely a
diplomatic centre and a centre of society; thanks to Montesquiou
it was also an artistic one. On 21 July 1891 she gave on the island
in the Bois de Boulogne a party inspired by her cousin. The
programme, which strikes us as delightful, and which attracted
Heredia, Moreau and Leconte de Lisle, consisted of: 'Pavane' by
Fauré; the Siegfried Idyll; 'Elégie de la Nuit', recited by Le
Bargy, and 'Bulbul', whose 'stream of melody enchanted silence';
and, for a conclusion, 'Clair de Lune' and Fauré's 'Berceuse'.

The Count was too visual really to be a musician; he made
great efforts, however, so that in spite of protests from the
League of Patriots, Wagner was performed at the Opera. He put
Mme de Greffulhe at the head of this campaign, the first of their
great artistic crusades. At less than thirty, Montesquiou was

* 'This is how he refers to this reconciliation of styles, of which I was so
proud' (Montesquiou).
† 'Not in the least' (Montesquiou).

already one of the stars of Tout-Paris society. Handsome, rich
and endowed with both a great name and an inexhaustible spirit,
he bustled about from *salon* to exhibition, from St Moritz to
Dieppe, from Boisboudran to Verteuil. However, he was haunted
by a melancholy from which he distracted himself by poetry and
the insatiable acquisitiveness which led him to rummage in
antique-shops; for he doubled the parts of aesthete and informed
connoisseur. But was there really not a minute to spare for
an affair? For transitory adventures, for the pursuit of an object
that could not be put in a show-case?

CHAPTER 7

Poetic Shopping

Features of days obscurely dim
On which at noon white smoke
Floats downward from the heavens' sombre rim . . .

Dear Jacques-Émile

ROBERT DE MONTESQUIOU had a warm liking for Jacques-Émile
Blanche, a young painter whom he met at Mme Aubernon's and
saw again at Manuela's feet. Not tall, with a round face, a pointed
nose, a quick eye and a sharp tongue, the son of a bourgeois
family well endowed with both money and principles, this
sensible young man had two passions, society and painting.
Each of these helping him in the other, he was destined to have a
delightful life and a failed career. His talent was thought to be
very modern: that is to say, he borrowed from the Impressionists
the brilliance of palette which was changing the muddy colours
praised at the Salons, and from the naturalist novelists the
subjects for his pictures. His first works seem as much like illustrations for Daudet as Roll's for Zola or Gervex's for Maupassant.
All these three were, incidentally, excellent painters, whom the
glories of Renoir and Monet have left in the shade. In the same
way Degas's genius has caused his friends James Tissot and
Alfred Stevens to be overlooked. Robert was passionately fond of
Tissot and Stevens, because he rediscovered in their paintings
Balzac's crinolined heroines, Japanese vases, screens and lyre-
shaped chairs.

The poet met other painters with Blanche. One of these was
Helleu, whose style of painting was still nearer to Manet than
Blanche's own; but in his case it was not society but women that
diverted him from pure painting. La Gandara, less gifted than

Helleu but a much better looking young man, was often visited by Montesquiou in his studio at Auteuil. Like Whistler, La Gandara wanted to paint in the style of Velasquez; but he was never to be more than the successor of Carolus Duran. Also in this group was the tiresome Bostonian, Sargent; though much the most gifted of the three, he too was to let his talent go to waste, seduced by commissions from millionaires.

Count Robert liked studios. He liked their disorder of tapestries and Chinese-style bric-à-brac, of bearskins and Japanese lanterns, of divans, piled high with cushions, where one rested after a sitting in order to listen to a guitarist friend or to a model singing a song. He liked to feel that he was near to the spring of artistic creation; to smell the unfinished canvases which awaited his criticism; to choose a dress or a bouquet for a beautiful woman friend. The author was at home among painters, whereas with writers he was merely a visitor—did he not himself paint in water-colour pale and meticulous sketches of interlacing thistles or flowing orchids in the manner of Gallé?

Montesquiou helped Blanche organise exhibitions at the Georges Petit Gallery, where he met again Charles Éphrussi, surrounded by such collectors as Cahen d'Anvers and Camondo. To the Rue Lafitte he lured all his women friends to explain to them the beauty of a picture. Later this female chorus would carry his opinions to the farthest corners of Paris. Jacques-Émile praised and bought Monet and Renoir; the more intellectual Count Robert preferred Degas and extolled Moreau. Blanche was a little lacking in youthfulness, and it may be that his paraded passion for Mme Potocka was merely a screen. He was a snob, a gossip and even a liar; all traits which Proust ascribed to the type of 'shameful homosexual'. Robert not only flattered the painter's snobbery but was also an endless source of amusement to him. Having become a witty diarist at the age of twenty-four, Blanche wrote: 'Out of nothing Montesquiou makes a story worthy of the Thousand and One Nights. Ludwig II and Wagner, George Sand and Musset at Venice—the tender Marceline Desbordes-Valmore at the market—each of these is transformed into a morality play, an operetta or an epic poem.'

Blanche's father was an alienist who had treated Nerval and Maupassant and knew La Castiglione. All that fascinated the Count; but he wanted this young man ten years his junior to be a reflection of himself. Did they not admire the same things and, more important, laugh uncontrollably at the same things? They mocked Bourget with his psychologist's monocle screwed into his solid, academic face and his guilt for the errors of his youth; they followed the first efforts in society of the Barrès couple; they imitated Mother Aubernon. With great interest they watched the intrigues of Mme Straus and Marie Kann to tear Maupassant away from Mme Potocka; but they did not like the sergeants-mess gaiety of the novelist, and with a simulation of alarm put about the rumour that he had staged, with men disguised as women, a short play entitled 'Rose-Leaf'. Together they went to concerts, escorting Mme Potocka or Mme Casa-Fuerte.

In September, Countess Greffulhe invited her cousin to La Case, her villa in Dieppe. Her husband had just gone off to hunt, leaving the place free for what he called 'The Japanese': that is to say, Montesquiou, La Gandara, Helleu and Blanche. The last of these was staying at Bas Fort Blanc, where he filled his house with Englishmen, painters and fashionable women, to whom strict elegance meant an imitation of the Princess of Wales. For the morning Count Robert launched out in white serge suits and a black straw-hat; he was one of the first Frenchmen to wear a dinner-jacket in the evening—but it was a velvet one, in scarab-green or claret. The two young men made sketches, they went on excursions by mail-coaches; they tried the society at one villa after another.

In his desire to remove Jacques-Émile from his abusive mother, Count Robert directed him as to what to read and what to admire; chose his models for him; and all but held his paint-brushes. In 1889 there was a quarrel. Angry words resounded from Mme Potocka's salon. . . . The Legrands said that Blanche had said . . . Forain would scoff . . . Each of the two friends trembled for his reputation and feared to be compromised by the other. An indiscretion of Blanche poisoned matters further, and Montesquiou then summoned him to the Iles des Cygnes, where the pavilions for the 1889 exhibition were being erected. Jacques-Émile had brought all the letters he had received from Count Robert in a sandal-wood box, and now, like a Bourget heroine, he threw it into the Seine. Montesquiou raised his hat to these souvenirs that were drifting away and then said: 'If you set such little store by my letters, then I will no longer value yours. I had ordered a casket from no less an artist than Gallé in witness of the price I attached to your thoughts. If you had understood the importance as a tutor of one who wished to make you understand yourself, you might have avoided the mistakes which you seem to have taken pleasure in committing. Since I propose to cease to see you, I will devote an hour to you. Let us go up the Eiffel Tower to look down on a panorama of the city, so that I can point out to you what places to avoid in it. . . .' There followed the time-server's Sermon on the Mount, Rastignac's* 'À nous deux Paris'. Montesquiou pointed his index finger towards the Étoile, around which the 'Jewesses of Art' gathered; towards the Plaine Mon-ceau, centre of terrible gossip with the Baignères and Mother Aubernon; then to the Faubourg Saint-Germain, where only a few rare souls truly understood the artist. He predicted to his former friend that these rich quarters would swallow him up and strip him of his talent. Robert was right. Blanche became the Gainsborough of the fashionable 16th Arrondissement. But what of the time that the poet himself had squandered in the smart quarters of the city?

Exquisite passions

The friendship of Blanche had turned Montesquiou in the direc-tion of England, where there were to be found, as much as in Japan, the roots of that art which Montesquiou helped and harried on to bloom with the impatience of a gardener who loosens the earth around bulbs. Blanche had gone to England as a child and was to return there constantly; Paul Bourget discovered Oxford and the tailors of Savile Row. All Robert's friends followed this movement westward. Helleu wrote to him from London: 'The exhibition was well arranged. The Princess of Wales bought three engravings. The Graphic is going to send me to the Queen's next reception so that I can do a drawing. I am bringing you back a sketch of a Javanese from Sargent, who is always the most charming of friends. It is slightly foggy and the sun is very soft. At certain times it is ravishing.'

Helleu—all the more pleasant because he too had just quarrelled with Blanche—was there to welcome the visitor to this empire of

* A Balzac character: an elegant arriviste who is in most of the novels of Paris society. Trans.

elegance and aestheticism. He took him to the Park to watch the
Princess of Wales and Lily Langtry (both equally becurled and
impeccable) pass by; to polo at Roehampton; to regattas at
Richmond. Robert also saw Lady Archibald Campbell again; it
was with her at St Moritz that he had made numerous spiritualistic
experiments. This strange woman, of whom there exist some
photographs in the costume of a page, suggestive of Elizabethan
ambiguity, re-enacted the pastoral plays of Shakespeare in her
park at Coombe.

In 1889, Montesquiou saw her play Pierrot in a pastoral
called *The Kiss*, composed by Watts-Dunton as a deplorable
imitation of Banville. Lady Archie claimed not merely to
have second-sight but also to commune with fairies. Whistler
painted a portrait of her, entitled 'Lady in the Yellow Buskin',
of which little is now visible except one brilliant yellow boot.
Being an ultra-aesthete, she was a friend of Baroness Deslandes.
But there were more serious reasons for Count Robert's visit to
England and he had more important introductions.

Since the 'seventies London had led the artistic movement in
Europe: a position from which it was not to be supplanted by
Vienna until the beginning of this century. Up-to-date people
bought at Galignani in the Rue de Rivoli picture-books by Kate
Greenaway and Walter Crane and Pre-Raphaelite reproductions
the fresh colours of which (lime, lavender and lemon) seemed to
be seen through a fog. Chosen maidens in waistless tunics were
depicted offering lilies to Botticellian students against a background of sunflowers and Gothic arches. In the margins of rare
editions and on upholstery the bramble stretched its tentacles,
recalling Celtic interlacing work and presaging fin-de-siècle
creepers. Furniture, which previously had tended to be Gothic
or fringed and tasselled, now under the influence of Maple
tended towards Japan or Sheraton. The first piece of Art Nouveau
furniture designed by Godwin and Whistler was shown at the
Great Exhibition of 1876. For the opulent red-haired girls painted
by Rossetti, for the thin and anaemic blondes dear to Burne-
Jones, William Morris covered walls, chairs and even dresses with
hieratic flora. Decorative art had never been so immaterial: chairs
were made for souls and not for posteriors. 'Souls' in fact multiplied rapidly in literature and even in society; so that the word
came to be used to designate a group of brilliant people who had

been instructed at Oxford by an academic and timid Plato, Walter Pater.

Montesquiou, himself prepared for the right kind of 'soulful' condition, by the furniture of des Esseintes, was to become, much more than Bourget or Schwob, the one French disciple of this philosopher whose work seems to have been entirely inspired by a dictum of Baudelaire which he had probably never read: 'All arts constantly aspire towards the state of music.' His 'Imaginary Portraits' charmed Montesquiou, who saw himself reflected in their handsome and fantastical heroes: men like Duke Karl of Rosenmold, a sort of Ludwig II of Bavaria, or Denys l'Auxerrois, haunted by ancient beauty. Pater had defined this beauty too precisely for the taste of his colleagues, who asked him to withdraw these lines: 'To grasp at any exquisite passion or any stirring of the senses, strange dyes, strange colours and curious odours, or the work of the artist's hands, or the face of one friend.' Only Beauty mattered, the beauty of a picture or of a face, but it was modelled by the soul. The essay on Leonardo da Vinci became the bible of aestheticism: 'It is a beauty wrought out from within upon the flesh, the deposit, cell by cell, of strange thoughts and fantastic reveries and exquisite passions.'

Robert waited for these 'exquisite passions' without pursuing them; did not his mirror tell him that he was worthy of them? On the other side of the Channel there were more bizarre passions: Swinburne celebrated them in his poetry and, it was said, even lived them. Was it true that the poet allowed himself to be beaten by a female circus-rider and that in Normandy, in a cottage named Dolmance, in homage to Sade he shared his passions between a she-monkey and a little boy? Maupassant averred that it was. Robert was too French to go to the extremes for which the English are famous; but, like old Goncourt, he dearly loved to hear tales of sadistic peers and little girl martyrs. Of these there would be enough in fin-de-siècle literature to fill, jumbled one upon another, a high room or, indeed, a whole boarding-house: the victims of Mme de Paur in Toulet; the Honourable George Selwyn in 'La Faustin' by Goncourt; Péladan's Sir Arthur Gloucester; and the scandals revealed by the *Pall Mall* in Villiers' translation.

'How amusing!' exclaimed the Count when he was told of the worst enormities, his grey-gaitered foot only two paces away from the mire. But, troubled, he followed the English poet in his magnificent erotic delirium, attempting to translate that passage in 'Laus Veneris' when, in the procession of perverse and heretical queens, Herodias passes by of course, but also Thomyris, Alaciel and Pasiphae. In ecstasy he repeated:

> I am the queen of Cyprides:
> Mine oarsmen labouring with brown throats
> Sang of me many a tender thing. . . .

There was Dolores, Our Lady of Pain, 'daughter of Priapus and Death' and both sacrilegist and flagellant. Robert, however, was not the only one to catch the ball thrown back by Swinburne, who had himself received it from Baudelaire: ten poets, from Péladan to Samain, were to quarrel over it. More wisely, Montesquiou also read Ruskin; he liked his fevered erudition, but much less his aesthetic socialism which, in France, was to be taken up by the confused Jean Lahor.

The theories, the ideas and even the sayings of Pater, Swinburne and Ruskin were disseminated in society and even exported as far as the United States by an Oxonian Alcibiades, Oscar Wilde. Dressed in velvet, his hair long and one hand holding a lily, this young man expatiated in languid tones on the art of arranging a house and for the ecstatic 'Souls' praised 'The ivory body of a rare young slave with the pomegranate mouth. . . .' Some lines from a Gilbert and Sullivan operetta introduced Oscar to the public in much the same fashion as *A Rebours* had introduced Montesquiou:

> A most intense young man,
> A soulful-eyed young man,
> An ultra-poetical, super-aesthetical,
> Out-of-the-way young man.

Perhaps it was these lines of Wilde's that made Montesquiou want to go to London:

> The Thames, nocturne of blue and gold,
> Turned to a harmony of grey.

Dear Mr James

In 1884, Robert, accompanied by Dr Pozzi and the Prince de Polignac, went to London to do his intellectual and decorative shopping, with the cry '*Vive le Liberty!*' This store had enchanted him and of it he was to write:

Liberty—blue, green, lilac, pink, cream foulard.

In Bond Street he was overwhelmed:

By a concentrated odour
Of the choicest lotion.

London offered the traveller everything he expected: the Duchess of Leinster, with her Burne-Jones profile; the guardsmen, their tunics brightened by highly-polished breast-plates; the streets of black brick contrasting with white colonnades; the charming young men, admirably dressed and just down from Oxford. His favourite guide was undoubtedly Graham Robertson, who in his autobiography *Time Was* described the Count's visit as follows: 'He was in England incognito (I cannot imagine why) and took much delight in gliding down unfrequented ways and adopting strange aliases; visiting me by stealth after dusk with an agreeable suggestion of dark lanterns and diguise cloaks. . . .' The poet was delighted. 'Within a milky, smoky crystal, the shapes and the colours dissolve; passing uniforms blaze up in a brief splash of red which is quickly extinguished. The hansom cabs glide along like harnessed gondolas, each roof surmounted by a gondolier-coachman whose oar is a whip. Through the narrow window, sights crowd one upon another: flocks of peacocks perched on the trees of the great parks, with soot-coloured sheep beneath them; from street-organs which one does not see music radiates. In the windows of Pre-Raphaelite shopkeepers one sees women dressed in olive-green, dying of love for sunflowers.'

On this first visit, it is true that he liked the Pre-Raphaelites with reservations: he very rightly found that 'the latest Rossettis are bizarre Bouguereaus', but Burne-Jones, whose 'Merlin and Viviane' he had admired at the 1878 Salon, pleased him greatly. It was this painter himself who took Montesquiou to the 'abbey-phalanstery' of William Morris, where he selected some stuffs, and to the studio of William de Morgan, whose ceramics were already more Art Nouveau than Persian. He discovered Blake and noted: 'Nowhere else but in some of Redon's faces, it seems to me, is one able lightly to touch so much of the stupefying unknown. And the girl-flowers precede both Granville and Wagner.'

Edmond de Polignac presented Count Robert to a young American writer, a friend of Sargent and Bourget, who, like them, was to be for a long time deflected from his true inclinations by a passion for society and a respect for its conventions. Henry James was then about to adopt England as his second fatherland. Through him Count Robert met the master who was destined to make him recoil from the Pre-Raphaelites and about whom there had been so much talk at the house of Mallarmé: Whistler. Montesquiou knew that this American, a friend of Manet and Degas, painted society women for exorbitant sums and had covered a whole drawing-room with golden peacocks on a blue background. Rossetti, Burne-Jones and their literature seemed old-fashioned when set beside this painter who, on the whole, was the first to be conscientiously and aggressively modern. But he must see everything, and so he addressed himself to Henry James who had arranged the meeting:

Dear Sir,

In haste I leave you these few lines, to ensure that you do not make any engagement, if that is possible, for the evening of the day after tomorrow, Friday, and to ask you if you are willing to postpone our dinner until then. I have just seen Whistler, who unfortunately is engaged tomorrow, but solemnly promises to come on Friday. I will expect you then on that day at the same place and the same time—the Reform Club, Pall Mall, at 8 o'clock. In the hope that this will be just as convenient for you. Meanwhile at 2 o'clock tomorrow we are going to see as many Burne-Joneses and Rossettis as possible. Your ever.

3 Bolton Street, Piccadilly.

These visits took the young men to Chelsea which, with its small gardens and studios, might have reminded Count Robert of his Passy. The trip was a great success and Henry James congratulated himself on having brought them together.

21 August, 15 Esplanade, Dover

Dear Monsieur de Montesquiou,

   I am glad to know that you also remember with pleasure your short stay in London and I send you this note to urge you to return here without fear of seeing you spoil your first favourable impression. I believe that the interest you found in many things will only grow with a more intimate knowledge and that, for you as for all those who end by becoming attached to English life, the rather dull surface which at first presents itself will prove to have been only a misleading mask concealing the joys in store for you. Be certain at all events that each time that you reappear you will give much pleasure to

Yours faithfully,
Henry James.

(These two letters are written in French.)

CHAPTER 8

Picture of a Dorian Gray

O moth of night, of mystery or morning,
Mysterious Whistler, butterfly that trails,
With wings that Phoebus gilds, that Phoebe pales,
From dawn to dusk, then back from dusk to dawning.

The malicious magician

In 1890 Robert de Montesquiou returned to London with a disciple more handsome and more devoted than Jacques-Émile Blanche. He wanted to see Whistler again. This great painter was also a brilliant writer. Mallarmé had just translated his *Ten o'Clock* for the *Revue Indépendante*.

They met each other at the Grosvenor Gallery, the London equivalent of the Georges Petit Gallery in Paris. The Nocturnes, the Symphonies in Grey and Silver, and the portraits that brought to mind Velasquez in their blacks and the fluidity of their touch had been hung, for ultra-elegant visitors, on Venetian damask. Robert was enraptured, much more than he had ever been by the Impressionists, whom he had always associated with naturalism and not with modernism; he almost forgot Moreau, the distant magician of the Rue de la Rochefoucauld. Whistler, the Brummell of painting, epitomised an impeccable elegance beside which the jewels of Moreau seemed theatrical. The American had carried taste to the point of genius; Degas, who admired him without liking him, grunted, 'Art is killed by taste.' Signing his work with a butterfly in illustration of Pope's paradox, 'Who breaks a butterfly upon a wheel?' he at once inspired the author of the *Chauves-Souris* with the idea for one of his most charming poems: 'Moths.'

Pastel shades, caught on moth wings,

Twilights, reflections of beige and grey
Charmed the monarch of all things transitory.

Whistler was like a butterfly, with his little sharp nose, hairy face and allusive rapidity; but his character was more that of a bird of prey. His career was marked by law-suits which he exploited with a typically American flair for publicity. He dragged into the courts first Ruskin, the patriarch of aestheticism, who had accused him of 'throwing a pot of paint into the face of the public', and then the husband of Lady Eden, a rich industrialist for whom he had devised the famous peacock room, and who found that the portrait of his wife had been executed too rapidly. Whistler was odious, witty, and as sure of his wit as of his taste; but to those who shared that taste he was delightful.

Robert was invited to the studio in Chelsea, then a near-suburb by the Thames; its eighteenth-century houses with gardens alternating with the Gothic or Dutch-style dwellings erected by Royal Academy painters or successful Pre-Raphaelites. Art and society mingled more easily in London than in Paris and the two friends came on a party similar to that described by Blanche in 1882.

When we arrived Whistler was in the middle of curling his hair, while a perfectly charming young male guest (an intimate friend) was busying himself with arranging some yellow flowers which, placed in blue vases, made a harmony of blue and yellow. The servants were putting the last touches to the table, which was laid with fastidious care. In the middle of it was a blue-and-white Japanese bowl in which goldfish swam among water-lilies. In the centre of the room was a large table, in the corners small ones. At about one-thirty the guests arrived. All were lords and ladies, with the exception of some Americans. Everyone spoke French and was as familiar with Paris as with London. Opposite me was a lady in black and yellow; for all the ladies wore a little yellow or a little blue to match the colours of the dining-room. The dishes to which the guests helped themselves were as follows: Smoked fish; curried lobster; pressed beef; creamed chicken patties; polenta; saffron eggs; Italian cakes; and a Moselle cup (the favourite drink of the Prince of Wales). Things were said that entirely defied the imagination of a writer of vaudeville: people went into ecstasies over a flower; a particularly round pea was passed round the table on a little plate. After the meal there was a big reception, with 'all' London filing into the studio. Whistler took me aside and opened for me whole boxes of drawings. I browsed over a series of drawings and pastels that were sheer master-pieces.

But Whistler did not allow Robert to see the doubtful wonders that Wilde had accumulated in his house in Tite Street; or else Wilde did not wish to receive them. 'What do you think about Oscar and his pipe?' Whistler wrote to Montesquiou—the idea of Wilde smoking a pipe being one that his malice could not fail to find comic. Another letter runs: 'Dear Robert, You are the sun and the only joy of life. The glitter of your beautiful jewel and the gleam of your ravishing song have succeeded in illuminating for us the profound night which has enveloped London in its sadness for the last two days. I can even believe that the nice things you said to me were all true. The result is that the idiots who surround me have become intolerable! And I have immediately engaged Oscar Wilde in battle! You will soon know the result. . . .' The Irishman and the American were completely at odds with each other. Whistler had written in *The World*: 'What has Oscar in common with us artists, except that he dines with us, and steals the plums from our plates to stuff the puddings that he goes and peddles in the provinces.' It was he also who wrote 'Oscar has the courage of the opinions of others.' All these insults were to be published in a book entitled *The Gentle Art of Making Enemies*. The painter declared and Montesquiou was to repeat the statement: 'My nature needs enemies.' For both of them friendship was no more than 'a stage on the way to a quarrel'.

Count Robert was also to imitate the intonation and the appearance of his new friend:

The voice drawls slowly, quickening to a kind of snap at the end of every sentence, and sometimes rising to a sudden screech of laughter; and all the while, the fine fierce eyes of the talker are flashing out at you and his long nervous fingers are tracing extravagant arabesques in the air. . . . Like himself, necessarily, his style was cosmopolitan and eccentric. It comprised Americanisms and Cockneyisms and Parisian *argot*, with constant reminiscences of the authorised version of the Old Testament. . . . (But) Whistler never failed to find the right words and the right cadence for a dignified meaning, when dignity was his aim.* 'And when the evening mist clothes the riverside with poetry, as with a veil, and the poor buildings lose themselves in the dim sky, and the tall chimneys become campaniles, and the warehouses are palaces in the night, and the whole city hangs in the heavens, and fairyland is before us. . . .'

As for Montesquiou, he saw Whistler in this light:

> Whistler is like a rare bird, his white locks being the crest, his little eyes shining like jet pearls, his beak curved, and his round tongue continually twirling around in a strident hollow to emit squeak-like words.

This description betrays Montesquiou's sudden rapture with his new friend. Is this Ludwig II meeting Wagner? Or is the emotion expressed something deeper than admiration? Unconsciously, did not Montesquiou change from being a ludicrous and hostile reflection of his father to becoming like the imperious but sympathetic painter? He, too, began to resemble a butterfly: he cut the ends off his moustache, grew a short imperial, dressed in check and the severer kind of tweed, raised his voice, sought fame. The exquisite young man, painted entirely in half-tints— 'epicene', 'willowy'†—now began to hold himself so erect that it seemed as if he wore stays; from being sinuous his gestures became jerky and comminatory; his voice became sharp and resonant; his wit became more biting, his taste more sure and far more simple. Thus the aristocratic pleasure of giving offence became a chapter in *The Gentle Art of Making Enemies*.

But beneath his dandy's armour of irony Montesquiou had for Whistler the same tender feeling of comradeship that united the Knights of the Grail. He had been initiated into a new theory of Beauty and he spoke of it in mystical terms; it evoked for him the Ivory Tower. 'To withdraw oneself and to collect oneself in the remembrance of that which, when we are alone, we cannot ignore and which dominates everything, seems to me an occupation worthy of the leisure which the Gods give to us.' The young man was impatient to serve a great cause, to be *initiated*—and this impatience explains much of his contempt. Whistler was the

* Max Beerbohm, *Yet Again*, pp. 115–16.
† These two epithets are in English in the original. Trans.

master of an order dedicated to Beauty. Those who neglected this god were no better than Saracens and deserved to be destroyed by the arrows of ridicule. Another letter shows the mystical tone of his attack:

> Mystery in all its forms is, I am sure, the one thing in life with which I am on the best of terms; so far from making me afraid, mystery charms me, for, as a noble epigraph expresses it at the head of one of my poems, there is nothing beautiful, grand or sweet in life that is not mysterious. Nearly everything of value is surrounded with mystery, but a mystery that vanishes at once when ineffectual things attempt to envelop themselves in it. . . .

But, as always, as soon as Montesquiou had Whistler's confidence, gaiety tempered ardour. He called Whistler 'dear angelic devil'; he assured the engraver that 'my dry-points will for you be only soft-edged'. While waiting to start engraving, Robert began water-colours and produced in sepia, some charming little Whistlers. Montesquiou well knew that artists have a greater need for some enchanting piece of nonsense, some useless luxury than for money; and it was in this spirit that he gave to the painter some pieces of the blue-and-white china he had made fashionable, lacquer decorated with his emblem, the butterfly, and, when Whistler set up house in Paris, a magnificent Empire bed. The American and Beatrice, the woman he had just married, were both profoundly touched by these attentions. Letters in French from the 'butterfly' to the 'bat' reveal a delightful Whistler:

> 'Bat! Dear Bat!* The butterflies are inconsolable and invisible tomorrow. Sunday they expect you at the same hour, the same twilight. . . .' 'The Butterfly,† who is alone, only crosses the Channel to try out his wings.' 'Your surprises are like those of Aladdin—the splendid present of the beautiful Empire bed, which could only have come from his magic-lamp, far exceeds any hopes that might have been suggested to us either by the cravings of friendship or the frantic avarice even of collectors like ourselves.' 'Only the sparkle of your pretty jewel and the rays of your charming song have been able to illuminate for us

---

* The superscription begins in English. Trans.
† In English. Trans.

the dark night that now, for several days, has enveloped London in its sadness.'

Recipe for a masterpiece

Once the portrait was decided on—it was to be that of a modern d'Artagnan—Robert journeyed to London for the first sittings. Fog and the caprices of the master delayed the sessions; but Whistler apologised so well:

'We have been absent from each other for too long, dear friend, and this has meant that "things" have, for the moment, got the upper hand. So let's not talk of it any more. It is always humiliating to recognise in life that there are circumstances over which one has not got absolute power.' 'I feel that I have become more mysterious and more enveloped in mist than all the mysteries undertaken up to the present. . . .' 'The cup of tea took a long time to drink, however, and the fog has been a match for you. Come, beautiful talker. . . .'

Whistler was pleased to see Montesquiou imitating his malice and plunging into quarrels. In Paris such affairs concluded in a duel, not in a law-suit.

I have heard that you were splendid the other evening, and that you are about to make 'gentle enemies'. You are getting ready, you are practising fencing, I am delighted about it! Summon me one morning and if ever you are in need I shall be proud to cross the Channel for you. Don't forget that, though I am a resident of good old Chelsea-les-Bains, I come from the South, a country whose exquisite humour has arranged that the lost celebrated code of honour was drawn up by a magistrate! A justice of the peace!

In numerous letters Whistler shows that he was eager to come to Paris. But curiously he never speaks of such friends as Degas and Mallarmé, appearing to be totally occupied with exhibitions at Georges Petit's Gallery, sending consignments to the Salon, and above all seeing Montesquiou, who arranged such agreeable days for him:

And then the evening at the countess's and her charming sister's* and the conversation, the prince and the pawns! And the story of Lady Archie's† spirit telephone! What a perfect day! Now I must see that the beautiful dish arrives intact and arrange for its official installation among its companion pieces.

Montesquiou became Whistler's publicity agent and the painter kept him informed about his work:

The experiments on the songs on stone‡ in colour have continued. . . . While waiting for all the rest, go and see the beautiful things which Goupil proposes to make commercial. It seems that in Paris people at last want to buy me! That would please me very much, for we like blue china and silver spoons. And, above all, that would annoy everyone here, where it is agreed that people will never buy me! You will find there two pastel-jewels! an exquisite red observation, a picture that you know, a nocturne; and a Saint Mark's that you do not know. Now that you have become relentlessly worldly, you can send all the beautiful women in Paris to see the little Pompeian Whistlers . . . Also there will be the portrait of my mother, but that is another matter.

Thanks to Whistler, Montesquiou entered into a world of clear and polished things. His first master, Moreau, had been '1900' since the Second Empire; Whistler had been 'modern' since 1880. There was a great contrast between these two men; between the dreamer and the fighter; between the studio in the Rue de Roche-foucauld and the studios in Chelsea and the Rue de Bac. In the one there was all the crowding of an historic theatre; in the other, well-waxed floors, some Empire furniture and a Coromandel screen to display the Chinese simplicities of the 'Études'.

It was said that Whistler had a baleful influence on Montes-quiou; and Jean Lorrain gave substance to this rumour by suggesting that Monsieur de Phocas (Montesquiou) was under a veritable spell cast by the sculptor, Ethal—a character in whom Whistler's malice was exaggerated into satanism. According to Goncourt, strange diversions took place in the studio looking out on to the garden of the Missions Étrangères: '5 April. When

* Countess Greffulhe and her sister, Caraman-Chimay.
† Lady Archibald Campbell.
‡ These three words are in English. Trans.

1. The Countess Thierry de Montesquiou with her four children. Robert is peering from behind his mother's skirt.

2. At Dieppe in 1880. Montesquiou with the Marquis du Lau (the friend of Mme Greffulhe), the Prince de Sagan, Prince Edmond de Polignac, Charles Haas (Proust's Swann), and an unknown person.

3. Montesquiou with three of his cousins, 1888. *Left to right:* Elaine Greffulhe (the Duchess of Gramont), the Countess Greffulhe (Proust's Princesse de Guermante), Montesquiou, and a Montesquiou cousin.

4. In the garden at Passy. *Left to right:* the Marquis du Lau, Mme de Broissia, Montesquiou, Charles Haas.

5. Montesquiou and Sarah Bernhardt in Renaissance dress.

6. Montesquiou as Louis XIV.

7. Montesquiou dressed in the Japanese style which, together with *art nou-veau* and the period of Louis XIV, he popularized in France.

8. Montesquiou and Gabriel de Yturri, his secretary, *chez* Madeleine Lemaire.

night had nearly fallen, a choir of men singing the *Laudate*, male voices rising aloft—Montesquiou supposes that this took place in front of obscene pictures representing terrible punishments in exotic countries—rising up and becoming exultant in front of images of martyrdom, as though the singers in the garden were themselves to be bloodily strung up.'

Goncourt was worried; he went everywhere saying, 'Whistler is pumping the life out of his model. Were it not that he has discovered a wine made of cocoa that is particularly tonic, Montesquiou would not survive these sessions.' But the real tonic was the wit of the painter.

Brilliant conversation concealed the spell. 'Why have you never painted Lady de Grey?' asked Montesquiou, and 'I find her altogether too beautiful a man!' came the answer. Another time the painter warned the model: 'If you continue to go about in society, your fate will be to meet the Prince of Wales'—that is to say, to become entangled in the dissolute world of horse-racing and banking, frivolity and vulgarity. But the painter was no less derisive about those of his colleagues who thought. Of William Morris's socialism he declared: 'It is as if I painted to persuade drunkards to drink nothing but water.'

In the portrait, Count Robert poses with one foot forward and leans on a cane; over his arm is an opulent chinchilla greatcoat, the subdued greys of which clash with the blacks of his dresscoat. The model was on the lookout for the painter's secrets: 'This odd fashion of delaying, of balancing the brush—of waving it in the air for long moments before placing it on the precise spot where the work demanded it—in order to get nearer to the throb, the actual breath of life. . . . One would say that Whistler drew the desired likeness out of the canvas rather than imposed it on the canvas; then when he seemed to recognise in what he had painted a meeting like those of Poe's Wilson and Shelley's Zoroaster with their doubles, the apparition made him shout out the most beautiful of all sayings that ever came from a painter's mouth: "Look at me again for a moment, *and you will look at yourself for ever!*" '

The picture was brought to Paris, but it needed some touching-up. The impatient Montesquiou yielded to the importunities of the genius who wrote to him after many difficulties: 'The visit was delightful and came just at the right moment. All goes well.

Now I have seen what was missing in your picture. Again just at the right moment, so that I could give it the dash and the perfect finesse which it must have before its future is sure.' The model decided that it was necessary to take the work from the studio, for it must triumph at the Salon of 1894. 'How right you are, dear poet! How mad I was! It is splendid, a true d'Artagnan, I shall never forgive myself for my unworthy modesty and fear. But what an inspiration to have sent for it—and just in time! For an ultimatum came from the Champs-de-Mars—the Chevalier Noir is gone.'

At the same Salon, Sargent also exhibited his famous portrait of Montesquiou's friend, Graham Robertson, with a cane in his hand and adopting the pose and expression of a half-fallen angel. Perhaps the success of this work, one of the painter's best, annoyed Montesquiou because it was at about this time that Graham Robertson passed out of his life.

In front of his own portrait Count Robert gave veritable lectures for the little group of society aesthetes which Barrès—who sometimes insinuated himself into it in pursuit of the Baroness Deslandes—termed 'the little class'; 'An unexceptionable cravat, childish mannerisms, a taste for Mallarmé, for Burne-Jones, for Gustave Moreau, the friendship of La Gandara and of Jean Lorrain, agreeable personal behaviour, and in the absence of wit three rather malicious little grimaces—that was the trousseau required to join the little class.' Montesquiou took Whistler to dine with the Duc d'Aumale at Chantilly and to have tea with Mme de Casa-Fuerte and Mme de Montebello. One of the two women asked how much it was necessary to pay Whistler. Montesquiou replied, 'One must give him more than one is able to!'

Some years later Blanche was to write: 'Whistlerism and Mallarmé-ism were the formulas that enchanted our youth—seeming then to be preciosities worthy of our disdainful persons.' Montesquiou expressed his indignation in a poem written on the occasion of the marriage of his old friend:

> Jacquetta is the legitimate wife of Jacquot:
> The couple will pay no tribute to Venus;
> Conjugal duty will confine itself to the table.

There was a question of a duel between Blanche and Yturri,

causing Jean Lorrain to wonder in *Gil Blas* (April 1895): 'When is the duel between Mr Oscar Wilde and Lord Alfred Douglas to take place?'

Scandalous cravats and delicious waistcoats

Inevitably one thinks of *The Picture of Dorian Gray* when reading of the influence of Whistler on Montesquiou. In the novel, the wicked genius is, of course, Lord Henry. Basil Hallward, the painter—who also exhibits his work at Georges Petit's Gallery—is an honest man; but both the nature of his talent and the décor of his studio are reminiscent of Whistler. As for Dorian Gray himself, he was born—if one can put it that way—out of an encounter between Lucien de Rubempré and the Duc des Esseintes.

Lord Alfred Douglas could not have been the model for Dorian Gray, as is often supposed, for the first fatal encounter between him and Wilde took place on the day that the book appeared. More likely it was John Grey,* a friend of the French Jew Raffalovitch, then resident in London, who lent his name and his beautiful face to Wilde's hero. But how can one not believe that Wilde, who so often came across Montesquiou in drawing-rooms and studios, did not reproduce a number of the traits of the man who had already been Huysmans' model? Dorian Gray's eccentric clothes are much more like Montesquiou's than those of a young man of 'Society'. Wilde must have read in a Paris review: 'Monsieur de Montesquiou visited Monsieur de Heredia, wearing a gleaming cravat, fencing school gloves and a sombrero. "Let us go and visit de Nittis" the poet suggested. "I cannot visit that lover of nuances dressed in such rich rhymes. I must put on dove-grey",† came the reply. The Academician waited ten minutes in his carriage; then Monsieur de Montesquiou appeared in opal—the subtlest Liberty shades. "Now I have the right nuances for him."'

Montesquiou, Wilde and Dorian Gray are all three of the

---

* He ended his life as a Roman Catholic priest in Scotland.

† The French reads: 'Je vais me gorger de pigeon', a pun impossible to translate. (Gorge de pigeon: dove-colour . . . se gorger de pigeon: to gorge oneself on pigeon.) Trans.

company of which Dante said: 'They wanted to become perfect by adoring Beauty.' They are above all, with Théophile Gautier, 'among those for whom the visible world exists'.

This world of appearances, as Mario Praz remarks in *The Romantic Agony*, impedes *Dorian Gray* by too often submerging its dramatic elements. Thus Praz criticises Wilde for introducing into a scene which he intends to be terrifying such a catalogue as: 'an opium-tainted cigarette, a pair of lemon-yellow gloves, a gold-latten match-box, a Louis Quinze silver salver, or a Saracenic lamp studded with turquoises' (*The Romantic Agony*, p. 344). The décor is more important than the drama; just as in Montesquiou's poems it becomes almost an end in itself.

Certainly this proliferation of knick-knacks could come directly from Huysmans and from a simple analogy of temperament between Montesquiou and Wilde; but there is a deeper tie between the two men—both were narcissists. Wilde could have seen in the houses of many friends portraits and photographs of Montesquiou; let us not forget that, when young, Montesquiou was very handsome. Moreover, the curious rapport between the poet and his portrait by Whistler—expressed in those words 'You will look at yourself forever'—was very near to that of Dorian Gray with his portrait.

Curiously, the years have produced on Whistler's canvas an effect similar to that produced by his crimes on the Picture of Dorian Gray. It is difficult to distinguish, on the bitumen-eroded canvas in the Frick collection, the traits of a dress-coated Mephistopheles, who is more like Whistler himself than Montesquiou. This sarcastic, even sinister work, has often troubled musicians invited to play in the gallery of this New York museum.

CHAPTER 9

The Mauve Peril

Themselves they tremble from the terrors they inspire
Filled by their endless vacancy with sick desire.

DID THE Parisian Dorian Gray yield to the admiration which his looks and his wit provoked?

Jacques-Émile Blanche was not handsome enough to hold Montesquiou, and in any case he had too much spirit to accept the leadership of a friend, even though that friend might be both dazzlingly brilliant and ten years his senior. Both were too much afraid of gaining a scandalous reputation. A bourgeois wisdom saved Blanche from having one; a prodigious insolence allowed Montesquiou to defy one. In this fin-de-siècle period, which seems to us to have been dedicated to women, there was little liking for homosexuals. Rarely was an epoch more obsessed by buttocks and bosoms. All stages of undress were displayed in posters stuck on walls, on the stage and in the pages of magazines which ranged from the worldly salaciousness of *La Vie Parisienne* to the crude bawdy of *Frou-Frou*. Courtesans were national figures, and adultery was as inexhaustible a theme for Feydeau as it was for Bourget.

However, many required a more refined eroticism than that provided by deplorable imitations of *Mademoiselle de Maupin*. In Rachilde's *Monsieur Venus* (1887), applauded by Barrès, a young girl of 'the highest social standing' becomes the lover of a very handsome workman: it seems an unlikely story. In *À Cœur Perdu* young Neba 'endowed the desire of the princess with masculinity'. Péladan praised 'the Uranian Eros' and recorded 'a bitter concern for phallic necessity'. Later, in Lorrain's *Monsieur de Phocas,* there was a maiden who presented a silhouette 'scourged by ephebism'. Rodenbach predicted: 'The next great success will be the novel of inversion.'

Romanticism had been strongly tinged with Sapphism; but the troubled hues of 1900 came from Sodom. This Byzantine Paris, in which society, libertinism and literature rubbed shoulders with each other was dominated by a tall, odd person, Jean Lorrain, who amused it by his bad form and who thought that he led it by his intrigues. In each generation some of those men who share women's tastes cannot resist borrowing their finery and even, by an extraordinary mimetism, the actual lines of female fashion. Thus, in 1900, such people made Sarah Bernhardt their model: their torsoes became narrow and prominent, they imagined that their voices were 'golden', their waistcoats were fashioned from Theodora's purple stole, and the gems of the Princesse Lointaine were mislaid on their fingers. To go out, they threw over these treasures l'Aiglon's cape. Jean Lorrain records how de Max* played Heliogabalus and Nebuchadnezzar and lived in such a fashion that both his appearance and his scandals became a terrible warning to others. Montesquiou met Lorrain first at Moreau's and then at the studio of another painter, La Gandara, a superb Spaniard with grey eyes. Montesquiou was fascinated by this Velasquez of the cocottes—as Lorrain was also—and entertained him with witty conversation while he was painting; but he was put to flight by the arrival of Lorrain, either in the company of his secretary, a former pedlar called Moufflard, and of some gunner on leave, or else, all out of breath, mopping his forehead with a handkerchief redolent of ether, and complaining that he had been badgered to the doorstep by a street arab he had picked up on the fortifications.

This solid Norman, mauve under his powder, pretended to be in love, one after another, with Liane de Pougy, Sarah Bernhardt and the Baroness Deslandes. In spite of the prejudices he aroused, he was received by the Goncourts and the Daudets, whom he supplied with scabrous anecdotes, more or less invented. He was, above all, a remarkable journalist. By turns he was Santillane in *Gil Blas,* Salterella or Mimosa in *La Vie Parisienne,* and d'Epremesnil and Stendhaletta for other reviews. Lorrain had lost all sense of shame. In *Modernité* he wrote:

* A Rumanian actor celebrated for the bizarreness of his playing and the splendour of his costumes.

At Cythera, at Lesbos, it is the feast of feasts:
The one at which, in an impure dream, the deluded senses
Mix effeminate blond youths with brown wrestlers
And jockeys from a club with a clan of lewd poets. . . .

This made one tremble, thought Count Robert, who mixed with
poets and whose father was vice-president of the Jockey Club.
Who knew if des Esseintes would not end up like the Herodias
of Sodom:

> Dancing, red rubies starry in his false red curls,
> A fairy in a *tutu*, mincingly he twirls?

A stanza of Lorrain particularly troubled Montesquiou:

> A low and narrow forehead, pupils large,
>   Features such as possess
> Those passive ones on whom the gods perverse
>   Lavish their tenderness.

He repeated the lines to himself at the house of Baroness
Deslandes ('Elsie', who also wrote under the name of Ossit)
while growing maudlin in front of some reproductions of
Leonardo's Saint John the Baptist.

But Lorrain and Montesquiou no longer bowed to each other;
for in 1882 Count Robert had refused to allow the other man
to dedicate to him a volume of poems, remarking that this kind
of compliment was more flattering for the donor than the
recipient. One appreciates the wisdom of this decision when one
opens Lorrain's book *Le Sang des Dieux* and reads of Hylas:

> And his naked arms, polished by the kisses of Hercules,
> Shine like two lilies in the midst of the reeds,

or of Bathyllis:

> Staring at the sailors, red with lust,
> He distributes to each his bunch of laburnum,
> Then extends the palm of his hand to be kissed.

These are personages from the world of Gustave Moreau and
it was Moreau who accepted the dedication.

For nearly twenty-five years the hatred of the journalist would
pursue Montesquiou and his friends; calumnies and sarcasms were

exchanged to the great delight of all Paris. Proust, bespattered by
the mud-slinging of this quarrel, was to fight a duel with Lorrain.
But Baroness Deslandes hovered about, twittered, and without
seeming to have anything to do with the matter, wafted their
boy-friends in the direction of her habitués.

Robert was interested and charmed; but Elsie was really 'not
quite quite' and if one did meet in her house some peeresses and
quite a few German highnesses, she was literally surrounded by
too many doubtful young men. In consequence the poet's fervour
was to abate. Did curiosity impel him towards Jeanne de la
Vaudière, the woman orientalist who lived in the bourgeois
quarter of Les Ternes and was authoress of *Les Demi-Sexes* and
Androgyne? Surely not. It was enough to read one of Jean
Lorrain's articles to know all about the woman. And again it was
Lorrain who described the terrifying Baron Doazan, cousin of
Mme Aubernon, who was known as The Widow. Robert fled
from such people as from the plague, murmuring these lines of
the columnist for *Gil Blas*:

> His ancient beauty steeped in paint for preservation,
> Still full of high disdain, of high ambitions full,
> Raised by Louise-Philippe to once exalted station. . . .

The Baron had the disagreeably aggressive manner of those who,
for fear of being thought effeminate, affect martial ways. When
someone turned his back on him, he had a pleasant saying: 'I
would rather lose my friends than my vices.'

The disenchanter

An even worse manner characterised Pierre Loti, who evoked
images now of his distant fiancées and now of his robust sailor
friend Yves.* Robert admired him: 'He operates through
thousands of brush-strokes, applied and then removed, as in a
Renoir. He is an effeminate Fromentin.' They met at Mme de
Casa-Fuerte's and were seized with the desire to know each other
better. The novelist awaited the poet at the Hôtel 'Bon La
Fontaine';

* *Mon Frère Yves* is the title of a book by Loti described by the author as
'une vie de matelot'. Trans.

Different messengers, successive and solemn, made me stand
about (to no purpose) in dark rooms. Then one of them guided
me along some brighter corridors and at last opened a door for
me from which burst a flood of light. At the same time I was
overcome by a strong smell of walnut juice, with which some
close friends were occupied in smearing the author of *Azyadé*
in order to prepare him for the role of 'an archer of Darius' for
an intimate fancy-dress ball. I am accustomed to find everything
natural in those whose merit exempts them from ordinary laws,
and therefore made no comment on an exhibition that was no
doubt intended to astonish me. I paid my respects, as if the
corkscrew curls of the Persian wig had been the stripes of a
soldier's cap and the crossbow of Madame Dieulafoy* some
sort of Cardan lamp; then I took my departure, shaking the
hand of the artist, whose tone had touched me and who had
seemed no less respectable under the finery of his fantasy than
Aurevilly under his in the past. I think that my indifference to
a display which inaccurate information had persuaded him
would please me must have both surprised my host and disconcerted him. At any rate, the next day I received from him a
very kind message, expressing the hope that our first meeting
had left in my memory an impression more precious than the
'mere recollection of a freak in the bedroom of an inn'.

The term 'freak' was what the crossbowman of the previous day
had used in making fun of Madame Dieulafoy. Perhaps, after all,
Loti did not like this trousered woman, for whom Dumas *fils* mis-
took him once in the subdued light of a hall. But Robert, or rather
his handwriting, had already surprised Loti. On the day of his
marriage Loti found 'a pink envelope, of an adorable pink,
resembling a flower-petal. Its edges—not scalloped as was then
the fashion—looked like mother-of-pearl that one could snap.
On it there was writing unlike anything one had ever seen before;
at first one would have said that it was cufic (the ancient
ornamental form of Arabic writing); however, if one looked
closer one could see that it was, in fact, French, with my name and
address inscribed. Who then, with laborious research, had learned
to change our vulgar writing into such harmonious twirls and
figurations? . . .'

* This woman archaeologist always dressed as a man.

This friendship did not advance. Loti returned on his high heels to his numerous betrothed in foreign parts, having done little more than glance round the salons of Paris with eyes ringed with *khol*, his sad look that of a man who has learned the secrets of Death and of Beauty. Some years later he sent Montesquiou a photograph of himself completely naked with the words 'Academician's academy'. Each time the traveller passed through Paris, he suggested 'coming to smoke a cigarette' with Montesquiou and wrapped himself in mysteries that were rather exasperating. Sometimes he was Monsieur Viaud de Pointe-à-Pitre, at others a Levantine, M'Asman Daney. There were a thousand misunderstandings between these touchy people. Robert, irritated, composed a malicious poem about Loti.

Indiscretions

Entertained by lovely women like the magician Klingsor among the flowers, Montesquiou often gave a side-long glance at this Sodom into which he dared not penetrate; and since he could not share in its pleasures, it was with all the greater verve that he exposed its oddities. People very much enjoyed hearing him tell two parallel after-dinner stories, from which he drew a lesson about the morals of society. 'Dear Count . . . incomparable . . . tell us . . . we beg of you . . . The story of the princess . . . and the story of the jeweller's wife . . .' After a few protestations, in which a fear of offending the canons of decency seemed to lend momentary strength to the modesty of the virtuoso, Montesquiou rested his elbow on the mantelpiece, the chorus of women closed in, and around them a hedge of black dress-coats formed itself. In the impeccable diction which we still admire in Monsieur Escande,* the Count began with some general remarks on the state of manners. Then the voice was raised, became fervent during the long descriptions, took on a shrillness in the dialogues: until, at the finest moment in the story, it completely went out of control, making the crystal chandeliers tremble, before once again moderating itself in a cascade of beautiful words, allusions and quotations, among which a moral could be found.

The first scene of the recital was a very beautiful mansion in

* The oldest actor at the Comédie Française.

the Rue de Grenelle, 'the woodwork of which, carved by a
tortured disciple of Caffieri, preserves in its blossoming rococo
a whiff of frivolous and empoisoned scent left there by that
duchess, my very, very distant great-great-aunt, who was so
extreme in her love of the beautiful that she even sought it in her
footmen—and found it there. . . .' A shrill laugh would follow.
This would bring to mind another duchess—unless she was in
his audience—to whom, according to Montesquiou, her coach-
man said, 'If Madame the Duchess would be so good as to move
a little further over to the left thigh, then I would have the honour
of giving Her Grace the more enjoyment.' The Count would then
proceed; and though he was concerned with historical personages
and heroes, he withheld the actual names. The Duke, who lived
in the Rue de Grenelle, had a wife, and a daughter engaged to a
Prince 'whose blood contained that *morbidezza* which Cardinal de
Retz had already experienced in one of his ancestresses'. The
duchess and her daughter went to Deauville shortly before the
marriage—here the narrator interposed a reprimand for the
people who took themselves off to this Second Empire watering-
place when they possessed three historical châteaux. In spite of
their frivolity the ladies got bored and returned home one day
sooner than arranged—'and that is as serious as opening a letter
that is not addressed to you'. No one was there to welcome them,
but they were drawn towards the great salon by the lights and the
sound of a piano. Hastening thither, they found the husband and
the fiancé both passionately waltzing in the arms of lusty footmen.
The duchess was on the point of fainting; but her daughter said
in a perfectly even voice, 'Really, papa is such a bore with his
men. . . .' 'And so, ladies, the incident was closed, the marriage
took place. It was a happy one; the young princely couple and
their progeny living in the family house and enjoying the service
of a staff devoted to them *body* and soul.'

Eddies of conversation in the audience: '. . . But you know of
course . . . What, him too! . . . Who can one trust? . . . The other
story, for pity's sake!' After some hesitation Montesquiou took
up his position again near the mantelpiece. 'Well—good heavens
—now we will pass on to quite another stratum of society. That
of rich merchants, jewellers, dressmakers. . . .' Here he enumera-
ted a number of arrivistes who had annoyed him and to whom he
ascribed a fortune gained from commerce and a crapulous past.

'Who can tell if a jeweller or a dressmaker will not be seen with
your daughter?' There would be shocked protests from all those
around him. 'The most wealthy family of this kind lives in
a mansion not far from the Bois, with the wife's father, a still
vigorous widower, whom we will call Monsieur Jocaste. The
wife goes to Deauville'—here the Count would quote,' "See who
has the folly to cross the planks from which a coffin will have to
be made for Madame Legrand". ' 'She—the shopkeeper's wife—
is not bored at Deauville, but she loses at the casino and comes
back a day early. She finds the mansion deserted. She goes to her
room and sees—er—two beards sticking up out of the conjugal
counterpane! Father-in-law and son-in-law, interrupted in a
criminal conversation, hide their shame.' The Count mimed this
scene, worthy of Feydeau. 'The shopkeeper's wife rushes out on
to the balcony and proclaims to the four corners of the earth the
opprobrium which lends, we must admit, a certain distinction to a
family that, until that moment, was very dull—if, at all events,
united.'

In these two anecdotes the natural reserve of the young
princess is contrasted with the outraged suffering of the
bourgeoisie. But in actual fact the upper crust, being both pious
and scrupulous, showed great severity to deviations of this
nature, and the Montesquiou family began to sigh when Count
Robert's name was mentioned, since his eccentricities seemed to
be a proof of the sin of which, in reality, they were only the
sublimation. No longer are we in the seventeenth century, when,
as the proverb of the time puts it: 'In France the nobles, in Spain
the monks, in Italy everyone.' The family were weighed down
with horror by this poem, written by Count Robert as an act of
faith:

> The effeminate fights, the effeminate avenges itself,
> The effeminate conquers.
> The effeminate works and thinks and over the morass
> Of the opaque and heavy male predominates and exults.
> In himself, the effeminate contains more than one race,
>   Yes, more than one sex also,
> He is indefatigable when others are exhausted,
> And deceit and anxiety only lend him strength.

But against the evidence of such lines we can set the opinion of a shrewd judge of character, Bernard Berenson: 'In my long acquaintance with Montesquiou, I never noticed the side for which Charlus is famous: sodomy. And Lord knows that at that time, young as I was, I made homosexuals' mouths water.'

Let us play with fire

The hostility of his relatives merely acted as a spur to Montesquiou's insolence, and he provoked and mocked them with spirit. He was the more annoyed, however, when one of the few people who intimidated him, Degas, gave him a lesson in public, since he admired this painter unreservedly. At an exhibition of decorative art, the poet, seated on a green bed made to his own design, caught the attention of the painter. 'Do you believe, Monsieur de Montesquiou, that one would have better children in an apple-green bed? Take care—taste can be synonymous with vice.' At the opening of Liberty's in Paris, Degas growled 'Liberty—which leads to penal servitude.'

He must have been thinking of his meeting with Wilde at Mme Straus's, at which the Englishman gushed, 'Ah, sir, you know how well known you are in England!' only to receive the answer, 'Happily, less well known than you.'

Montesquiou often came across Wilde: with Sarah Bernhardt, whom the Englishman claimed to adore; at the Baignères; at Blanche's; and at the house of Marcel Schwob, who, in spite of his ugliness, imitated the Englishman's waistcoats and cravats. For Wilde was handsome, even if his looks were soon to grow heavy. His hair was too long, he wore too many rings, and his frock-coat flared too extravagantly. Montesquiou shuddered: 'The Antinous of the horrible.' The Englishman personified the homosexual decadence that awaited des Esseintes; Montesquiou wished to have nothing in common with him. Besides, when he was present, no one else had a chance to utter a word. Decidedly, one met him too often: at the Duchess of Richelieu's; at Lady de Grey's; at the English Embassy; at Reginald Lister's;* and certainly at the feet of Baroness Deslandes.

* An elegant attaché at the British Embassy, who also claimed to be an admirer of Sarah Bernhardt. A combination of amiability and unorthodox tastes earned for him from Lorrain the nickname 'The Cordial Aunt'—a pun on 'L'Entente Cordiale'—'La Tante Cordiale'.

Wilde, like Lorrain, represented degradation and scandal; but also that abandonment of one's rightful element which so much attracted Montesquiou—shop-assistants' and apaches' balls, at which Huysmans would slip a note-book into one's hand; walks with some horseguard on the deserted alleys of the Champs-de-Mars; all that mysterious and labyrinthine side of Parisian life of which he loved to hear. Lorrain and his disciples acted like Rudolf in search of a hulking Fleur de Marie; later this Fleur de Marie was to be called Notre-Dame des Fleurs.*

Huddled in the depth of his brougham as he returned from an evening party, Montesquiou would begin to muse, the chestnut trees of Passy or of the Esplanade des Invalides above him, on the shadows whose weavings reminded him of the bats at Courtanvaux—*Hybrids sigh for those that will devour them*—and with melancholy he considered the passions he renounced.

Stiffening into a shameful reserve, he would recount this moral story to the young: 'A headwaiter, in every other way respectable, was arrested one evening in the Champs-Elysées *in flagrante delictu,* while conducting a homosexual "conversation". Locked in a cell, he broke his pince-nez, crushed the glass and swallowed it so as not to have to live with his disgrace.'

Montesquiou was not himself consumed by the fires of Sodom; but he smelled them burning and his malice was directed to fanning the flames of slander. Was it not in those same Champs-Elysées that he had once strolled with the novelist Paul Bourget? 'Calumny', this friend of his youth had written to him, 'draws both of us into its net, tipped at each of its knots with poison. A journalist has commented, "I see Bourget incessantly in the Champs-Elysées in the company of a very well-dressed young man. Why?" The supposition of some monstrous liaison has burst forth.' It seems almost as if Montesquiou stayed pure in order to be able to mock. Insolence is a luxury for which one pays with one's pleasures; just as a politician remains honest less from virtue than from the determination to be in a better position from which to insult his opponents.

The poet forged for himself a breast-plate to protect him from the flames; but it was more like the bronze corset of the dragonfly.

The Wilde scandal justified this wisdom and put a check on some Parisians who were a little too showy in their behaviour.

* The title of the first of Jean Genet's novels.

Forain drew a picture of young aesthetes in front of the ticket-office of the Gare du Nord, with the caption: 'They are going to disgrace themselves in London!' The similarities between Dorian Gray and des Esseintes were stressed. Whether in irony or chauvinism, the journalist Baüer proclaimed: 'The darling sin of Wilde does not find any practitioners here' and further on, recalling *A Rebours*, adds treacherously: 'The legend which ascribes to a nobleman who does not much like rumour the distinction of having been the model for the hero of the book, must be disputed.'

The quarrels first with Bourget and then with Blanche are merely the forerunners of innumerable others throughout Montesquiou's life. Willingly he assumed the role of a prince who is equally arbitrary in his apportionment of favour and of disgrace. In a manner very like that of Ludwig II, he would allow a sudden disgust abruptly to terminate his enthusiasm. He had a craving to educate some protégé or other up to his own level; but not infrequently he soon dropped the object of his choice. So, in spite of his charm and quaint humour, Montesquiou would have remained a lonely figure, if he had not met an absurd and charming person, whose admiration overcame the trials which friendship and even love could not withstand. What part did each of the two men play in a liaison which was to defy malice and prejudice for fifteen years? If it was love that they felt for each other, sensuality had little part in it. Frail, nervous and imaginative, the poet knew no greater pleasure than that derived from the eyes when they are focused on some beautiful face or perfect object. Thus the aesthete who seems to outrage conventional morality by his attachment to a young man with a Botticelli profile, in reality respects it much more than the man who, though discreet, looks for pleasures more solid than those of mere contemplation.

A lovable person appears

On Monday, 16 March 1885, the day of the opening of the Delacroix exhibition at the School of Fine Arts, a tall young man, with a fine moustache, black hair, burning eyes and expressive hands, dressed in a drooping cravat and becoming frock-coat, was presented to the poet. 'Ah! County, soubleem admiathion!' Graciously, the prince's hand checked the genuflexion. His expression changed rapidly from haughtiness to curiosity, then to amiability. He made the young man repeat his name: Gabriel Yturri. Discreetly, Montesquiou then discovered that he was a young Peruvian, who had been brought up by English priests in Lisbon in order that he might be removed from the temptations to which, in the hotter climate of his native land, his good looks might have exposed him. The Count took Gabriel's arm and led him to 'Sardanapalus', where he quoted Baudelaire's *'La Jeunesse Retrouvée'* at him, before throwing Heliogabalus, Joan of Arc, Zoroaster and Gilles de Rais pell-mell into a dazzling furnace of historical exposition. Women rushed up and the young man was introduced—'Don Gabriel de Yturri!'—to the Duchesse de Rohan, to the Chimays, to Mme Straus. Then he was taken off to have a cup of tea in the Japanese garden.

For those in the know, this introduction was a little like that of Madame Du Barry at Versailles. Montesquiou and Gabriel could in fact have met each other several months before at the Carnaval de Venise, the shirt-maker's in the Boulevard de la Madeleine where Gabriel sold astounding ties. Already Baron Doazan had evinced an interest in the Peruvian; but the Count's prestige easily enabled him to get the better of his ruined and faded rival. That same evening Gabriel wrote: 'I am devoted to you, body and soul, for life. I will give everything I possess to spare you a moment of sadness.' Robert had once expressed the wish that admiration for his poems would go as far as physical desire. Here the wish had been fulfilled.

Very quickly Gabriel had moved into the Rue Franklin, a mere two steps from his friend, having given up cravats in order to become his secretary. With admirable courage Montesquiou imposed Yturri on his friends. Certainly the Peruvian looked a bit like a shady adventurer; but his manners were delightful and only he knew how to appease the master's rages. 'I should like to put under your dear tired steps a carpet of thornless roses.' He had to extend this carpet to place it under the steps of all those whom Montesquiou annoyed or hurt. He mollified the robust Léon Daudet himself by averring that no one had been as sensitive as Montesquiou when he was in trouble. The diarist has left this portrait: 'Yturri changed rapidly from sweetness to anger. When anxious, he played with the hair on a mole on his chin. . . . He saw everything in the darkest colours—such a passion expended on nothing.' This 'nothing' must for Daudet have been the society of the most affected people. At once Yturri took over all the tastes of his master: helping him in his hunt for antiques and supporting him on social occasions. The female chorus was delighted to welcome a young man at once so handsome and so aggressively correct in the manner of Levantines or South Americans whose shiny top-hats rival in brilliance the flashing of their teeth and of their eyes. Mme de Casa-Fuerte doted on him; the excellent Duchess de Rohan, who was excited about literature, found him 'a beautiful soul' and started a correspondence with him.

Other houses at which Robert was an accustomed visitor had to be stormed: Verteuil, for example, where Count Aimery de la Rochefoucauld saw that an atmosphere even more ceremonious than that in his mother's house prevailed—and his mother, like Montesquiou's, had been born a Duroux. La Rochefoucauld spoke constantly of his ancestors and his illustrious cousins, to such an extent that one of his club friends said to him: 'How bored you must have been for nine months!' He made exact gradations between the respects paid to a serene highness and those owed to a simple member of the nobility of the Empire. Montesquiou stormed this citadel of the upper crust. 'Cousin,' he declared on arriving, 'I have joyful tidings! . . . Monsieur de Yturri is arriving by the next train.' What could one do in such circumstances? To object would have meant both depriving oneself of a guest whose vivacity would brighten the evening and making a redoubtable enemy. It was necessary to pocket the affront. At Charnizay, at the house of Count Robert's father, things went off less well. As soon as he saw the secretary, Count Thierry growled insults, of which 'shady adventurer' was the mildest. Yturri took the train back, while Count Robert remained in his tower without speaking to anyone, unless it was to little Aude, daughter of Passiflora. He had to economise that year. He was seen in the park, cloak blown by the wind, and at Sunday Mass, holding, disguised as a missal, the *Visions de Catherine Emmerich* or the works of Swedenborg.

If they had not been too extravagant, they would go to Algeria, Naples, Venice. Everywhere they were photographed—'at Triana,

St Moritz, Venice, on the cursèd terrace at Monte Carlo'; dressed
as Tunisians, as shepherds, as devotees of the turf, as cyclists and
even as Englishmen—'frockcoat by Poole, with a large button-
hole of Parma violets such as the English are accustomed to wear
on Sundays when they go to church'. Sometimes Yturri travelled
alone, as the ambassador extraordinary of Montesquiou: to see the
Pope, the Rothschilds, Duse. The Peruvian went on little bicycle
excursions, 'with someone who has a very bad influence'—whence
some scenes. But happily 'at the same moment our two hearts
blazed out for each other'.

Before this meeting, so decisive in the fates of both of them,
Yturri had knocked about a good deal and had become familiar
with the intrigues of the homosexual world. Montesquiou wished
to know everything and to be involved in nothing. Yturri would
make a tour of the antique-shops before his master visited them.
To Montesquiou he would bring stories of tea-parties (these
gentlemen used to drink enormous quantities of tea under pink
shades) at the home of John Audley, a friend of Wilde, who lived
in a mezzanine in the Avenue Montaigne where a curious mixture
of peers and boxers could be met; of the mortifications endured
by Gordon Bennett, the proprietor of the *New York Herald*; of
the latest conquests of Monsieur de Schlichting, a collector of
eighteenth-century works of art who was famous for his white
whiskers. But when Count Robert went to the house of this last
in order to admire Watteau's 'L'Indifférent', the baron hid the
gigolos. Up to his death in 1905 Don Gabriel (Montesquiou
ennobled him) followed the Count like a shadow; a sententious
shadow that lifted its finger to command silence: 'Listen to the
County, he is going to speak to you!'; a deferential shadow,
gathering the pearls that Count Robert scattered as he talked; a
shadow so music-mad that, in order to underline some particularly
sublime passage, he would start to beat time.

Such an extraordinary couple needed a wider field. So it was
that they visited London, the Mecca of aestheticism, to be photographed in their pilgrims' garb of overcoats lined with vicuna,
and astrakhan hats pulled down over their ears.

Under this picture Count Robert wrote, in tribute to Walter
Pater, *The Passionate Pilgrim*. However, there were gales of
laughter in editorial offices when this poem by the dreadful
Lajeunesse came to be repeated:

Ave, Caesar Morituri
Te salutant!!! Mort? Yturri!
Oh! Dis! Tu ris? mon Yturri?*

* Literally:

Ave, Caesar, morituri
Te salutant!!! Dead? Yturri!
Oh! Say! You are joking? My Yturri?
But it is impossible to find an equivalent for the puns 'salutant—salue,
tante', 'morituri—mort Yturri', 'Dis! Tu ris?—D'Yturri'.

CHAPTER 10

The Poet's Teachers

A curio is what I wish these lines
To be—unique, particular and strange:
Around its edge a flash of colour shines
From time to time to dazzle and derange.

The magician of the Rue de la Rochefoucauld and the connoisseur of Auteuil

THERE WERE more painters among Robert de Montesquiou's teachers than there were poets. Moreau had revealed his treasures to des Esseintes, Whistler had clarified his taste and hardened his wit. This wit was that of a painter: since for a poet, the exercise of malice, such as resulted in Montesquiou's sayings being quoted with those of Forain, ought never to become a pleasurable act. The virtuous Gabriel sighed, 'If you really wished it, people would like you'; to which Montesquiou retorted, 'Don't frighten me!' At the approach of his fortieth year, Montesquiou began to dry up, becoming a two-dimensional figure, as elegant as a Hokusai drawing. He lived surrounded by other drawings, graceful or comical, in which he did not attempt to find a third dimension. A narcissist, he did not see beyond the mirror. The mirror that Whistler held up to him was the dandy's in polished steel. Moreau, on the other hand, showed him the magician's cloudy crystal.

Gustave Moreau cast aside his habitual reserve for this new disciple; he was touched by his vivacity, and perhaps between them we can also guess at two ties other than painting. The first of these was spiritualism: had they not just each discovered the interest that transports the solitary into the Beyond? A letter from Moreau to Montesquiou, dated January 1888, seems to be partly couched in the language of magic. 'It is inevitable that from springs of generosity as noble as yours an artist must imbibe much painful exhaustion', he begins; then goes on to say that Montesquiou both needs and deserves far wider success: 'But don't wait too long, I entreat you; don't put off the act of creation, for I am sure that in it you will find satisfaction and joys you have never suspected. . . . Your admirable poems, dear great poet, have a super-terrestrial mystery that goes straight to the soul, enchants it and troubles it deliciously.'

The second bond, which most probably remained unspoken between them, was homosexuality. It is now known that Moreau lived with a young man called Rupp, and that when young he had an affair with Fromentin, the author of *Dominique*.

Moreau was too reticent to allow Montesquiou to achieve the same intensity of friendship with him as the poet had with Whistler and later with d'Annunzio. None the less there existed a profound affinity between the poet and the artist. When Montesquiou was walking beside Degas in the master's funeral procession, Degas remarked to him: 'Moreau was one of those men who always begin by drawing back his foot for fear that someone is going to step on it.' The most accurate judgment on Moreau, perhaps tinged with irony, is Odilon Redon's: 'What marvellous embroidery in old and out-of-date silks on the cushions of this old lady, whose dreams are of luxury and whose past has no faults except that her eyes are always shut to poverty!' These lines could also serve as an epitaph for Montesquiou.

We have seen that Japan had created a bond between Edmond de Goncourt and Robert de Montesquiou. The old writer was interested in the young man, who was such an artist—'hartist' as the women who imitated Sarah Bernhardt liked to pronounce it. This fin-de-siècle period has made us as disgusted with the word as the eighteenth century was with 'heart'. The Goncourts invented an 'artistic' way of writing and lived in an 'artistic' house in the Boulevard de Montmorency, where Montesquiou visited the writer with whom he was to have the closest affinity. Edmond de Goncourt looked every inch a gentleman; but his jealous and often smutty mind committed superficial judgments to the *Journal*.

On the first visit, the naturalist was on his guard: 'Young Montesquiou-Fezensac had put on trousers made of Scotch plaid and had prepared an *ad hoc* mind in advance for his visit. A cracked and deranged literary figure, none the less gifted with that supreme distinction that characterises aristocracies when they are on the verge of disappearing.' Three years later the impression was better: 'I find that he has a humanity that is entirely superior to that of des Esseintes, who is only a caricature of him. It is not necessary to say that he is an extremely distinguished, over-ornate person and that he may well have real literary talent.' None the less the legend of des Esseintes created havoc and Goncourt recorded a very improbable episode, which must have been the invention of that pest Lorrain: 'One hears tell of his love-making with a woman-ventriloquist who, while Montes-quiou was labouring to pleasure her, threatened her noble client by imitating the drunken voice of a pimp.' But Montesquiou knew how to flatter the old Marshal of Letters: 'To apply aristocratic judgments to works and personalities of literature, he [Montesquiou] recognises only Chateaubriand and me.'

Robert again met in Blanche's studio the Bonnières and Forain, alike implacable in their witticisms and their unscrupulousness, Abel Hermant, Paul Adam and Octave Mirbeau. All these attended open-mouthed as Zola and Daudet vied with each other in boasting about the numbers of their editions. Decidedly, objects were here worth more than conversation. Robert could not get over the fact that a man as distinguished as Goncourt could be sufficiently interested in the adventures of a prostitute called Elisa to write a book about them.

In the 'nineties Montesquiou was constantly being mentioned in the *Journal*. To Sarah Bernhardt he committed the task of delivering for him the following bouquet of friendship to the writer at the house of the editor Charpentier:* '3 March 1895. At 11 p.m. Sarah Bernhardt, leaning her elbow against the mantel-piece of the great drawing-room, lorgnette raised, read non-chalantly in her golden voice this tribute to Edmond de Goncourt by Robert de Montesquiou:

> "The snow-white peacocks roused in Faustin's dreams
> Glide gently through our minds, but gentler yet
> The grace, dear master, of your heroines seems—
> Girls like your Renée, Marthe or Manette . . ."

* Renoir's superb painting of Mme Charpentier and her daughters in a Japanese-style drawing-room now hangs in the Metropolitan Museum.

'While Sarah recited these lines, I followed them in a copy
written in Montesquiou's hand and illuminated by Caruchet;
the paper was buff, decorated with peacock's feathers painted in
gouache with so much discretion that they seemed to be no more
than elegant watermarks on it. I went up to thank Sarah, who
with her idol's clothes and her seductive manner looked like some
sorceress. Thereupon Montesquiou presented me "to his
women": to those beautiful ladies of the noble faubourg who are
always in attendance on him. . . .' After these precious minutes,
realism returned with Yvette Guilbert, who sang 'La Saoularde'
('The Drunken Woman').

Flowers for the poets

It must be confessed that curios were for Montesquiou a far
stronger tie than poetry. Thus he was much less intimate with
Mallarmé than with Goncourt. But as we have seen, a genuine
esteem existed between these two aesthetes. Sometimes at the
evening parties in the Rue de Rome, Count Robert seemed a little
intimidated by so much simplicity; a little irritated at having to
give his hand so often to people; a little bored when an exhausted
Villiers de l'Isle-Adam got muddled up in a story which he had
started so well—though Montesquiou admired the man who had
written 'Everyone understands what is familiar to him.' In order
to conceal his embarrassment on these occasions, Montesquiou
was far too ingratiating and was only natural with the poet's son.
His stories and his imitations used to make this sickly little boy
laugh. One day he brought him a bird from the West Indies, in a
golden Chinese cage. The poet thanked the Count for 'the
parakeet, whose stomach glitters as though enflamed with a
whole orient of spices'. A little later, 'My little boy smiles up at
you from his bed like a white flower remembering the departed
sun.' When the boy died in December 1879 Montesquiou received
from Mallarmé this beautiful letter: 'You are one of those that I
shall always be happy to see. Our minds move in harmony, but
that apart, there are, I know not why, many other ties of intimate
sympathy between us. But yes! I tell myself how, with your real
perspicacity, you derived so much pleasure from the delightful
being who was our treasure.' After that the relationship slowly

cooled. But twenty years later, in acknowledging a collection of poems, Mallarmé wrote to Montesquiou: 'My dear poet, In this surprising book *Parcours du Rêve au Souvenir,* you delightfully illustrate the belief that certain people think in verse exclusively and are incapable of not doing so.'

In the relationship between Montesquiou and Verlaine there is further proof of a kindness which was often stifled in order to shine at another's expense. Count Robert was really very good and very patient with the old poet; and for one so afflicted his attentions must have been more than a prince's bounty.

The sixty-six letters written to the Count from Verlaine read more like those of a beggar than those of a master. They are written on coarse hospital writing-paper, on pink or mauve prostitutes' cards, or on the back of wine-merchants' accounts. Always they smell of pipe tobacco. The old man's Maecenas piously had them bound in dark brown moroccan leather, writing on the title-page this direction by Molière for a ballet: 'Men and women afflicted, singing and dancing.' With some friends, among them the Countess Greffulhe and the Duchesse de Rohan, Montesquiou and Barrès guaranteed Verlaine a pension. But that was not sufficient, and Verlaine sold to his admirer manuscripts which he failed to deliver because of 'felonious intrigues by a landlord assisted by a whore'. From hospitable Broussais he begged for 100 francs to 'buy some clothes' and then for 'the means to rent a hovel, to which only my work would call me. . . . I am in a quandary.' In 1893 he sent some poems 'recopied in the bad handwriting of a fever-patient and a skeleton. The people who give me money are slow—slow. God! How bloody all this is!' At once Montesquiou despatched Yturri with help. Thus it came about that this charming boy earned a sonnet, ending as follows:

> How exquisite a gallant, bringing alms
> To succour one he conquered by his charms.

The Count had earned compliments still more flowery:

> The thinker and the avid aesthete I admire,
> His thoughts a-flutter like swift bats above:
> But the enchanter, fine and sweet, I love.

Verlaine participated in all the recitals and parties arranged by Montesquiou in order to have a statue erected to Marceline

Desbordes-Valmore: 'I am happy to see you embroider my name on the noble and poetic oriflamme which you wave so beautifully in honour of our friend.' The committee had to meet and dine at Foyot's* and Verlaine asked for some shoes to take him there— 'not a farthing at home'.† Then came the end in the house of the good woman who had sheltered the poet. Several times Montesquiou visited her to encourage her to support the sick man—it would be to her ultimate glory. Another faithful visitor was Gabriel Fauré, a dear friend of Montesquiou, who brought help on behalf of the Princesse de Polignac and kept her informed of the poet's condition. Would he have the strength to write the poems which Fauré needed? The musician sent to his protectress a drawing of the old faun in his hospital bed. Express letters from Dr Parizot kept Montesquiou constantly advised about the illness and he was present at the last consultation.

Verlaine's last letter is dated 2 January 1896: 'Monsieur de Yturri brought me 100 francs on your behalf.' Count Robert was again there on the last day, when Verlaine shouted in his delirium: 'The wreaths are suffocating me . . . take away the wreaths.'

Gabriel Fauré had met Verlaine through Montesquiou, and to him he wrote: 'How I should have liked to acquaint you with the last melody—*Votre âme est un paysage charmant*.‡ My publisher is in a state of confusion over Masques and Bergamasques. In succession he consulted his wife, his children and all his friends; then he told me triumphantly, "You see, no one knows what it means!" ' In the days of his friendship with Blanche, Montesquiou had Fauré's quartet played in the painter's studio and asked him for a portrait of the composer. Perhaps Verlaine was one of those invited. But let us return to the death-bed.

Thanks to the intervention of Mendès, the Ministry sent 50 francs to pay for those wreaths on the day of the funeral. The cost of the ceremony was divided between Montesquiou, Barrès and Mendès. Robert and Yturri followed the procession; but it was Barrès and Coppée, Mallarmé and Mendès who held the coffin-ropes, and one can imagine Montesquiou, draped in his greatcoat with his back against the rusty iron railing, impatiently tapping a foot while listening to the orations to which he had not

* A famous Left Bank restaurant.
† In English in the original. Trans.
‡ The line in fact reads: 'Votre âme est un paysage choisi'. Trans.

himself been asked to contribute. 'Goodbye, Verlaine! Goodbye, child of genius!' sighed Coppée in an over-emotional voice; Mendès's roaring sobs shook his yellow mane of hair; Mallarmé murmured something vague; then it was the turn of Moréas, that Greek who imitated Montesquiou's ways and his style of dress.

Did Count Robert ever meet Rimbaud? Such a possibility cannot be excluded; for when quite young, he knew Forain, Father Papillon's protégé and, at one time, a close intimate of the poet. It is perhaps permissible to attribute to Montesquiou a sonnet signed 'Ludwig II' and addressed to 'the brother of Baudelaire, to Arthur Rimbaud', since in the first place the epigraph is a quotation from Saint Joseph of Cupertino, dear to Montesquiou because, like his grandfather, this saint practised levitation, and in the second these last lines seem to have come from *Les Chauves-Souris*:

> Ah! made not for the surly heaven of our nights,
> But like some Etna which a moon unlooked-for lights.*

Léon Daudet was right when he said that 'Montesquiou goes to literature as others go to the people'. His relations with genius remained on the plane of ordinary social intercourse—friendly words were exchanged, as were little presents. He brought the same bland grace to his intimacies with academicians or outcast poets. Leconte de Lisle—'fine-featured, but a quill-driver' (Léon Daudet)—received him often, encouraged him and attended the party in the Bois de Boulogne at which *Les Chauves-Souris* was recited for the first time. To Montesquiou he confided, 'It is annoying at the end always to seem to have written things that no one understands'—wise advice that one would rather have expected to emanate from Mallarmé.

As for Heredia, it was he who, from the day they met at Mme de Poilly's, ran after the young man. Count Robert would pass from the smoking-room in the Rue Balzac, where the poets discussed rhymes and contracts, to the drawing-room, where the beautiful Mme de Heredia and her ravishing daughters would entertain him. Did they not think of him as a possible son-in-law? The author of the *Trophées* waxed tender: 'Louise, little Louise said to me, "That smells of Montesquiou". We were passing by a villa in front of which there was an avenue of carnations.' The

* Cf. Verlaine, *Pléiade*, p. 1000.

master thought of the young man as his successor in the Academy, and in the meantime introduced him to Edmond de Goncourt. He agreed to compose the Preface to one of Montesquiou's collections—indeed, he doted on it, writing to him: 'I have a sudden vivid, intense, immoderate and immediate desire to have some poems by you. It's essential. Send me the *Flûtiste sans Tête* and others as well. As a result of repeating "It is the Persian jugs . . ." I have become haunted, ill, and if you do not wish me to hate you, you must give in to me unremittingly, without delay at once, immediately, instantly.' The man whom Anatole France called 'the runaway horse with a respect for knick-knacks' was a little too apt to encourage Montesquiou to cultivate such trivialities himself.

Montesquiou was so well received by the leading writers of the day that he did not deign to frequent the editorial offices of the influential reviews. Certainly as a Maecenas he subscribed to *Scapin*, to *Décadent*, to *Vogue*, which published the first drawings of Grasset and de Feure, to the *Revue Wagnérienne* of Théodore de Wyzewa, who supported Moreau and Redon against the Impressionists. Did he expect to be begged to contribute to these publications? Or did he wish to reserve his poems for the delectation of an élite? We do not know. At all events he was much nearer in spirit to the *Mercure,* over which his friend Marcel Schwob reigned as editor.

To Schwob who, like Walter Pater, wrote *Imaginary Portraits*, well informed and, in his case, as far-fetched in their erudition as in the vices they depicted, Montesquiou seemed to lead, in this Paris of carriages and the Eiffel Tower, a quite imaginary life. With his immense appetite for culture, Montesquiou paid attention to Schwob's accounts of The Rome of Petronius and The London of Defoe; and he noted the titles of strange and forgotten books, the vocabulary of which was destined to enrich his own poems. The ugly and generous writer willingly welcomed Montesquiou into his apartment on the Ile Saint-Louis. He lived there with Marguerite Moreno, a tall girl with brown plaits of hair twisted round her head and wearing dresses that were totally straight and had full sleeves; she was called the Muse of the Symbolists. Count Robert preferred her intelligent diction to the uniform and naïve moaning dear to the interpreters of Maeterlinck. This couple, too, had been very good to Verlaine.

They were served by a Chinese manservant of dubious charms. The master of the house only became animated between two shots of morphine; then he compared Montesquiou to both the Duc de Lauzun and to an Arab poet in *Près des Jets d'Eau*. The author of *Roi au Masque d'Or* delighted in the poet's erudition and when in 1897 the first collection of Montesquiou's articles *Les Roseaux Pensants* appeared, he devoted to him 'a precious article in *Le Figaro*'. At each visit Robert brought a present; an English engraving, a very much alive Japanese dog, and one day a 'devoted cat', with a collar that Gallé had engraved with the titles of Schwob's works. At this house Montesquiou met a number of young men—some, like Gide, serious Wildeans, and others, like Valéry, disciples of Mallarméan elegance—but both groups he eluded. Young men of letters are on occasion ironical: Jules Renard, who believed Sarah Bernhardt when she told him that Montesquiou had had a real tear enclosed in a ring, noted after being introduced to him in 1896: 'Montesquiou has an aged face and uttered "Very flattered" through the beak of a bird of prey whose only food is vanity.' As for Léautaud, he recorded (June 1903) that it was Yturri who wrote for the Count, since he had overheard him say to Montesquiou, 'I shall have to shut myself up at home'; after which—since everyone seemed to be wondering what this might mean—Montesquiou attempted to explain, 'Yes, my poor Yturri is ill, very ill indeed.'

Those who on summer evenings saw along the quais the figures of Montesquiou, his cape billowing around him like the wings of a bat, a felt hat over his eyes and a cane in his hand, and of Yturri ever close behind him, imagined that some suspicious rendezvous was about to take place. Not at all! They were simply taking the same walk that Restif de la Bretonne used to take, before reaching Schwob's, passing as they did so under the balconies of the dwellings where Baudelaire, Delacroix and Chopin met each other. It was not a double life but a number of imaginary lives that Montesquiou lived—the lives of those he admired. But a hunger remained (if one can put it like that), and in the manner of Herodias he 'waited for something unknown'. He would visit poets, as one visits a clairvoyant, ready for sublime revelations; with thudding heart he climbed the narrow and well-polished staircase to Mallarmé's flat in the Rue de Rome or the sordid flights that led up to Verlaine, or the stone steps at the end of which he would find Schwob. Poetry, spiritualism and mysticism sometimes got confused in his head, as in the works of his master Ernest Hello: 'a man of genius with lightning flashes of mediocrity' (Léon Bloy).

A multitude of poets

Spiritualism and satanism floated like malarial mists above the Symbolist marsh, which was fed from such beautiful sources: Mallarmé, Verlaine, Moreau. . . . In those mists, grotesques and magicians often tended to get confused, so that vague shadows were taken for poets. Thus in the year 1890 poets pullulated—to be grouped for that season into Hydropaths, Zutists and Hirsutes. A report on poetry written by Catulle Mendès at the command of the Ministry of Public Instruction dizzies the mind with its endless list of names. It resembles a herbarium of exotic plants collected from a lagoon in the middle of which stood the splendid ruins of Ludwig II, the Byzantium of Sarah Bernhardt, the Middle Ages of Huysmans, the orient of Moreau. Magnificent flowers could there be gathered, like those of Rollinat:

> I give myself as prey to whores to cup:
> But with its tortuosity refined yet more
> I feel my fever's gimlet deeper bore.

Or Mallarméan colocynths such as: 'The defoliated rhythms of the divine young man resemble the golden nails which the Hippogriff, when he couples with omnipotent Boeotia, scatters as he strikes her soil with his foot.'

There, too, grew the creepers that were to clamber over the buildings of Guimard and Van de Velde, the orchids that were to decorate the vases of Gallé and the furniture of Majorelle. Gallé, the gardener of these new forms, described their evolution as follows: 'Phantoms, fuliginous symbols of empiricism, and of a disregard for causalities, monstrous forms of chimerical doctrines —these begin to appear in my conception of decoration. Then on to the paper will hasten the notations of intruding forms, of the bizarre adaptations of certain beings to their natural state— strange faces of nocturnal animals, a cyclopian eye, the white gaze of ghosts, pteropuses wrapped in Procinian cloaks, spectres and lemurs, vampires and noctules.'

Some painters, happily less numerous than the poets and unhappily less inspired than the glass-maker, were to find in these troubled waters vague, equivocal or splendid subjects with which to decorate the Mount of the Holy Grail of Art Nouveau. These were Lévy-Dhurmer in Paris, Troorop in Holland, Klimt in Vienna, and above all the incomparable designer Aubrey Beardsley, whose elegant monsters Wilde's *Salomé* introduced from England into France. And what did Count Robert do among so many poets? Well, like a heron rigid under its grey feathers, so he observed the swamp around him, pecked here and there at a delightful picture or a fashionable subject, sometimes took the croaking of worldly frogs for the goodwill of the public, and then, softly unfurling his wings, he would make for the bats coming in to meet him from the towers of Courtanvaux or even from China.

CHAPTER 11

The Poet

Where does the bird of Paradise alight?
My arms, half-open, are a living lyre.

The bats disappear into the Symbolist forest

AT THE beginning of 1892 Whistler and Mallarmé, the Countesses Greffulhe and Potocka, together with others famous for their genius or beauty, each received a box wrapped in a piece of silk on which bats had been embroidered. In this casket there was a stout volume printed on China paper, on the fly-leaves of which bats, grey on mauve, once again fluttered. It was these bats that gave their name to Robert de Montesquiou's first collection. The 'happy'* were indeed 'few',* for this edition with its vignettes by Whistler, Forain and a Japanese artist and its fly-leaves of silk figured with a yellow Whistler motif, is more a work of art than a book. To study poems recited in fashionable *salons* people required a more accessible edition. With this request the Count gracefully complied; and henceforth he was to offer his works to the public with a prodigality that was to continue until the day of his death and even beyond it. A Preface clarified certain obscure points, certain refinements. The dedication is enigmatic:

TO
L.T.B.F.A.F.B.C.
Sidereal personage
I present this ZAIMPH
R.M.F.

The zaimph is the cloak of the goddess Tanit in Flaubert's *Salammbo*, invisible to mortals, and the 'sidereal personage' was

* In English in original. Trans.

the affected Flavie de Casa-Fuerte. A quotation from Baudelaire sets the poet 'among those whose spirits have been "touched with pensiveness"* from their infancy—action and intention, dream and reality always remaining separate, with each one prejudicing the other, each usurping the place of the other'. Robert explained his work as a Japanese painter unrolls his *kakemono*: with the florid and sometimes macabre verve of a Hokusai. Like Victor Hugo in his *Orientales* he tries his hand at the oddest of forms. Certain lines flutter about like birds of good omen:

> Wasps
> Of the night
> Twirlings
> Contacts light
> No buzz,
> Noiseless flight
> Wasps
> Of the night.

Other poems show the unmistakable imprint of Lamartine:

> The mystery of night exalts chaste hearts.

Often he murmurs like Verlaine:

> The pale moon
> Seems like an opal
> That a changing sky
> Has mounted in silver.

Sometimes in the manner of Banville the poem is a mere literary exercise, to which he gives the brazen sonorities of an Heredia:

> O son of Anabaxore or of Anacydaraxe:
> You feel your powers waver on the balance of their axe.

One cannot help thinking, as one reads poems so deeply influenced by the period in which they were written, that they must have been known to those witty parodists of Symbolism, Vicaire and Beauclerc. In *Les Deliquescences* by 'Honoré Floupette' (published 'au Lion Vané à Byzance' in 1885) one reads:

> My heart is a Carylopsis from Japan. Pink
> Spangled with tawny gold . . .

and a little further on:

* In English in the original. Trans.

For a petunia makes me incorruptible.

The sonorous heroics of Heredia were not enough for the young poet: he also wanted his *Legend of the Centuries*. From it he selected the heroes for his fin-de-siècle Valhalla: Heliogabalus and Sardanapalus became the neighbours of Gilles de Rais and Henri III; but it was Ludwig II—towards whom Robert felt like a brother—who dominated the whole strange company. In contrast with this King of Dreams, the poet also glorified the Prince of Diamonds—that Duke of Brunswick who inspired Elémir Bourges in *Le Crépuscule des Dieux*.

An aesthete of the fin-de-siècle

In spite of these romantic images and symbolic trappings, the critics did not deceive themselves: Montesquiou was a *précieux*. In this poet who culled his laurels from the *Guirlande de Julie* they recognised the same exuberant pedantry, the same flowery gongorism that characterised the writers of the time of Louis XIII, exhumed by Théophile Gautier in his book *Les Grotesques,* the first lines of which describe the Wivern: 'Taloned, rough, sprinkled with scales, its wings like a bat's, its hind-quarters coiled.' It was in that company that Robert found his ancestors: the absurd Scalion de Virblumeau, Cyrano de Bergerac, Saint-Amant or Théophile de Viau. He was often to imitate Scarron's drolleries, and his pictures of society were often to have the obscene virulence of the Mazarinades.* How near, too, he seems to Scudéry, when one reads these lines by that first of the aesthetes:

> A heron's plume of black more sharply throws
> Into relief the white that ermine shows.

Gautier more than Baudelaire, whose name the young poet was to invoke so often, was the true master of Montesquiou. Both of them were aesthetes, their heads crammed with bizarre conjunctions of objects with words. *Mademoiselle de Maupin* satisfied Montesquiou's passion for the equivocal; *Le Capitaine Fracasse*

---

* Lampoons written against Mazarin during the wars of the Fronde. Trans.

his taste for display. He was near to Gautier through his friend Judith Gautier, and perhaps he was also distantly related to him, since the Priest-Duke may have asked Mme Gautier, whose husband was a civil servant at Auch, to brighten up his stay in the Pyrenees. In any case, the old man had taken notice of the youth and had interested himself in his education, writing to Gautier's parents: 'Don't put any more obstructions in the way of M. Théophile. His replies are unanswerable, since they are inspired by such a pronounced taste and such a consciousness of his powers that they suggest that he is a genius.' In short, if it is not certain that he owed his existence to the priest, at least Gautier owed to him the fact that his vocation was not opposed.

In any case a kinship of minds, if no other, is evident between the two poets; and there is a passage from Gautier quoted as an epigraph in the volume that followed Les Chauves-Souris, Les Hortensias bleus. This latter collection includes poems written before those in Chauves-Souris and contemporary with Les Illuminations, Rostand's Les Romanesques, the first poem of Francis Jammes and Sully Prudhomme's Reflexions. The curiosity that des Esseintes aroused irritated the critics as soon as he began to publish regularly. Doumic wrote: 'What M. de Montesquiou possesses in his own right and what no one will contest is an admirable fertility.' As for Gustave Khan in the Revue Blanche: 'How is it that his nullity annoys us more than other nullities? Because it is more profound? No: because it is more affected. It is a broth for the culture of the microbe of frivolity.' Rémy de Gourmont, who wrote in the Livre des Masques, is fairer: 'With half of the Hortensias bleus one could make another very thick volume consisting almost entirely of delicate, high-spirited or gentle poems.'

Count Robert set out his verses with as much taste as an interior decorator arranging china in a show-case; but there is much trash among all the curios.

When the poet recalls his youth in the châteaux, then the work of art becomes authentic:

Sleep, room! Your eyelids, which are curtains, veil your eyes,
While slowly on your panelling mirages rise
Of faery things, to make for you a world of sleep,
Of fleeting vision and of furtive peep.

Montesquiou is a kind of poet-collector: he is led by words as by things, but rarely by thoughts, or at any rate by thoughts on which he has reflected sufficiently profoundly to produce that quasi-algebraic crystallisation of a poem demanded by the Mallarméan ideal to which he sometimes aspired.

Certainly some stanzas in praise of Edmond de Goncourt seem to rise up clear above the shelves encumbered with over-decorated and fragile objects. It was these that Sarah declaimed when the old collector was being awarded a prize at the house of his editor, Charpentier. The naturalists of Le Grenier* were exasperated by these refinements, which did, however, bring Montesquiou a new friend, Georges Rodenbach, a Belgian poet. Montesquiou called him the 'brugeois gentilhomme' or the 'shepherd of the swans', invited him to a tea that 'could not fail to be aesthetic' and, highest praise of all, had himself photographed while reading *Bruges-la-Morte*, Rodenbach's then famous novel. Certain poems from the *Hortensias* emanated from the northern mists which, with the Seven Princesses and Mélisande, had begun to shroud the Byzantine follies of the time.

Proust said that Montesquiou often spoke as Maeterlinck wrote; here are some lines that are certainly like extracts from *La Princesse Maleine*:

> She told a tale, the little maid,
> Now that she had to die,
> A story, while the sombre shade
> Rose over her so high.

Two years passed before another collection, *Le Chef des Odeurs Suaves,* appeared. This title derives from a person in *Salammbo* and it did not take long before it was applied ironically to Montesquiou himself. His affectations have grown more extreme and his vigour has diminished in this monotonous herbarium, resembling a Japanese album filled with a thousand delightful drawings. Some of the poems have titles that are pleasing puns: for example, *Urbi et Herbae—Ce Que Dit La Bouche d'Ambre*. The opening words are a reply to the young Anna de Noailles:

> A noise of secateurs within the gloomy orchard,
> This small grey net the shade of mountain-flax . . .

* The house in which the Goncourt brothers lived. Trans.

The volume is divided into a dozen floral games, with Rosatinums, a House of Perfumes, a Florilegium. These are allusions to the catalogue of the florist Vilmorin and to the celebrated Jeux Floraux of Toulouse.*

Malicious people thought that it was rather absurd for a man to busy himself with making such dainty bouquets, but the female chorus, drowning all critical murmurs, fervently repeated the flowers in the catalogue:

> Hearts-ease, pansy, anemone, columbine,
> Heliotrope, ageratum, iris, wisteria,
> Violets schooled to be glad or repine,
> Mallows deflowered and lilacs growing wearier.

People hastened to La Baudinière to hear truly remarkable lectures on painting; but Montesquiou went too far in over-loading his poems. He still recited his verses in the drawing-rooms to ladies and young men thirsty for Beauty. A girl in the back row began to whisper and the Count broke off with an 'I see that I am boring you', which froze their hostess. The chatterer's name would be entered on a black list. But Montesquiou's fervour carried him beyond the target of his animosity. It would often happen that by uttering some offensive epithets too loudly he would confer fame on some person who would otherwise never have emerged from obscurity. Sometimes the poet entrusted the task of bringing out every nuance of his poems to some celebrated voice. Mme Bartet recaptured the accents of Iphigenia to hymn the falling of petals; her gradual lightening of the sonorities was a triumph of imitative harmony:

> Petals come, go, fall, shower down, settle.

Every celebrity had to work for the glory of the poet. Leconte de Lisle introduced *Les Chauves-Souris* at a festival in the Bois de Boulogne; a sonnet by Verlaine welcomed *Le Chef des Odeurs Suaves*.

> *To Count Robert de Montesquiou*
> The poet whose infinite vision doubles
> Each nuance, deep into our scruples probes,

* Jeux Floraux, Academy of Poetry founded by the Troubadours in Toulouse in 1323. Trans.

Bursting our faulty reasoning like bubbles—
A puff alone destroys their fragile globes.

Verlaine helped Montesquiou to organise a fête in honour of
Marceline Desbordes-Valmore, to whom a rather mediocre
monument was unveiled at Douai on 13 July 1896. Several years
of lectures, recitations and stirring people up had been necessary
to gather together the money and the personalities. Caran d'Ache
portrayed Montesquiou as the postilion of a coach on the roof
of which all the celebrities can be picked out. The minister
proposed a speech from Armand Sylvestre, whose scatological
sonnets made him worthy of the cognomen 'perdomaniac'. After
paying a thousand compliments to Mme Arman de Caillavet,
Montesquiou managed to enlist Anatole France; also Sarah
Bernhardt, 'the great Guitry, the beautiful Brandès and the blue-
stocking Moreno'. This consecration was the fulfilment of a vow
made at the bedside of his sister-in-law to drag poor Marceline
out of oblivion. In conducting his campaign Montesquiou
displayed all the ardour of a knight intent on delivering Angélique
from the grotto of forgetfulness.

It was also in the guise of Christian knight that Montesquiou
composed a work destined to be received far more favourably
than the one which had preceded it, since both the ludicrous and
the exquisite were omitted. The gardener and the antiquary have
now become the thinker, sometimes, it must be admitted, with
the nobleness of Sully-Prudhomme or the tremolo of Coppée.
This collection consisted of: *Eight sets of ten rosaries—for the use
of artistic fingers and distinguished hearts*. If one has the courage to
go beyond these forbidding adjectives and if one averts one's gaze
from Madeleine Lemaire's illustrations, one can find some
beautiful poems in the *Prières de Tous*, of which the best known is
La Prière de Serviteur:

The house is set in order, I have barred its doors:
But still I guard its treasures while my master lies
In sleep. Like me, the hound which on the flagstone snores
Dreams through the long, slow night with only half-closed
    eyes.

The fountain now is silenced and the lamp alight,

The clothes are folded and the cups and plates are cleared
Where in the dark the stair-rails vanish out of sight
Tears force their silent runnels down on to my beard.

Except at last beneath my gravestone, master dear,
I shall not know repose. There like the dew
A summons will for once fall sweet, and from my bier
'Master!' I shall reply—and it will then be you!

Montesquiou, who in his hours of melancholy turned towards
the Beyond, often believed himself to be a thinker; but with the
exception of the poem quoted above, the most beautiful subjects
were for him only pretexts for decoration. Thus, in another
collection entitled *Les Paons, La Cité Mystique* is little more than a
jeweller's display:

Cornelian and sardonyx, amethyst and sapphire bright,
Hyacinth, chalcedony and jade all gave delight.

As almost always in the case of aesthetes, thought is of less
value than vision. Montesquiou's eyes made out all shades, all
details. He gathered the impressions received on his travels into a
collection which, though it received scant attention, contains
some pretty things: *Le Parcours du Rêve au Souvenir*. This is like the
notebook of a painter, with sketches of Brittany, Holland, Venice,
Algeria and England.

On a background flax-blue, sky-grey, pearl-azure,
The dune vanishes into a hue of fine yellow.

His Venice is that of Whistler's water-colours, lightly rubbed in
on bistre paper.

Venice—
Flavour of aniseed,
A bluish-white reflection—
Is tinted
With absinthe,
Dies of softness.

At St Moritz he parodied the naïvetés of Baedeker:

The chief aim of this book should now be clear:
To show its readers how best to enjoy
The marvels of a land without a peer.

It is possible to trace the influence of Montesquiou on Apollinaire, for these lines from *Le Chef des Odeurs Suaves*:

> Here are the antique lampreys, queens whose greed
> Demanded flesh of slaves on which to feed,

find an echo in the *leitmotif* of Apollinaire's *Chanson du Mal Aimé*:

> I who know songs for queens, the hymns of slaves
> To lampreys . . .

And what a number of coincidences exist in the evocation of
Ludwig II in *Mal Aimé*. . . .

When Montesquiou went to Algeria he was as susceptible as
Gide to the charms of youth:

> Orange-tree buds like living pearls distil
> Their drops of perfume on their outstretched fingers;
> Those who desire me pursue me still—
> Upon my clothes the scent of jasmine lingers.

The resemblances between the poetry of Montesquiou and
Stefan George are even franker; it is known how much the
German admired Mallarmé, but the themes which he treated were
nearer those dear to Montesquiou. In the *Jardin d'Algabal* there
are many flowers and precious stones, and the emperor in it,
'beautiful as Satan', is the brother of the Heliogabalus of whom
Montesquiou made one of his most frightening 'Lunatics':

> The stone upon his forehead starts to tremble,
> Because he dares a woman even more resemble.

Les Perles Rouges do not belong to the gimcrack treasures
plundered from Sarah Bernhardt's wardrobe; they are worth
more than that because they were formed by everyday aesthetic
experiences and, as we read them, we follow Count Robert on his
walks at Versailles.

The facility of Montesquiou's output, already condemned
by his first critics, has subsequently discouraged readers. If
we look again at Catulle Mendès's report on the situation of
poetry in the France of that time, we can imagine Montesquiou's
irritation as he went through page after page of that incredible
catalogue of names, before he at last came on the one that was

devoted to himself. True, Rimbaud is only named in passing: 'What seems to me to distinguish him is little except the vileness or the nastiness of the subjects to which he devotes himself'; but it is necessary to endure paragraphs of praise for Moréas, Viélé-Griffin, Gustave Kahn and even Ephraïm Mikhael, before reaching Montesquiou, 'who in his early poems pushed the fantastic to the verge of eccentricity'; but 'little by little he repudiated his former buffoonery. *Les Perles Rouges* contains some almost perfect sonnets; *Les Prières pour Tous* show an almost genuinely religious soul.' At that the author of *Sainte Thérèse, courtisane de Dieu* concluded with a pun: 'Robert de Montesquiou's penitence should be to say the burial service, exquisitely, at the altar* of Rambouillet.'

Rémy de Gourmont, a critic of a different class, says in his *Le Livre des Masques*: 'After all, M. de Montesquiou exists. He is one of those flowers which one inspects with curiosity in a flower-bed, the name of which one asks, and which one remembers. His originality is excessively tattooed. The beauty of this bard comes as a reminder, not without melancholy, of the complicated patterns with which the ancient Australian chiefs liked to decorate themselves.' Finally, with a two-edged compliment, the critic sums up the opinion of the time:

'C'est une précieuse!'

* 'À l'autel'—'à l'hôtel'. The pun cannot be reproduced in English. Trans.

CHAPTER 12

'Marie-Antoinette Pensive, and Louis XIV Knowing'

I trace my portrait under the shadows of the park,
Nobleman and smiling, young and of an ancient stock.

Return to the Grand Style

ONE FINE afternoon in May two gentlemen dressed with dazzling discretion, one all in grey and the other all in a beige of a shade scarcely darker than his tawny complexion, went once more on a pilgrimage to Versailles. Perhaps they went to see their friend Pierre de Nolhac, who wished to give back to the château, at once saved and destroyed by Louis-Philippe, its pristine glory; or their friend Lobre, who painted the deserted salons of the Trianon and the thickets to which the red trousers of members of the garrison added a touch of colour. In these years of the 'nineties Versailles was the Venice or the Bruges of France. Since Musset and 'the stairs of pink marble', a romanticism weary of the exotic and a symbolism eager to escape from softness and delicacy found there a more classical inspiration. The works of the Goncourts on the royal favourites, the early articles of Lenôtre, and above all the writings of Nolhac attracted attention to Versailles. Count Robert had never stopped going there since his childhood, for one of the Montesquiou aunts lived in the pavilion once inhabited by Mme Elisabeth.* At Versailles his taste for the antique sharpened, his nostalgia for vanished grandeur blossomed.

The carriage which conveyed the two friends to Versailles passed, in the Avenue de Paris, an iron gate to which was fixed a notice 'To let'. 'Let us look inside,' cried Montesquiou, who

* The sister of Louis XVI.

could never resist his desire to enter an empty house. He already saw his furniture miraculously transported like the *casa santa* of Loretto, and was even considering what pieces he would have to buy. As usual, Yturri tried to curb his enthusiasm; but on this occasion he was won over and the friends left the house in possession of the lease. Let us leave to Montesquiou the task of describing this house, intact to the present day: 'Two noble gates, with posts crowned with baskets in worked stone and decorated with fruit, commanded the double entrance, each of them dwarfing the two pavilions of a less imposing construction which faced them and between which, extending along the façade, there was a terrace. Two symmetrical paths, on the right and on the left of which there was a regular slope of lawn, led towards some central steps which, in turn, led to a fairly large enclosure, half-garden and half-orchard.'

Montesquiou now abandoned Passy with as much speed as he had once abandoned the Quai d'Orsay. Japan was finished: it had become too common, all the cocottes had bamboo furniture and Buddhas in their winter gardens,* and the Bon Marché had begun to manufacture imitation Japanese embroidery pictures. The two friends retained nothing but some lacquer boxes that looked so well on chests-of-drawers, some guardian lion dogs and some bronze cranes for the lawn on which scampered Tama, a pekinese that had been the gift of the Princesse de Sagan. There was a salon in the Empire style to please Whistler. The Vigée-Lebruns went well on the panelling and the young painter Helleu helped to hunt out some easy-chairs by Jacob and striped wallpapers. Helleu had just moved into an apartment in the Porte Dauphine district. His dry-point etchings, which had become fashionable, had enabled him to buy Marie Antoinette furniture and to bring together a whole collection of picture frames, which he hung, some inside others, on the apple-grey silk of his salon. Pale-grey silk, armchairs covered with lilac damask, flowered Savonnerie carpets, woodwork painted white on white—all these things could also be found in the Montesquiou pavilion. However, reproaching Helleu for his frivolity, Montesquiou made him come to Versailles to paint the fountains and the thickets in order to prove to himself that he was also a great artist.

If Helleu was the Minister of Taste, Yturri was the Floral

* See the description of Odette de Crecy's house in Proust's *Swann's Way*.

Chancellor* to the Commander of Delicate Odours. This last nickname, derived from the over-exquisite title of the over-copious collection which followed *Hortensias Bleus* far too rapidly, nevertheless personified Montesquiou. Daudet had already called him 'Hortensiou'; Forain 'Grotesquiou'; *La Vie Parisienne* 'Thankiou-Coursensac'. . . . All this made the common herd laugh, and Montesquiou congratulated himself that it should be so. To know that one is a source of ridicule but to persist in the behaviour that makes one so, becomes one insolence the more.

Nolhac lent the poet the keys of the park; surveying the deserted views, he could imagine himself to be Ludwig II at Herrenchiemsee, and his walks here inspired him with some of his best poems, '*Les Perles Rouges*'. In autumn he sees:

> Faro, lansquenet, reversi and cavagnol
> Are being played with dead leaves for cards
> In the cold heart of the groves.

Perhaps round a thicket he saw Jean Lorrain—felt hat turned down and a cape enveloping him—deep in conversation with some non-commissioned officer. Montesquiou himself preferred the statues:

> Now Ganymede extends this cup from which is shed
> The death of the princess . . .

He read carefully the descriptions of Versailles in Piganiol de la Force. The custodian took him on a tour of the intimate apartments; declaiming Saint-Simon in a trumpeting voice, Montesquiou went through his whole shrill gamut of grandeur and insolence. At the Trianon he recited Chénier:

> O Versailles, O woods, O porticoes,
> Living marbles, ancient bowers . . .

But, curiously, carried away by his admiration for Michelet, his judgments on the last Bourbons were as severe as those of the historian and not at all those of an aristocrat. His sonnet on Mme de Maintenon, *Servante-Maîtresse*, is famous:

---

* In French 'le Chancelier de Fleurs' in allusion to 'Le Chancelier de Fer'—Bismarck, the Iron Chancellor.

She mingles boldness, ecstasy and spite,
No nasty secret holds for her offence,
And though obsessed with faith and penitence,
Yet she grows amorous at fall of night.
The ancient cripple now is nothing to her;
She stays to hear some verse by Racine read,
Meanwhile the Setting Sun sets in her bed.

There are, of course, some insipid fancies about Marie-Antoinette; they had begun with *Les Chauves-Souris*:

The gardener of the Trianon presents
The scenery to you:
Kerchiefs of lawn from royal breasts
Still cloud it from the view.

Montesquiou and Yturri would spend whole days in the park of
the Trianon, attracting to it both poets and elegant women who
came to listen to Nolhac or to Montesquiou himself. Mme
Greffulhe organised a fancy-dress party for charity in the Dairy.
The two friends were so very much at home there that it is
possible to suggest an explanation for the strange encounter
which two extremely rational English women dons at an Oxford
college experienced in the park. These ladies published, under the
title *An Adventure*, an account of how they both witnessed the
apparitions of people in bygone costumes and heard mysterious
music. Perhaps, however, the 'ghosts' which they took for Marie-
Antoinette and her courtiers were, quite simply, Mme Greffulhe,
dressed as a shepherdess, rehearsing an entertainment with some
friends. Or 'Marie-Antoinette' may have been Mme d'Hervey de
Saint-Denis, of whom Montesquiou possessed several photographs in the costume of the queen. The description of one of the
apparitions by Miss Moberly exactly corresponds to Yturri: 'Tall,
with large, dark eyes . . . crisp, curling black hair . . . large sombrero hat. His face was glowing red as though through great
exertion—as though he had come a long way. At first I thought
he was sunburnt, but a second look satisfied me that the colour
was from heat, not sunburning. He had on a dark cloak wrapped
across him like a scarf, one end flying out in his prodigious hurry.
He looked greatly excited as he called out to us, "Mesdames,
Mesdames", (or "Madame", pronounced more as the other), "il

ne faut (pronounced *fout*) pas passer par là." He then waved his arm, and said with great animation, "Par ici . . . cherchez la maison." [*] Did the visitors intrude upon one of those re-enactments of the past that the poet devised for a rigidly exclusive circle of chosen friends? That would explain the panic of the more or less disguised participants and the manner in which a short young man slammed a door in their faces. Perhaps the part of Marie-Antoinette had been entrusted to someone who had the queen's profile and wore the queen's clothes, but whose sex was different from hers, and perhaps at the moment when the English spinsters were about to burst in, a photographer was in process of capturing a moment of bizarre beauty. There is also the possibility that the strange appearance and the stranger voices—of another century and of another country—of the two friends stirred the imaginations of the two Englishwomen and induced hallucinations. The pavilion may have been reorganised for a party, so that the reply of the custodian, 'Impossible, unless they were masqueraders', causes no astonishment. The green liveries could have been those of servants. The man in an enormous hat, which seemed to them sinister, and with a face pitted with small-pox, might have been Montesquiou himself, whose face, after his fortieth year, was deeply lined with furrows which he had the habit of covering with paint much as men used to do in the time of Marie-Antoinette. It is extremely rare in the whole history of apparitions for two people to see the same images and to hear the sounds at exactly the same time. Who, indeed, can say that Montesquiou himself did not experience on the desolate paths encounters similar to those caused by his passage?

> Speech made from silence in which lutes have sighed,
>   A puff of wind from breath where roses grew,
> A glance from mystery where things had died,
>   A word checked on the lips of one I knew.

These lines exactly express the tension that seized the Englishwomen a short time before the phantoms appeared to them in a place thought by them to be deserted, yet peopled with memories and haunted by a poet.

---

[*] *An Adventure*, by C. E. Moberly and E. F. Jourdain. In the French original a summary, rather than a translation, is given of this passage. Trans.

The first of the great fêtes

Versailles became a place to visit for those who hoped to meet
Montesquiou; a centre of social excitement for those he invited
there. He knew well that people of fashion admire only those who
come to their notice through fashionable entertainments. He
therefore entertained on a scale remarkable for Versailles—to
launch artists he admired, to give recitations of his poems.
Only intimate friends had known the Quai d'Orsay; the Japanese
of the Rue Franklin had given only tea-parties among his curios.
But at Versailles, the blood of generations of court chamberlains
and ladies of honour awakened in his veins, so that during the
summer his parties not merely filled the pavilion but spilled over
into the garden. Lace and feather-boas circulated among the blue
hydrangeas; plumed hats rivalled the bunches of lilacs and budd-
leias. In autumn, ladies were asked to dress like the autumn leaves.

In the spring a huge party brought Sarah Bernhardt back,
to declaim some of the host's poetry. She was sheathed 'in
glittering silver silk, decorated all over with irises'. Mme Bartet in
her tailor-made costume by Redfern still suggested the veils of
Iphigenia; but for reciting works by the Count, Marguerite
Moreno changed into a virgin's waistless dress, the essence of
Rodenbach. Under ornate umbrellas that billowed as much as
their skirts, swooning ladies were propped up by delightful young
men, in morning-coats, grey spats, striped trousers and waistcoats
as subtly variegated as their souls. Depending on whether he was
impersonating Ludwig II or Plato, Montesquiou needed pages or
disciples. One of these, drunk on high society, rushed forward at
the conclusion of a party to kiss the gloved hand of the master of
the house. Proust, the cleverest of these flatterers, wrote to him:
'Will you be returning soon to Versailles—of which you are the
pensive Marie-Antoinette and the knowing Louis XIV?'

Great men flocked there. Barrès came in the company of his
wife, who, peering through her lorgnette, gave all this fine
society a stare in which disapproval and snobbery were at odds
with each other. Anatole France let himself be brought by Mme
Arman de Caillavet; with his long nose and his little eyes he
resembled an elephant in the charge of a keeper disguised as a
lampshade. Mme Daudet apologised for her ailing husband—'But,
dear and great friend, he will come next time. That is a promise.'

Her voice almost inaudible, but straining towards these aristocrats who fascinated her little Lucien, she was introduced to right and left. Countess Greffulhe invariably arrived late, to receive the respects of those guests among whom she scattered her perfunctory greetings much as one throws sugared almonds to the poor at village baptisms. She made a tour of the party on the arm of her dear Robert, but not all were greeted by name. It was necessary to earn this favour by an ingenious compliment or a charming profile.

When the guests had gone, Montesquiou kept back two or three favourites: perhaps a highness who was passing through, or some new recruits whom he wished to dazzle by leading them through the deserted palace to see the sunset from the gallery of mirrors. There he would declaim: 'Skies of Gethsemane and Golgotha, skies of Leucadia and of Cayster: Gustave Moreau found them in this Versailles, united in a mystic paganism and in the fountains of the Sun-King playing every day on the mirrors of water of the King-Sun. I muse there sometimes, amidst the evening blaze, when the remains of storms and celestial eddies whirl through the atmosphere like splinters of light, like heads of hair of fluid gold, like flounces of salmon-coloured gauze or of orange muslin.' The magician arranged for the fountains to be played for his guests; the improvisation began again—or was it a recitation? . . . 'Daily fireworks the flying rockets of which let fall their sparks to meet the silky and coralline bouquets of sensual laurel blossoms. One might call it a massacre of doves, stabbed to the heart in the wide spaces of the sky'—the cleverest of the flatterers makes a note of those doves at that point—'their imaginary down mingling with these borrowed gems, with these artificial petals. Sham flowers and false feathers, illusory rubies are absorbed into the broken smile of the horizon, which closes like the lips of a wound.' This spectacle and his comments on it had left the guests in a trance: now came the moment to give orders. 'Helleu, leave the ladies from the Avenue du Bois to that syrupy Flameng and come and paint this fountain. Cousteau's Diana has even longer legs than Miss Deacon—and at least she does not talk. Paul, be serious. Promise me to come tomorrow!' Montesquiou called Versailles in summer 'my marble beach' and affirmed that the palace and the garden had cost exactly 457,518,478.35 francs.

When the last carriage had disappeared at the end of the Avenue de Paris, the poet, surveying his lawns pocked by women's heels, his disarranged furniture and his tired bouquets, thought up some malicious comments. Decidedly, he told himself, he was far too amiable; he always invited far too many people. At that, he would take his revenge in verse. On his cousin, Prince Giovanni Borghese, for example:

> A plate is all Batista's patron chooses
> To give him, and this plate the poor man uses
> Both, when he begs for food, as begging-bowl
> And as an alms-box to contain his dole.

Friendship was no more immune from this mockery than was the family, and Poland provided some comic rhymes:

> To poor Countess Potocka
> Potocki proved a shocker

or

> Madame Bernardak—
> Y is a property shark.

Someone took the liberty of bringing along the grotesque Mrs Moore, whom Montesquiou found both flat in character and protuberant in person and whom he dismissed as 'a bed-bug afflicted with elephantiasis'. 'Gabriel, do come and hear my comment on Mrs Moore!' 'Divine, dear Robert!'

Introduction of Marcel Proust

Montesquiou was then a scintillating—and for some people even a burning—star, surrounded by Yturri as Saturn is surrounded with its whirling ring. He drew into his trajectory some stars in the process of forming: stars destined to be planets reflecting his sun in what the journalists called 'the firmament of Parisian life'. On the eve of the new century the poet reached his zenith; he adjusted his gravitation to the gravitations of stars of the first magnitude—Bernhardt, Anatole France, Barrès—but at the same time hurled confusion into less important galaxies, by annexing to his own system some of their lights. In 1892 the most shrewd of the society astronomers could not have foreseen that sixty years after the meeting of the star Montesquiou with one of the lesser satellites of Mme Lemaire's salon, the first would have become a dead moon round the second, who by then had become a sun.

The glittering of this Lemaire galaxy seems to us today to be one of the most absurd phenomena which could ever have dazzled our grandparents. We are so often surprised by the success of some of our women today that it seems almost impossible for us to understand the success of Madeleine Lemaire. Even odder is the alliance between the Commander of Heavenly Odours and this flower-painter of whom Dumas said, 'No one, after God, has created more roses.' These roses as heavy as cabbages, the colour of slaughter-houses, showed themselves off on the fans of grand-duchesses, on the menus of the Rothschilds and around the poems of Montesquiou. At each Salon, Marquisettes received them from the hands of gallant Musketeers; or, spread out at the foot of the altar on the occasion of a Pompadour wedding, they made one think that the bride must have succumbed to indigestion. The Empress of Roses, as Montesquiou called her, could not have put a higher price on her roses if each petal had been a bank-note. The stars could show great tolerance among themselves, and Montesquiou frequently wrote in praise of the talent of this woman who so often entertained in his honour:

The flowers in our gardens, you have perfected them in paint,
Fairy with the brushes steeped in amber and honey.

Madeleine Lemaire wore big hats to hide her acne and trains on her dresses to hide the size of her feet. When she dressed, she put on fancy-dress, and so as not to be the only person thus attired, her balls were always costume ones. Tall and bony, she was conceded to have chic; painstaking and tame in her workmanship, she was conceded to have talent. Undoubtedly she was witty, with the satirical wit of the Baignères or of Forain's stories, to which an endless flow of society gossip was added. She knew the exact circumstances of everyone, the debts and the expectations, the liaisons and the quarrels. She was always accompanied by an unmarriageable young girl called Suzette, who also painted flowers. Everyone was seen at the house of 'our old clear-starcher', as Forain called her. Her house, a modest little mansion with a small garden in front, was in the Rue de Monceaux, in the shade of the chestnut trees of the Murat property. At the end of a

courtyard there was a Louis XVI-Venetian studio. It was through
this small courtyard, with an awning above it, that guests made
their entrances to her famous balls.

Once each year Mme Lemaire invited all the names on her
great register: this reception she called Majora Canamus, an
allusion to the marriage at Cana. But nearly every day she gave a
tea-party and every Wednesday in the spring she held open-house
—all this apart from the poetical and musical parties to which a
more select list of guests was invited. This lady, a solid bourgeoise
launched into Bohemian society through an affair with Dumas *file*,
forced herself by her gift of the gab into the luncheons that went
with openings at the *salon* and exhibitions by Carolus Duran or by
Detaille. She allied herself with Béraud, the portrayer of clubmen
—the only painter invited into high society. Rapidly she extended
her conquests; and so it was that she put her drawing-room at
Montesquiou's disposal and introduced him to artists and writers;
in return for which services he could not do otherwise than bring
along his chorus of society women. Towards 1890 her salon had
become smart, offering, as it did, on the one hand, an opportunity
for stepping down from one's class in the exact degree that was
calculated to please the Faubourg Saint-Germain and, on the other,
the mob of people who had given significance to the term 'Tout
Paris'. 'The world and his wife' were to be seen there, even more
than at Mme Straus's; but in addition the Princess of Orléans, the
Grand Dukes, Bernhardt, and Pierre Loti—in short, a jumble
ranging from anyone who could afford to order a fan costing a
hundred louis to anyone who promised to become famous (for the
lady water-colourist had a flair). The parties given by Mme
Lemaire for Montesquiou were like fish-hatcheries from which the
poet chose those specimens who were worthy of attending his own
receptions. He frequently shone there: either by scattering *Les
Perles Rouges* before a herd of ecstatic women, or by choosing as the
listener to one of his more scandalous poems some female guest
who, at first delighted, would slowly be made uneasy by the
favour. Had she laughed at the right moment? And would people
repeat to the victim the fact that she had laughed? But Montesquiou was to take his revenge on reticent compliments. He
began pianissimo:

Maguelonne has painted flowers for sixty years,

On them a mass of paint she piles and smears

—his voice threatened to overwhelm the hubbub—

The same paint from her old face also oozes.

Once and for all Madeleine Lemaire had decided not to hear anything on such occasions. She would cry, 'A chair for Madame La Duchesse de Chartres!'; then she would shriek at Mme de Chevigné, who wished to present her to a grand-duchess, 'Oh, my dear, you're humbugging me!' Another twirl again: 'Ah, my dear little Reynaldo, when the Good Lord has satisfied our appetites, you will sing us a madrigal.'

On 23 March 1893, while Julia Bartet recited some of Montesquiou's unpublished poems, he sat with his eyes fixed on the door. Since he had put on a good performance, dear old Madeleine Lemaire could be satisfied. . . . She approached, pushing before her a very dark young man, with admirable eyes in an elongated and completely white face. 'He is dying, yes, literally dying. He ought not to have come out to meet you. You make him so frightened— do promise to be nice to him. This is my delightful page— Monsieur Proust.'

CHAPTER 13

A Professor of Beauty

I am the lord of transitory glory,
    A courtier of the subtle and the rare,
Of the Infinitesimal the heir;
    Now of life's changes I shall tell the story.

A delightful disciple

IN THIS introduction the fervour of the aesthete and the flutterings
of the snob became confused; confronted with his ideal, Proust
saw the nobleman and the poet at one and the same time and
exaggerated his compliments to the first to the same extent as he
revered the second. The words jostled each other on his lips as
they forced their way out; but these were not the fatuous compliments uttered by the foolish young men who craved to be
invited to Versailles. Amiability blossomed on the face of the
Count. He asked some questions: 'Do you write, Monsieur
Proust?' 'Some prose poems in a little review called *Le Banquet*.'
'Ah, yes, I know . . . Jacques Bizet, Mme Straus's son, and
Gaston de Caillavet, Mme Arman's son, collaborate on it. . . . An
intelligent set. You must come and see me. But, hush, here she
is. . . Proud Julia Bartet, imperishable diseuse.'

Shortly after this party Montesquiou received a letter, the
intelligent compliments of which confirmed the good impression
already made by the young man.

> . . . For a long time I have observed that there is much more
> to you than the exquisite decadent (a type which has reached
> perfection in your case, but which is usual enough in these
> times) that people would have you be. . . . Has Corneille
> written a more beautiful line than this one: 'By waning lights
> she sees within herself more clearly'? Or one more typical of

his style than 'Those whom proud modesty has doomed to tearless lashes'? . . . All that for the greater good fortune of your very respectful and grateful . . .

The messenger came back to Paris with a huge photograph of the Count, taken at Otto's and inscribed with this line:

I am the lord of transitory glory . . .

A little later this poem, written on pink paper, arrived:

Pilgrimage
And all Viroflay still sleeps

Banville

Come now, dear Monsieur Proust,
As birds fly home to roost.
Please do not count the coust.*

Beneath my lilacs steal a
Moment to read and feel a
New El Filasoufilas.

Sky painted by Helleu
And neither rose nor blue,
We'll call upon Saint-Leu.

The siege of Montesquiou began. It was to prove more fortunate than Proust's earlier siege of the Countess of Chevigné, but infinitely more difficult than that of Mesdames Strauss and Lemaire. These women, the young man had very well understood, suffered from an extreme loneliness in the midst of so much social activity. Messengers no longer brought them anything but invitations and letters of thanks. Marcel could fill this void with lengthy epistles and presents of books and curios. His adoration rejuvenated these women whom society had desiccated. He smothered them with flowers, nestled at their feet, listened to their secrets and went on errands for them. . . . He was so *nice*! Nice—he used this word a little too often and the Count did not care to have it applied to himself—he might be magnanimous, kind or merely polite, but this being 'nice' he left to the lower orders. Still, this useless 'nice' was only a single thorn in a bed of

* In the original, the rhyme is also 'Proust . . . coust'. Trans.

roses. At every turn Proust compared Montesquiou with his
favourite writers; nor did he forget to flatter Yturri.

> Your Venetian tumblers, your goblets in shapes at once
> so sad and so proud, are of those shades which, as Michelet
> remarked of pearls, 'make the heart delirious'. . . . [There
> follows a postscript aimed at Yturri:] I have fallen under the
> spell of his spiritual charms. What a delicate, civilised person
> and yet how like a wild cat! So much sweetness combined with
> so much vigour!

Yes, this little Proust was charming: he had read a lot and even
knew a fair amount about painting. Of course he was devoid of
taste; but where could he have acquired any? Not from those fine
people, his parents, certainly. But it was astonishing how well this
boy was known in society. Henceforth, the poet met him almost
everywhere, with other young men equally taken up with
pleasing: one, Lucien Daudet, by his looks; one, Reynaldo Hahn,
by his voice; others, Albert Flament and Coco Madrazzo, by their
pencils. All were witty; all had charming manners and first-class
tailors. From a distance the Count followed their little intrigues,
their little passions. Sometimes they irritated him, for they were
thoughtless, elusive and tied to each other by an exclusively
private code of jokes, followed by mysterious convulsions of
laughter.

It was at the Daudets that the little group appeared to be most
natural. They amused the novelist, who looked like Christ with a
monocle. A charming talker, Daudet would be suddenly convulsed
with horrible pains which the voice of Reynaldo, his 'musico', could
sometimes soothe. Mme Daudet, who was worried about Léon's
violence and her daughter's ugliness, lavished her affection on her
youngest son, Lucien. It was the thought of this young man with
oriental eyes that no doubt prompted Daudet to refuse to sign a
petition in favour of Wilde with the words: 'I have sons.' Lucien,
in spite of his immense consideration for Montesquiou, stole
round to the house of Mme de Casa-Fuerte, where he was introduced to the Empress Eugénie, of whom they then chattered
without cease. Very quickly from Versailles there came this
couplet:

> The young Lucien Daudet
> Is now a princely toady.

One day the Count, who had come to tea in the Rue de Belle-chasse, placed, as was his custom, his hat on the ground. While Lucien was handing round plates, he tripped and the *petits fours* fell on the green Russian leather that adorned the top-hat. The traitor, thought Montesquiou; he had done it on purpose! A little later the poet wrote to Mme Daudet: 'You are a rose—and your children are your thorns.' Did Montesquiou know that Lucien had described him as 'varnished for eternity' and that he had compared him to 'a child's magnifying glass, through which a knick-knack seems as large as a Michelangelo'? Mme Daudet who, with one eye wept over the humble and with the other squinted in the direction of the Faubourg Saint-Germain, set great store by Montesquiou's friendship. One day, when the visitor had scarcely left, she exclaimed: 'But this Montesquiou—one must admit—he is really a Fairy Prince.'* 'Mother lets herself get carried away—she knows so little of the world,' explained Lucien, for once losing his composure, before he ran off to the cloakroom with Proust and Flament in order to conceal his uncontrollable and, to his poor mother, inexplicable laughter. 'He is sublime—divine!' gasped Marcel in a fit of choking during which asthma and admiration contested with each other. 'That description of Mme de Janzé's hat! . . . I adore him!'

A difficult master

Marcel had never been so astonished as by Montesquiou. Very soon the Count made it his habit to reserve for this intelligent and flattering listener his bawdiest stories about the upper crust, many of them mythical scandals that went back to the crusades. The young man could not resist the temptation to imitate his illustrious friend. He imitated him both consciously to make the little group laugh and also unconsciously in his letters and even his gestures. Thus Proust, whose teeth were excellent, now began to raise a hand to his mouth when he laughed, since this was what Montesquiou, who had terrible teeth, was in the habit of doing. To stress either the expression of admiration or the delivery of an ultimatum Proust would now tap his foot in the

* The actual word used by Mme Daudet was 'tapette', Provençal for a chatter-box and slang for 'fairy' or 'pansy'.

manner of the older man. However, enthusiasm did not rob him of perception; after a lecture at La Baudinière* he wrote as follows to his friend Robert Dreyfus:

> At first I did not realise that Montesquiou was aware that he was ridiculous; until at his first lecture—when everyone expected him to be dressed in pink and green and he appeared, on the contrary, in the black suit of a lawyer's clerk—he said to me: 'I was intent on arousing this feeling—"the expectation of something ludicrous disappointed".'

It is during one of these lectures that one should picture Montesquiou, well-set and glistening, aggressive yet charming, advocating his Crusade for Beauty. This Beauty was always represented, in the front row, by Mme Greffulhe. She alone took it upon herself to say to her cousin before the lecture: 'Make it simple and short.' The enthusiasms of this generous woman were always at the service of her knight, to support and defend him. In 1904 the two friends organised a great Gustave Moreau exhibition, inaugurated by a lecture. After this occasion the Countess wrote to Montesquiou:

> You know that I do not believe in animal youth but in the youth that comes with the years; thus you seemed younger and more handsome than ever yesterday. I have suffered from the rather too personal praise addressed to me by the brilliant advocate that you are; but you have also been the source of praise that is enshrined in the depth of my soul. The latter kind of praise, reserved but luminous, you awarded to me in the middle of the exhibition; but it is the other that stays with me, struck like a medal or coin of our mutual love for the great poet. To you profoundly.

It will be seen that Proust had guessed the nature of this relationship, for later the romantic princess (de Guermantes) who was modelled on Mme Greffulhe was to love the fictional caricature of Montesquiou.

At the slightest summons Proust hastened to Versailles or even as far as Engadine, where the Count was sharing a chalet with Mme Howland, a close intimate of a number of celebrities but especially of Charles Haas, whom the young man was burning to

* A small hall used for lectures and concerts. Trans.

know. But whom did he not burn to meet—this man who, with his bewildered but shrewd civilities, pretended to be shy? His appetite for social activities seemed to be infinite.

'I will ask you also to do me the kindness of showing me some of those ladies among whom you are most often to be seen (the Countess Greffulhe, the Princesse de Léon).' Soon it was to be the Duchesse de Rohan.

But the citadel which was Montesquiou could not easily be taken by storm. Again Proust attacked, in his eagerness that Countess Greffulhe should be surrendered to him. He saw her 'with a hair-style of a quite Polynesian grace, mauve orchids descending to the nape of her neck. I wanted very much for her to know that she had impressed me greatly'. Montesquiou had to be pressed, he did not like to present young men; but if he met Proust on neutral ground, then he would benevolently introduce him to some of the ladies of the chorus. Above all he replied to all Proust's queries about the upper crust, for example recalling the adventures which caused the disgrace of Mme de Beaulaincourt, née Castellane, whose affair of thirty years' standing with an ambassador had at last begun to turn respectable, and underlining her rivalry with Mme de Chaponay, who dressed like Marie-Antoinette, and with Mme de Janzé. From this particular story Proust was eventually to distil the character and life of his Marquise de Villeparisis. All three of these women quarrelled over celebrities, but where the upper crust was concerned they had to content themselves with the company of their own families. He showed him the elegant Mme Legrand, who was to become Mme Leroy, a woman so circumspect that she refused to set foot in the house of any of the great ladies who had fallen. He explained that nothing could be more chic than Mrs Standish, a cousin of the Noailles, who went each season to Sandringham. He taught him to open his eyes: 'Since Mme d'Haussonville had the kindness to invite you, look at that beautiful portrait by Largillière of an abbess of Remiremont at the time of Louis XIV and that divine Ingres of Albertine de Broglie. . . .' Thereupon he imitated the little curt greeting of the daughters of this worldly couple. The mentor warned his protégé against false relationships that would lead to nothing: with Mme Aubernon, for example. He forewarned him against Blanche, 'the badger of Auteuil', 'he will embroil you with everyone, he is an ingrate'.

Proust was warned. In the eyes of his friend there was no greater crime than ingratitude. At the least sign of neglect, the intimate became a pariah, exposed to the most biting sarcasms and singled out as the hero of innumerable ludicrous or scatological anecdotes. Either because this seemed to Montesquiou the French style in bygone days or because a certain vulgarity of speech struck him as a sign of virility, he used against his enemies a vocabulary of Rabelaisian crudeness. It was in this that one saw his Musketeer ancestry. He would rattle off an anecdote in the manner of Tallemant des Réaux, his truculence all the more astonishing when it emanated from the Commander of Delicate Odours. Proust, who would laugh till he cried at these tales, shared the poet's fervour for Marceline Desbordes-Valmore and asked the Count to recite to him:

> I wish to die on shores where I was born:
> The tomb of Albertine is near my cradle.

We will come across this Christian name in a novel which the young man was soon to think of calling 'The Murdered Doves'.

Little Proust was useful for the organisation of the Douai parties. In a Paris that was both verbose and worldly, flies were necessary to move forward the coach of renown.* The capricious friendship of Montesquiou alternated coldnesses and favours. Sometimes the Count was irritated by Proust, sometimes he feared that the young man's bad form would compromise him. He was displeased when, reading an article by Jean Lorrain on *Les Hortensias Bleus,* he found Proust named among 'those pretty young men of society who are pregnant with works of literature'. Nor did he like it any more when there appeared in *Les Plaisirs et les Jours* a reference to Proust's love for Lucien Daudet. There was another cause for irritation; Proust was too often ill to be always at the poet's disposal—though it is true that he apologised amusingly. One day, miraculously, he was, however, ready: 'Since eleven in the morning, up and bathed like Esther to appear before a sovereign-king.' That this sovereign was a tease the following from Proust witnesses:

Dear Count,
    I have just forwarded to Reynaldo the letter you inflicted on

* A reference to the fable by La Fontaine 'La mouche et le coche'. Trans.

me as a charming torture of Tantalus, addressing it to my house where the sight of a fascinating and loved hand caused to be at once born in me the desire to read further; whereas I had to dispatch this present, at the same time offered and forbidden, without having been able to learn its secret or taste of its charm. . . .

It is even more difficult to assess the degree of self-interest in a friendship than in a love-affair. But the presence of ambition does not exclude a liking between the exploiter and the exploited. Just as courtesans are often extremely happy in the arms of the men whose substance they are devouring, so Proust plundered Montesquiou and yet truly liked him. What emotion when, because of an error of taste, a quarrel threatened! He ran to Mme Arman de Caillavet for her help and then wrote to his mentor: 'Monsieur France would like to add to this letter a little postscript in which he tries to incline you in my favour further than justice may deserve. It is on the subject of my taste, to which I attach such importance (since without it I could not love you) and which you were cruel enough to deny yesterday.' France's addition went: 'Dear Poet, How can you not see that Marcel Proust has taste when he speaks so well of your poems?'

Montesquiou kept this letter and most of those he received from Proust. In the margin of one he wrote, 'Full marks being 20, this little piece of epistolary homework deserves only minus 15.'

Evidence of long aesthetic discussions between master and pupil is provided by the following letter, which Proust wrote after the appearance of his translation of Ruskin:

As to the innumerable complaints about Ruskin's attitude to Whistler, Karr and Sue, I should like to point out, if you will allow me, that the criteria by which we reach our judgments are all-important and that these criteria inevitably vary from country to country and from period to period. Thus we can read in Goethe that French literature had never produced anything to equal the songs of Béranger; in Stendhal that the Gothic cathedrals are the shame of France; in Tolstoy that Wagner's innovations are ludicrous and a thousand other absurd judgments on our contemporaries. As for his comparing himself to Karr, Ruskin does that partly in humour, partly perhaps for reasons of policy, and also perhaps partly from that sublime unconsciousness of Genius, which only recognises as masters those who are, in fact, infinitely inferior. . . .

One can imagine that the friend of Whistler had little regard for Ruskin. In his Preface to his translation Proust had drawn a comparison between the English critic and Montesquiou, without mentioning the latter by name, however. In Montesquiou's copy of the translation he inscribed the following: 'I am afraid that I let you think yesterday evening that this translation was not entirely my own work. On the contrary, it was I alone who did it in its entirety. Here and there I asked Humières for his advice, but the whole is my work and I revised it at least twenty times.'

Proust tried every expedient to remain in favour. He wrote an article 'On the Simplicity of Monsieur Montesquiou', but no paper wanted it. Then he had recourse to more audacious kindnesses, introducing a charming young musician to Montesquiou. But this youth overshadowed the friend who had sent him and Proust was then obliged to despatch to Versailles some Liberty cravats, followed by a Neapolitan cradle angel of more or less the eighteenth century. Its nose was broken; and in any case it could never have attained, as Proust put it, 'the passionate finesse of the nose of our little musician'.

'*Ours*'! It was really too much. At a party at Mme Lemaire's, Montesquiou extended only a finger to the provider of angels and then summoned him to Versailles. The subsequent rebuke made so profound an impression on the young man that, twenty years later, echoes of it were to be found in a famous scene of his novel:

'Put yourself in the Louis XIV seat', and as though rather to force me to move away farther from him than to invite me to be seated. I took an armchair that was comparatively near. 'Ah! So that is what you call a Louis XIV seat, is it? I can see you have been well-educated!' he cried in a shrill scream of rage. 'You can't even tell me what you are sitting on. You offer your hindquarters a Directory Chauffeuse as a Louis XIV *bergère*. . . .' You would have called him an Apollo grown old; but an olive-hued, bilious juice seemed ready to start from the corners of his evil mouth. . . . He gave a disdainful smile, made his voice climb to the supreme pitch of its highest register, and there, without strain, attacking the shrillest and most insolent note: 'Oh! Sir,' he said, returning by the most gradual stages to a natural intonation, and seeming to revel as he went in the oddities of this descending scale. 'I think that you are doing yourself an injustice when you accuse yourself of having said that we were *friends*. . . . And who says that I am insulted?' he cried with fury, flinging himself into an erect posture on the seat . . . his voice became alternately shrill and grave, like the deafening onrush of a storm. . . . 'Do you suppose it is within your power to insult me? You evidently are not aware to whom you are speaking. Do you imagine that the envenomed spittle of five hundred little gentlemen of your type, heaped one upon another, would succeed in slobbering so much as the tips of my august toes?'

In brief, they were reconciled. Proust, having understood Montesquiou's adage, 'Never explain yourself, prove yourself', was invited once again; and when the last *petit four* had been swallowed, he rushed to report these splendours to *Le Gaulois*.

Alas! in the article that appeared the next day about the party at Versailles, the description of Mme Potocka's dress and the names of Mme de Broissia and Mme Howland had all been cut, as well as the name of Proust himself, included, by his own pen, 'among those whom one also noticed . . .'

In any consideration of the friendship between the two men, Bernard Berenson's wise comment ought perhaps to be recorded: 'A novelist's best inspiration is not that which comes directly and immediately from whatever happens to him, but is that which comes from narrated facts passing through the screen of another voice. . . . This was the sort of inspiration Proust derived from his mentor, Montesquiou.'

In which the aesthete becomes a critic

It must not be thought that social events constituted the basis of the friendship and of the conversations between master and disciple. A common passion for Balzac was a solid bond. Montesquiou helped Proust to identify several people in the *Comédie Humaine*. Thus the Duc de Decazes had lent his fine southern face and his ruthlessly ambitious character to Rastignac—at the realisation of which Proust burst out laughing: 'In that case Louis XVIII must be the model for Madame de Nucingen!' Was the Princess de Cadignan the Duchess of Dino? Du Sommerard cousin Pons? Both of them dreamed of having in their service that fiery groom of the late Baudenord. One day Montesquiou commented that Proust had put on trousers 'of a Balzacian grey'. 'Yes', replied the other man, 'those of Lucien de Rubempré, but not those of Pierre Grassou, who was conceited.' Montesquiou gave an account of all the Talleyrand part of the *Comédie Humaine,* describing the châteaux of Valençay and Rochecotte, with their splendid façades and squalid basements. There was the Castellane woman who married Fouché, and the Castellane son-in-law of the Duchess of Dino who compelled Talleyrand's old mistress to dine with a steward who was altogether too much loved. He exposed the unscrupulousness of the last representative of the Marsays, the Prince de Sagan.

Proust was not one of those sanctimonious snobs for whom each duchess opens the door of a paradise. Despising his passion and loathing the humiliating steps which it forced him to take, he liked, in compensation, to see his idols disgraced, in much the same way as the sadist likes to witness the humiliation of the object of his affections. Montesquiou, subject to crises of hatred and bearing a thousand grudges against his own class, was for Proust a mine of abominable anecdotes. Thus Proust's great ladies, because of the existence of this cruel and monstrous side to his character, were to be far more life-like than those of Balzac, whose robust faith respected the Faubourg Saint Germain as legitimacy.

No less effective than Balzac in soldering their friendship was the aesthetic fervour which they shared. The History of Art suddenly acquired a far greater importance in the 'nineties, largely due to improvements in photographic reproduction. Alongside the old *Gazette des Beaux Arts,* directed by Charles Éphrussi, there had appeared some new magazines: *Les Arts* and *Les Arts de la Vie.* In these, Montesquiou could express himself on furniture and painting; and the critic often proved superior to the poet. Certainly his taste tended to the bizarre, and his judgments were subject to fashion (though most of the time it was he who initiated the fashion); on the other hand, his erudition was prodigious and he reached his opinions in complete independence from cliques and, of course, dealers. He suffered from blindspots—the Impressionists meant nothing to him; and he tended to favour those painters who had illustrated his own works: Madeleine Lemaire, for example, and Arthur Chaplin, though the latter's meticulous still-lifes are certainly remarkable. None the less, one keeps coming across brilliant statements, and phrases as profound as that about Ingres which so much delighted Proust: 'And like another Prometheus he paid the penalty for the strange crime of having stolen the cold, by being chained to his Angélique for ever.'

The first collection of Montesquiou's criticisms, *Les Roseaux Pensants*, appeared in 1897. Certainly the article which begins this collection is written in pseudo-Mallarméan gibberish: '. . . Thus it could be pointed out that the suppressed or deferred emission of delectable knowledge may for ever deprive the mind of its harvest due.' But the article on Ingres seems to show that Proust was right when he declared that he found the critical articles of his friend 'never abstract, superior to those of Fromentin'. Montesquiou writes of how 'the drawings are of pearl-grey'; the Louis-Philippe fittings 'contribute to the discomfort of the portraits'. Both men liked the passage: 'the arms of the Indian princess, whose flesh acknowledges the caressing kiss of the stuff that is a sister to her'. Proust admired Montesquiou for knowing as well as Ruskin the names of the flowers in a painting by Pisanello. Today we can find many affinities between this collection of essays and surrealist taste. Thus, the writer dotes on Grandville in whom he discerns 'a frenzy of degradation', 'a predecessor of Odilon Redon' and even of Gallé, another Nancéen, 'a gramineous talent, like that of the inventor of Animated Flowers'. He championed, as we shall see, Art Nouveau in 'Mobilier Libre', at once a veritable philosophy of furniture, and a vindication of Gallé and Tiffany; and, even more interesting, he thought up a Son et Lumière spectacle for Versailles, which might have been the centre-piece of the 1900 Exhibition. As for the Surrealists, everything bizarre aroused his enthusiasm. Thus he went into raptures over the miniatures of M. d'Aramon, who portrayed more than 100 queens of France, among whom were the four sisters of Caribert: Ingoberge, Miroflède, Marcovelde and Theodechisilde. Such childishness discouraged critics, who otherwise shared his point of view. The Doumics and the Brissons of the art world might sneer when reading the descriptions of opulent clothes and exquisite jewels; but a better informed critic, Bernard Berenson, read Montesquiou's articles with admiration and impatiently waited for August when they met at St Moritz: 'I have missed you these days and have so much regretted your departure; as I have never regretted anyone else. I am your devoted slave, the true disciple of the parable.' When his attack on the great American portrait-painter appeared in 1905, Berenson congratulated Montesquiou: 'Your article on Sargent enchanted me. It perfectly expresses all that I think and all that I feel about this "artist". Admit that your exquisite politeness is much more malicious than the brutal criticisms of us others. I am infinitely grateful to you for having been the first to attack this idol of the Anglo-Saxons.'

Proust, eager to redress the injustices inflicted by the established critics, wished to thank the aesthete for all that he owed him in an article that was unfortunately marred by excessive flattery. This study appeared only in *Art et Vie* (1905) and is entitled 'A Professor of Beauty'. For modern taste he dwells too much on Montesquiou's descriptions of flowers: 'These blue hydrangeas, the leaping pale-green corymbs of which are reflected in these silver trays like bouquets of lustreless turquoises.' But he was right: Montesquiou approached life with his arms full of flowers. It was the 'Commander of Delicate Odours' who taught Proust to plait garlands of hawthorn around his work and to pin to it cattleyas and tuberoses, so that it was adorned like a cathedral porch on some fin-de-siècle Corpus Christi day, the grimaces of its gargoyles all but hidden. Again it was Montesquiou who provided the details which set those monsters in relief.

The Professor of Beauty sometimes deigned to give lessons at the Proust house. What a to-do then! Mme Proust would harass the cook; Marcel plundered the florists, multiplied the express letters and proposed guest-lists to the Count. Charles Éphrussi? Mme Cahen d'Anvers? But could one risk the Brancovans? Another list, with substitute names, was proposed to Chancellor Yturri. Then came the task of discovering which lady of Robert's chorus was most in favour at that moment, and whether the handsome Illan de Casa-Fuerte or his mother should be invited. There was always the fear of a quarrel at the last minute, which would transform the dining-room into a tilt-yard. The Count was besought to give a lecture at dessert, since this prospect nearly always kept his temper under control. Usually all went off well. The illustrious guest treated Marcel's parents kindly—though, for some curious reason, they were placed at the bottom of the table.

9. Jacques-Emile Blanche by Montesquiou. They were great friends in the 1880s, but then became enemies.

10. Montesquiou by Whistler.

11. A cartoon by Sem of Montesquiou, Forain, and Yturri.

12. A drawing of a plant given by Montesquiou to Gustave Moreau in 1887.

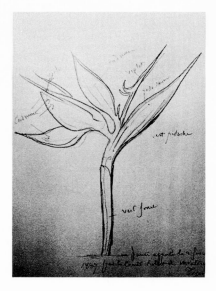

13. A vase carved out of willow-wood.

14. Montesquiou *(right)* and his secretary Gabriel de Yturri in their travelling cloaks.

15, 16. Palais Rose at Le Vésinet was Montesquiou's last home. *Above:* the steps. *Below:* Mme de Montespan's bath, which Montesquiou discovered in the grounds.

17. Léon Delafosse, the pianist, on whom Proust modelled Morel. Proust introduced him to Montesquiou at Versailles in 1894.

18. Robert de Montesquiou.

In a low voice he remarked to Marcel with a mixture of wit, insolence and good taste, 'How ugly it is here!'

Wilde had treated Proust's parents with greater contempt. The Frenchman had met the English writer at the house of his friends the Baignères, and by dint of paying him innumerable compliments had prevailed on him to accept an invitation to dine at his house. That evening Proust arrived back late and at once asked of the family valet: 'Has the English gentleman arrived yet?' 'Yes, monsieur, ten minutes ago. He is in the bathroom.' Proust hurried to the door. 'Mr Wilde!' he called. 'I hope that you are not ill.' Wilde emerged: 'Not in the least, dear, charming Monsieur Proust. But I was under the impression that I was going to dine alone with you, and when I saw the drawing-room and your good parents awaiting me in that drawing-room, I realised that the ordeal would be too much for me. So goodbye, dear Monsieur Proust—goodbye!'

After dinner the Count read some amusing pages about Mme Aubernon or a remarkable paper on Gobineau. On the next day, the readers of Le Gaulois were treated to this report, the work of the master of the house himself: 'An audience restrained, comprehensive, select . . . rare and precious good fortune, the surprise of an admirable reading. . . .' Flowers arrived at the Montesquiou pavilion in gratitude to the Professor of Beauty.

These flowers we find again, sown by the hand of Madeleine Lemaire, on each page of an elegant collection called Les Plaisirs et les Jours, for which Anatole France wrote the Preface. Montesquiou read these poetic essays of his disciple with favour. There was praise in them for 'this witty seriousness, this pregnant and subtle eloquence, this rigorous discipline which in him [Montesquiou] recall the seventeenth century'. The Count smiled on recognising several of his own characteristics in the exquisite Balthazar Silvante, who, like a white peacock perched on a chaise-longue, languished in beauty with a theorbo at his feet. He laughed freely at the quotations from the Imitation of Christ with which 'Violinte ou la Modernité' is stuffed, and also at the pastiche of Bouvard et Pécuchet. The master very much wanted to keep these verses near to his own:

Van Dyck, you triumph, prince of gestures calm,
In all the lovely beings doomed to die.

Montesquiou spoke of the little book to Barrès, whom with a lively step he accompanied on his walks in the Bois, and the 'great Frenchman' replied with indulgence, 'He will always be our young man!'

Montesquiou's patronage as much as France's Preface exasperated those who were jealous. 'This preface', wrote Jean Lorrain, 'has turned the heads of all the little Montesquitoes—the lesser or greater poets who frequent Mme Lemaire's. Could not M. de Heredia have signed his name Herediou in hallowing the author of *Hortensias*? At any rate, the salon of Mme Arman de Caillavou offers us this substitute for M de Fezensac—until now unique of his kind—the young and charming Marcel Proust. Pooh and Boo!'*

* In French 'Prout et Brou'. Trans.

CHAPTER 14

A Piano, a Cane and Some Swords

—————

His tuneful fingers stir the keys and so impart
Shiver on shiver to them from his icy heart.

The introduction of Morel to the Baron Charlus

'YOUNG MAN'—this was how Proust was to remain to Montesquiou until the latter's old age. The fifteen years that separated
them, the differences of social standing, and the period in which
they lived, all explain why the younger man's respectful manner to
the older was never to flag in the course of a long friendship
cemented by innumerable common experiences and attitudes. In
order to keep a favour which owed nothing to his appearance,
Proust acted like a maid-of-honour who has failed to arouse the
desire of the prince: he proposed another object for the prince's
delectation, thinking that in this way he would have a claim on
Montesquiou's gratitude through the compliance of a Ganymede,
who would, in his turn, feel himself to be under a bewildered
sense of obligation.

Proust found this pawn in one of the few *salons* of that period
which does not seem to us either pretentious or absurd: at a
musical reception given by the Count and Countess Henri de
Saussine in their beautiful mansion in the Rue de Saint-Guillaume.
The host—an excellent composer, who was a friend of Fauré,
Widor and the great women singers of the day—was the man who
introduced to the public the first piano pieces of Debussy and the
first songs of Reynaldo Hahn. One of Proust's first literary compositions was an *Eventail* for Mme de Saussine. Montesquiou had
been on cold terms with the Saussines ever since an evening
entertainment given by these charming people who had a vivid
admiration for him. Berthe Brady, the noted tragédienne, had

recited some of his poems, but being on edge after a scene with her lover, the poet and dramatist Henri Bataille, she massacred them. *Les Chauves-Souris* had inspired Saussine to write a symphony, of which he rehearsed the parts with one of the colts of the salon, Léon Delafosse. Blond, slender, with delicate features and the profile of one inspired, this young pianist was very much the ideal interpreter of Chopin. In this year, 1894, worried by the caprices of the Count, Proust advised Delafosse himself to put to music several poems from *Les Chauves-Souris*. The young man, only son of a widow who was herself a teacher of the piano, lived in the narrow and laborious world of the virtuoso. Proust knew very well the importance of contacts in this sort of career: having once performed at Montesquiou's house, Delafosse would receive the highest cachet and the best concert halls in Paris would then be at his disposal. The decision was taken. The pianist would become the delightful and docile instrument used to re-strengthen the bonds of friendship between the novelist and the Count. Lucien Daudet was too much the spoiled child; Reynaldo Hahn was already launched; Albert Flament had too many bourgeois prejudices and was interesting himself in Mme Henri de Rochefort in order to hide his true liaison with a newspaper proprietor, Léon Bailby; none of these three intimate friends was in a position to bring the affair to success.

Before the concert, during which M. de Saussine's *Fantasie* was to be played, Proust took to Versailles the person whom he had christened 'the angel' and of whom he had often spoken. The Count decided to foil the clumsy intrigue: No, he could not listen to the piano that day; he preferred to go for a walk. So for a walk they all went in the woods of Viroflay. From a distant fair came the din of a barrel-organ and Montesquiou was enraptured: nothing was more romantic, he declared, nothing more delightful than *Le Temps de Cerises*. Yturri, always kind, pitied the young man and reproached the poet: 'You are going to wound this poor boy cruelly; he is charming. Haven't you got enough enemies already?' For once Montesquiou listened to the voice of wisdom and they returned to the Pavilion, where Delafosse seated himself at the piano. Twenty-five years later the poet, now an old man, was to recapture the scene:

The punishment for my rudeness was to hear the pretty musical inventions suggested by my poetry. These the voice of the composer, though resembling that of a squashed cat, could not succeed in spoiling, since the sound it produced was sufficiently like the squeaking of bats not to be out of place. Besides there was a sincerity about the whole performance which, allied to the clever originality of the rhythms and the incomparable virtuosity of the accompaniment, persuaded one to overlook a vocal deficiency marked by faulty intonation. Never with any other virtuoso have I experienced such emotion as with this performer; and this emotion must have had something supernatural about it, since I have every reason to believe that it was foreign to his nature. How else can one explain how this little face, with its silly smile, should become transfigured with superhuman beauty (to such an extent that it assumed the pallor and expression of death), as though godhead had suddenly descended on him as it used to descend on the Pythonesses in ancient times?

The tartness of the recorder of the scene seems to have made him forget a friendship of several years, in which music was to be only one of the subordinate elements. Soon the master deigned to visit the musician: 'In an apartment that was rather low but large enough, in the Antin district; gloomy enough and sad enough too, with ordinary furniture among which the immense Erard piano appeared like a rosewood cromlech, coloured with the black and shining blood of the victims of the public concert.' Instead of any picture there hung on one wall a vast plan of the Erard Concert Hall. Proust and Lucien Daudet had also been invited but they had declined—the mere thought of seeing the Count at the Delafosses was enough to make them burst into uncontrollable laughter.

What did Delafosse mean to Montesquiou? Or, rather, what great model did the Count set before himself in embarking on the friendship? Was it the passion of Carlos Herrera for Rubempré, with the consequent desire to make a Paderewski of the youth? Or was it the passion of Ludwig II for the actor Kainz, who, transformed by the king's love, became an incomparable Hamlet? One could claim that Delafosse saw in this attachment no more than a means of self-advancement, were it not for the existence of his letters.

These letters are, in fact, much more like those of an anxious admirer than of a capricious friend. Of course one must make allowances for flattery; but the self-interest doesn't go further than to ask (in nearly every letter, it is true) for an introduction to the Princess of Monaco or Lady de Grey. '. . . It is difficult to appreciate how moral qualities can go with a sensitive and superior soul like yours. We are not worthy of such qualities; we admire them more than we understand them. But we reserve for ourselves the most desirable of privileges—which is to love you . . . tenderly. . . . The day on which I had the good fortune to know you was like the beginning of a new existence.' Delafosse recognised all that he owed to Montesquiou: 'The constant dedication to you of my talent, which manifests itself most completely when it is addressed to you.' Of course there were difficulties and jealousies; but there were none of those sordid dramas which were to come between the violinist, for whom Delafosse was to serve as model, and the fictional caricature of Montesquiou. 'I assure you that I do not confuse the King of Hearts with the Knave of Diamonds,' replied the pianist, with some humour, to reproaches the nature of which we can imagine.

After the fashion of those who are not really musical, Montesquiou liked music for the image which it evoked in him. It was a gentle opium, to carry him into a world of reverie and to refine his imagination. Outstretched on his chaise-longue, embroidered with bats, the poet listened to the musician. His Persian cat escaped from his lap to jump on to the shoulders of the pianist, whose profile, illuminated by the light filtered through the pink shades, stood out in relief against the shadows of the garden. 'Play Fauré's Barcarolle once again,' Count Robert would urge. 'It is a real embarkation for Cythera. . . .' 'Divine!' Yturri echoed. 'Tomorrow we must send Verlaine's poems to Fauré. . . . "Green —Turn, Turn, O splendid wooden horses . . ."'

Once again Montesquiou defied public opinion; he paraded his friendship with the pianist. At the opera and at exhibitions they were watched by Jean Lorrain, who was to become the chronicler of the friendship in *Monsieur de Phocas*. Here is the portrait of Delafosse: 'Thin, ethereal, cornflower-blue eyes in a face of diaphanous whiteness; the cheeks so lightly and sparingly touched with pink that one would have thought them made up; the hair as fresh and light as wild oats. Fresh and delicate, a Saxon, he insinuated himself into the group of enraptured society women. Count de Muzarett, who was shaken by an imperceptible shudder when the new arrival entered, hardly disturbed himself to make room for him. . . .' Later, at the opera: 'Muzarett, thin and fair, a poet and a nobleman, sat arched in his seat, his trunk having the appearance of being corseted. His little face was lined and anxious. Le Delabarre, the musician whom all the women adored, was his companion.'

Monsieur de Phocas

Jean Lorrain hated Montesquiou with the hatred of a middle-class woman who has lost her reputation for a great lady who is above scandal. This animosity has given us at one and the same time an amusing caricature in the character of Muzarett and a sinister one in *Monsieur de Phocas,* alias the Duke de Fréneuse, a des Esseintes who has fallen into the sewer of Byzantine Paris. But there is as great a difference between the writing of Lorrain and Huysmans as between the paintings of Moreau and Mucha. 'Tightly fitted into a suit of myrtle-green cloth and sporting an extremely high cravat of pale green silk sanded with gold, Monsieur de Phocas was a frail and elongated young man with a face that seemed anaemic and extraordinarily old under crinkly short brown hair. I had already glimpsed somewhere this precise and fine profile, the deliberate stiffness of this long, thin body. Standing near my work-table, Monsieur de Phocas slightly leant forward in a graceful pose and with the extremity of his cane—a Malacca cane, worth at least 10 louis, the green ivory head of which, strangely carved, had at once caught my attention—with the extremity of this cane Monsieur de Phocas turned the leaves of a manuscript and carelessly read it aloud.'

This novel appeared in 1902, the cane here described recalling a somewhat absurd incident and a terrible slander. Montesquiou had a whole collection of canes, which awaited, in a huge Chinese vase, for the honour of supporting him on his walks and of underscoring his gestures. There was one in green lacquered wood, intended for a woman, with a porcelain rose for handle on which a Chinese could have read the inscription: 'The beauty of a flower exhorts.' There were some all in ivory; others decorated with turquoises

or enamelled peacocks; yet others the handles of which were
netsukes. It was with a cane in the form of a serpent that Montesquiou, according to Pierre Louÿs, picked at a chaise-longue that
had become unstitched in the house of the Bonnières. Recently he
had bought a Malacca cane with a gold handle into which had
been set a turquoise reputed to have belonged to Louis XIV. With
this cane in his hand he posed for Boldini's masterpiece, exhibited
at the Salon of 1897. Lorrain commented on this picture: 'This
year Monsieur de Montesquiou has entrusted the task of repro-
ducing his elegant silhouette to Monsieur Boldini, habitual
deformer of over-excited and grimacing women and otherwise
known as "The Paganini of the peignoir".' The chronicler of
Gil Blas sneered again when an article entitled 'Table d'Harmonie'
and devoted to Delafosse appeared in *Le Figaro*.

Montesquiou did not wish to hear the croakings rising from the
bog of Lorrain, at whom he would, from time to time, cast a
glance of amusement. He had refused the dedication of a collection
that this bulky creature had offered to him in about 1880 and did
not deign to take up his challenge to a duel, as Proust had done.
The descendant of d'Artagnan required an adversary of better
quality. A catastrophe gave Montesquiou the chance to show his
courage.

On 4 May 1897, a fire at the Bazar de la Charité plunged society
into mourning. Many kinswomen and women friends of Montesquiou must, assuredly, have perished in the furnace, and staying
at home stricken with anguish, he excused himself from attending
a dinner which Madeleine Lemaire had not had the tact to cancel.
Yturri, despatched to garner news, came back with the names of
those dead and a description of the cries and terrible scenes.
Among other things, it was said that male members of the three
most exclusive Paris clubs, frenzied with terror, beat out a way of
escape for themselves by striking with their canes the women who
impeded them.

The news spread all over Paris; everyone thought with anguish
of loved ones; old attachments revived. Sarah Bernhardt wrote
immediately on this occasion: 'My very dear and very tenderly
loved Robert, On arrival I learned about the terrible catastrophe.
As I got out of the carriage, my maid greeted me breathlessly,
"Don't worry, none of those you love is among the dead. And by
good fortune—worthy of the genius who protects you—I passed

the Count de Montesquiou on my return." I adore you, my
Robert.'

Lorrain now returned to the subject of the Boldini portrait,
remarking that in it Montesquiou seemed to be in a trance of
adoration before his cane. 'This cane which . . . this cane . . .
Cudgel for living women and tongs for women dead, henceforth
sadly renowned in the annals of masculine elegance!' Lorrain
received no challenge as a result of this slander; and Montesquiou's
resentment crystallised around a person of quite another class:
Henri de Régnier.

The Symbolist Musketeers

It is necessary to go back ten or twelve years to see the first clouds
forming; at Mallarmé's house, on the one hand, where young
Régnier aroused sympathy through some beautiful poems and a
somewhat formal dandyism; and on the other hand at the
Heredias, one of whose daughters he soon married. It will be
remembered that Montesquiou had been warmly patronised by
the author of *Les Trophées*; but it may be that this favour was no
more than the bait to a matrimonial trap, with the result that
Montesquiou's total indifference to the superb and ardent
Heredia girls caused the friendship to cool. He invented this
motto for the Academician: 'Long may he Régnier' and gave to
the imposing Mme Heredia the nickname 'The Breasted Tower'.

Soon after the Bazar de la Charité, Baroness Adolphe de Rothschild, who was very fond of Montesquiou, acceded to his request
to open her palace in the Rue de Monceau to some of his artist
friends. The baroness, who habitually wore a red wig and carried
a cigar in her mouth, was a great friend of the Empress of Austria,
who was to be assassinated while on her way to visit her. 'The
Rothschilds', declared Montesquiou, 'are not so much members
of the aristocracy of money as patricians of wealth.' To lend
additional substance to the reception, Delafosse was to give a
recital when the collection had been seen. Among those present
were Lobre, Gallé, La Gandara and Sem; 'and our hostess, who
liked assortments as do all collectors, thought she had done well in
adding the poet Henri de Régnier, who came accompanied by his
wife and his two sisters-in-law.' When Montesquiou was in the

process of explaining the pictures and picking out the curios, Mme de Régnier attempted to interrupt him; but he crushed her with a look. Later, when the women in the Régnier party began to murmur during the music, the situation became extremely strained. Here is the account of the subsequent incident given by Henri de Régnier himself:

> On our entering the hall, Mme la Baronne de . . . brought us the canes we had left there. I took my own. Monsieur le Comte de Montesquiou, who had kept his during the visit, stood in the middle of a group of people. His cane, which was made of horn and was adorned with a porcelain handle, attracted the attention of Mademoiselle de X.
>
> MLLE DE X: You have a beautiful cane there. How heavy it must be! It's a real bazaar cane.
>
> MLLE DE Z: Yes, but the pieces seem to have joined together again quite easily.
>
> M. LE COMTE DE MONTESQUIOU: Do you imagine me to be capable of hitting a woman? At all times, I know how to do my duty as a man of honour.
>
> M. HENRI DE RÉGNIER: One would perhaps strike a woman with a sword, but not with a cane.
>
> M. LE COMTE DE MONTESQUIOU: I would not hesitate to chastise a woman who was unfaithful to me. . . . But it is a pity that fashion has deprived men of what used to be one of their embellishments.
>
> M. DE RÉGNIER: Yes. There are two things that I should like to have: a fan in summer and a muff in winter.'

Montesquiou claimed that Regnier's reply had been: 'A fan would suit you much better' and that he then retorted, 'I use only one weapon, the sword.'

At that they went off in search of seconds, leaving the baroness in consternation and the guests peddling the news to the four corners of Paris. Montesquiou chose Maurice Barrès and the fat Marquis de Dion, who was passionately fond of motor-cars, as seconds. He preferred a duel with pistols, so as not to kill his adversary through clumsiness; he was quite willing to be victim, but not assassin. 'Dion was angry about this, declaring that he would not lend himself to supporting a sham fight, and that if he was to accept the role of second, with its responsibilities and its burdens, then I must promise to fire "as though at a target"—that of my safety and my pride.' The press got mixed up in the affair, each paper taking sides. Régnier wrote some half-hearted excuses, to which Montesquiou answered with such scant courtesy that, from being the offended party, he became the offender. Régnier preferred swords. His seconds, the historian Houssaye and the painter Béraud, came and went, drawing up the proceedings. Aimery de Rochefoucauld was anxious—was his cousin about to cross swords with a gentleman? 'From what house is this Régnier?' he demanded. 'From 16 Rue de Boccador,' answered Yturri, with a false naïveté.

The great day arrived: Montesquiou was wounded in the hand, thus disappointing the pious friends who had provided a confessor hidden under the arch of a bridge. 'I have a magnificent doctor, the most handsome of all, our dear and great Pozzi. Quite a few people were present at the occasion, but nothing about it was displeasing, troublesome or ridiculous. The recollection of it will be as of one of the best parties I have ever given and it will stay with me for a long time. I don't know how many people came to see me, many of them counting it to my credit that I had had my rights and, without being personally concerned in the matter, had called a halt to the backbiting that was aimed at almost everyone.' But the prettiest bouquet was the admirable pastiche of Saint-Simon by Marcel Proust that appeared on the front page of *Le Figaro* on the morning after the duel:

He was the son of Thierry de Montesquiou, and the wittiest man I have known, with a princely air like no one else; a most noble face, sometimes smiling and sometimes grave; the figure, at forty, of a man of twenty, not merely slender but arched as if bent backwards, inclined forward again only at the dictates of whim, with great affability and every variety of courteous expression, before returning quickly to a natural position full of pride, haughtiness and the intransigent determination not to bend before anyone, not to cede anything, but to walk ahead without thought of whether the way is clear or not, jostling others either as though he did not notice that they were in his passage, or otherwise, if he wished to give annoyance, showing that he had seen them but paying them no heed; around him always a great bustle of people of much quality and wit, to whom sometimes he would bow to the right and the left, but whom more often he would leave, as one says, to hoe their own row, both his eyes looking straight ahead, while he spoke very loud and very well to his intimates, who would laugh noisily at all the funny things he uttered, since he was much wittier than one would imagine. Allied with this wit was the most serious, the most unusual, the most brilliant mind, characterised by a grace that was uniquely his and which all those who approached him attempted, often unwillingly and unawares, to copy and to adopt.

This praise touched the wounded man; but what touched him more was the following sentence in a note that accompanied the article, the most characteristic of all the words of homage accorded to him: 'You rise above enmity, like the seagull above the storm, and you would suffer from being deprived of this upward pressure.'

This duel inspired yet another great writer, Maurice Barrès, who wrote in his Cahiers:

> The Montesquiou-Régnier incidents lead me to think this with disgust: There are no secrets; the transports of the heart become, at a distance, the steps, whether adroit or clumsy, in a continuing process; it is always dangerous to treat someone as if he would always be the friend one expects him to be. This has been put magnificently: 'Treat your friends as though one day they must become your worst enemies.' The absurd thing, but also one of great significance, is that I was, with Régnier, a witness against Yturri.

What had happened was that Yturri had challenged a journalist after an accusation of immorality.

Charlus crushes Morel

And Delafosse? . . . Well, he played for the Count, inspired him, gave recitals here and there and repeated from time to time, 'How dull it must be not to be well known!' Count Robert would mutter between his teeth in reply: 'The most curious thing is that the *arrivistes* not only do not arrive but they never get started.' In fact the handsome pianist had begun to bore him; on the one hand

he found the protection he extended to him both time-consuming
and not very effective, and on the other hand he detected germs of
ingratitude. The two men went on a journey together; but that
was no solution, since they stopped at Amphion, at the property
owned by the Brancovans on the shores of Lake Leman. There,
each season, there gathered round the beautiful princess a company
which included Proust, Abel Hermant, the young Bibescos and
two dazzling young girls, of whom one, nicknamed by Montesquiou 'Anna the Syrian', astonished the guests with her word-
play and extravagant appetite for books. The princess, herself an
excellent pianist and a friend of Paderewski, welcomed Delafosse;
the prince was, according to his distant cousin Montesquiou, 'a
Rumanian braggart with a raucous voice; an old bogey with eyes
flashing with simulated fury; the eldest son of a hospodar, who
was rather jealous of his paste-board prerogatives'. Delafosse had
a far more enjoyable time at the Brancovans' than at Montesquiou's. The yacht took the guests to have tea with elegant
friends who lived on the lake; each day the applause came from
real connoisseurs.

On his return to Paris, Delafosse did not leave the Brancovans.
The abusive mother, who had pushed her son as far as the
Conservatoire, encouraged him to reduce his visits to Versailles—
did not the Count treat him like a maid who had been with the
family for years? Suddenly Montesquiou decided to make a break.
Yturri begged him to think it over: never would he find so gifted
an interpreter to explain his moods and calm his tempers. In vain
did the Chancellor mention pleasure and wisdom; it was necessary to keep the minister of music—Fauré liked him very much. 'I
have known Fauré for ever!' 'But he is a friend of Debussy.'
'You irritate me. I no longer wish to see him.' The quarrel was
ready to break; all that was needed was to wait for a pretext as one
waits for a fine night to let off fireworks. The young man wished
to dedicate a piece of music to the Countess Greffulhe. He was
astonished at having a refusal; and Robert, in one of his superb
scenes which none the less 'left him shattered', made him realise
both the immense space which separated them and the treasures of
kindness, of knowledge and of poetry that he had expended to fill
that space: 'Little people never see the efforts one makes to
descend to their level and never climb up to one's own! . . . All
the houses that have been opened to you by my sovereign

protection will be shut to you and you will be reduced to strum-
ming some Moldavian or Bessarabian clavichord for a pittance.
You have only been an instrument of my thought, you will never
be more than a musical mechanic. . . .'

Delafosse was crushed. Shortly after this scene, he happened to
pass the Count, who without returning his greeting declared: 'It
is natural that one bows when passing the cross, but one must
not expect the cross to return the bow.' An outcry supported
Montesquiou's rage. The chorus of ladies, jealous perhaps of one
or the other of the two men, resorted to the most facile kind of
vulgarity. For Mme Howard the pianist became 'this little fosse'
and for Mme de Broissia 'the cul-de-fosse'. From the 'angel' he had
been in the early letters of Proust, Léon fell to the rank of 'scram-
bled egg' or even 'scoundrel'. The Brancovans and the Marquise
de Saint-Paul, who supported the musician, were at once also put
on the black list. At Montesquiou's pavilion, Delafosse had caught
an illness that is particularly serious for musicians: snobbery. It
was inevitable that his frivolous nature should succumb. Thus it
was that he refused concert after concert in the United States, a
country without any duchesses. Sargent's affection for him won
him several engagements in London, and less and less famous, but
always handsome, he was to end his days soon after the last war
living with a Swiss spinster.

After the affair of the Bazar de la Charité, society was again put
to the test by the Dreyfus case. Dead people are buried, but
quarrels remain. Montesquiou, who was not interested in politics,
kept his virulence for aesthetic problems and did not quarrel with
anyone. In opposition to the upper crust, which he found stupid,
and even to Barrès, whom he admired, the poet leant more to the
pro-Dreyfus side under the influence of Mme Greffulhe. This
lady, because of her connections with the German courts and her
friendship with the English ambassador, was sure that Dreyfus
was innocent. Montesquiou jeered at Bourget, who suddenly
turned his back on the Artistic Jewesses, previously so much
courted and liked by him. As for himself, he remained faithful to
Mme Straus, to Charles Éphrussi and to the Alphonse de
Rothschilds. Perhaps one day a sarcastic remark about the Chosen
People escaped his lips in front of Proust, who told him in a very
dignified letter that his mother was Jewish. Of course, he chuckled
when Mme de Ganay, née Haber, proclaimed, 'I dine with the

Rothschilds. I find that this is not the moment to abandon them.'
But at one of these dinners, seeing an anti-Dreyfus sponger stifling
his scruples under truffles, the Count said in an extremely loud
voice, 'One would think that he himself had gone rooting for
them.'

From this time dates Jean Lorrain's most ferocious attack:
'M. de Montesquiou has relied, with a profound knowledge of the
human heart, on the vanity, flabbiness and weakness of a society
bereft of defence against anything which is bright enough or
noisy enough, to the extent that the word hierarchy has become a
dead letter for it, as have the words honour and dignity.' It is
always amusing to see the flag brandished in order to cover the
failings of the colour-sergeant. Forain was also to sneer, but he
did not dare to attempt any caricatures, for he went out in society
and, at bottom, his ferocity respected the malice of his old friend.

CHAPTER 15

Nineteen Hundred

The scarf turned liquid by the precious stones . . .
The gems that dawn within the folds of silk . . .
The flickers, undulations, coils and pleats . . .
(Loie Fuller)

The providers of Art Nouveau

THE PROFESSOR OF BEAUTY, the Commander of Delicate Odours, should be remembered less as the model for scandalous characters in fiction than as the gardener who planted and tended the blooms of Art Nouveau. He gathered the seeds at Gustave Moreau's, at Sarah Bernhardt's and in England. He searched in the decadent bog for the terrain where these forms could best expand; he asked Whistler, whose natural taste was for the unadorned, to act as prop for them. Montesquiou's reputation has suffered because he paid so much attention to a style which in France remained minor and decorative; a style the roots of which were English or Scandinavian and which quickly faded after the 1900 Exhibition, having enriched the French with only a few delightful artists and works of art: Gallé, Lalique, buildings here and there, the staircase of the Grand Palais and the entrances to the Métro. To set up against such innovators as Beardsley, Klimt, Munch or Hodler, the French can produce at best certain groups by Rodin (who unfortunately thought that he was Michelangelo), some of Redon's lithographs and the less good paintings of Van Gogh. In architecture there is no Frenchman of the stature of a Gaudi or a Van der Velde. During this fin-de-siècle period the French bourgeoisie was trying to assimilate the Impressionists and to appreciate good painting; 'Modern Style' flowers seemed just right for decorating curtains or calendars. Thus Montesquiou had to struggle less against the traditionalism of society—snobbery was succeeding in that already—as against good sense supported by nationalism. One of his friends, an excellent judge of painting, Octave Mirbeau, wrote that Art Nouveau was due to 'the vicious Englishman, the morphinomaniac Jew, and the cunning Belgian— or a pleasant salad of the three'. Since 1895 there had been an offensive against the English influence. Burne-Jones's exhibits at the Salon were ridiculed—'The poor man's Mantegna,' commented Forain.

Thus France under Loubet missed this prodigious flowering, and even today confuses its ramifications with a neo-rococo just good enough for the stucco decorations of an exhibition. In his articles, in his poems and above all in his talk from the end of the 'eighties onwards, Montesquiou strove to direct the public towards the centres where the marvellous flower was beginning to bud. The strelitza given to Gustave Moreau in 1887 was the first example of it.

Of all the establishments that Montesquiou recommended there was none more important that that of Bing. Samuel Bing was a German ceramist; after a sojourn in Japan he brought back a host of objects which dazzled the disciples of Edmond de Goncourt. Then he founded a magazine with Gonse, *Le Japon Artist-ique*, the format of which became the model for all such luxury publications for the next forty years. The plates, reproduced in shades of pistachio, salmon or lilac, were to offer every kind of example to artists: of stylisation to Gallé; of composition to the *nabis* (that school of painters which included Bonnard and Vuillard); of ceramic design to Carries; of caricature to Sem. In 1892 Bing associated himself with Tiffany, the New York jeweller, who had just adapted the use of stained glass for shades and screens. At the opening of their shop, 22, Rue de Provence, contemporary artists had supplanted oriental art; later, the name Art Nouveau was given to an exhibition in 1895, which brought together, among others, Whistler, Mary Cassatt, Bonnard and Aubrey Beardsley.

Montesquiou went into transports of delight over the illustrations by the young Englishman for Petronius, Wagner and Wilde; and with him a whole generation was carried away. Toulet compared him, very rightly, to the Mannerists, and little Mme Willy (Colette, already the author of *Claudine*) congratulated

Montesquiou on the article he had devoted to this unusual
innovator, whose work was characterised by 'geometric lines and
curves which, seeming to have been traced with a compass,
suddenly take the place of an arm or a drapery, with a baffling
sense of ornamentation and without one's knowing whether the
artist is making a reform in decoration, slurring over a difficulty or
trying to astonish the world. He had a sinful love for peacock's
feathers, Louis XIV wigs, untied shoes, candle flames and their
obscene tricklings of wax, puffs saturated with rice-powder,
black velvet masks and vine-leaves acting as masks lower down the
body.' Set beside the cruel Beardsley, the mauve tricklings, the
greenish sea-weed of De Feure, Grasset or Mucha (who, admittedly, captured the public more easily) betray a sickening senti-
mentality. Montesquiou did not have a word for them.

Bing's great decorator was Hoentschell, who 'has gracefully
entangled a veritable rose-garden of briars in iron, silk and wood
to make a whole suite of furniture, in a style that is truly *nouveau*'.
Montesquiou, brought up among the *bergères* and the consoles of
Courtanvaux, sighed when he saw some of Majorelle's creations;
none the less he commissioned the decorator to make a strange
sofa-bookcase, an ancestor of the cosies of the Faubourg Saint-
Antoine. He also deigned to invent some pieces of furniture or
rather some 'furniture-poems', like that cheval-glass surrounded
by wisteria which inspired Proust to a reverie. 'This pensive,
blind, calm gaze, fixed beyond the mauve flower that was moist
with the tears welling from his pupils, dispersed infinitely, dispersed irreparably, not so much by any arrogance but by its very
perfection, dreams of ours at once captivated by it and yet
unworthy to be reflected in its depths. A distraught young woman
rushed forward to make certain that the tricolour ribbons that
tightly encircled her ignoble throat were in place.'

Even more than wisteria, blue hydrangeas, first popularised by
Montesquiou, became the flowers of 1900. They are to be found
sewn on to the covers of the thin notebook in which Marcel
Proust jotted down a confusion of reading notes, sketches of his
famous acquaintances and the addresses of gigolos. Caran d'Ache
proposed for the poet: 'a waistcoat embroidered with a procession
of muses on fields of wild hydrangeas.'

Montesquiou even encouraged what seemed to him to be bad
taste, for 'the most excessively ugly things, bizarre inventions, and

motley reminiscences, which burst or become dislocated, amaze or scandalise, may perhaps play a preponderant role in this future genesis. . . . They will have opened the channels with a bombard-ment. They represent the Club des Jacobins of style, the Théâtre Libre of decoration.'

Gallé and Lalique

It has already been noted that Gallé was an old friend; and with him, too, there were to arise coolnesses from the day when success began to distract him from the perpetual task of showing gratitude to his patron. According to Montesquiou, it was once again the Brancovans who monopolised the potter and 'decided not to have their coffee served in anything but vessels shaped like calceolarias'. The poet very rightly distinguished such commercial products, such vases as might be offered to ethereal mistresses or to doctors who dabbled in the arts, from those others 'the paste of which, prepared by Gallé himself according to secret formulae, is tinted with hues corresponding to the symbolic plants even-tually engraved on the length or the breadth of the crystal. Such vessels are signed by the master, under the hexagonal and decor-ative cell of the waxy honeycomb, and are lambent with the internal radiation of the gems crushed into their pastes.'

Montesquiou and Gallé had the same Japanese eye for detail and shade, and if lines from *Les Chauves-Souris* are often carved on the sides of vessels, so too the name of the glass-maker often appears in the Count's verse.

A Gallé vase where spangles glitter mauve
Gapes like an orchid:
A cave in which there flicker twilights mauve.

Lalique was also a poet of objects, though less oriental than Gallé. Bending the female body to the requirements of the work of the goldsmith, he is, at least superficially, even more '1900'. 'Heads of hair became one of Lalique's obsessions, one of the favourite motifs of his decoration. He coils hair round faces in sinuous, fabulous billows, bewitching the colours until they become almost green, according to the prescription of the great Albert. . . . It was Sarah Bernhardt who first had set in flower-beds of gold-work the lunar lotus-blooms of Cleopatra, the pearled lilies of the

Princesse Lointaine.' Montesquiou gave Mme Greffulhe a diadem of fuchsias and to Lady de Grey a peacock-feather ring.

Montesquiou also liked Carries' stone-ware and in 1881 he bought a head of Othello that was in sentiment very near to the misty faces of Carrière; he also bought pins made by Falize. For a whole season he raved about Loie Fuller, whose skirts and whose methods of stage-lighting influenced the design of everything from ash-trays to lamp-shades:

> Waves which are only eddyings of net,
> Flames which are only flecks of chrysoprase,
> A plash, a splash, a rush, a pirouette,
> Within a great convolvulus a blaze.

No less than this famous dancer the orchids that came from des Esseintes' hot-house inspired the artisans of the period. In May 1895 Montesquiou invited his beautiful ladies to admiration at the Flower Show:

> The orchids dedicate
> Themselves to contemplate
> The strangest fantasies.

On the last day of the show Octave Mirbeau, who was writing *Le Jardin des Supplices*, met Lorrain in front of 'an equivocal still-life of withered flowers. The mauve and yellow orchids had become like crumpled pieces of silk-paper. The most curious gems were provided by the irises, the browns and the sombre blues of which, alongside the putrescence of the yellows, created the splendours of the charnel-house.'

There was a certain amount of necrophilia in the taste of 1900. It is to be found in Barrès' most beautiful book, *Amori et dolori sacrum*, as in this account by Lorrain. Montesquiou was not immune from it. His most frequently requested poem during the recitals which Sarah Bernhardt gave in her Gismonda dress of 'velvet of a faded hydrangea-pink that shaded into blue' was *Le Coucher de la Morte*. The tragédienne confided to Lorrain that she had 'rolled and battered under the presses a length of dawn-pink Venetian velvet. Then, when the stuff was shiny and tacky, she had had it fumigated with sulphur and saffron so as to alter the nature of the colour. Finally, with a vaporiser, the designers had awakened on the dead velvet heraldic flowers limned in perverse shades, making the whole gown a rainbow.' The only thing that remained to be done was for Mucha to draw the poster.

If Montesquiou scorned to speak of Grasset, whose pictures imitated Walter Crane, or of the fashion designer de Feure, he let himself be dazzled by Besnard, this 'painter Trismegistus of fusible gold and liquefied glass'. As early as the 1900 Exhibition he saw clearly the direction which Art Nouveau was taking in France and denounced the absurdities which allowed it to be supplanted so quickly by the Ballets Russes style:

> The threads of vermicelli that interweave with each other, the excreted tape-worms that today do duty for the Modern Style, have caused to fall into discredit inspirations that were formerly more inspired. The sinuous tendrils of William Morris's honey-suckle, spiralling in a German scroll pattern, are scattered like foliage around the necks of Mucha's women; with the result that here is the sky of decorative art all furrowed with curves without end and without name, with demented G clefs, with epileptic ellipses.

What was said by the voice from the shades

Mention of these follies is the cue to speak about the connection of Art Nouveau with rococo; but the rockwork, the lace-work and the *chinoiseries* of the eighteenth century never had any aim other than to cover a surface as pleasantly as possible. The sources of Art Nouveau were more serious and more profound. With William Morris, Gallé or Horta we find a resurgence of Celtic interlacing-work and of the ancient Scandinavian forms. This kind of modelling has always seemed foreign to the French with the result that its resurgence had been understood only by poets before it declined into superficial decoration. The other source of its origin has been expressed by Mallarmé as 'the ambiguous world of the indeterminate'.

The Dutchman Thoroop, in his mauvish canvases, supplied poets with visions of the vague entanglements of foetuses and succubi, much as, twenty years previously, Redon's lithographs seemed to come as the answer to the quests of Flaubert and Mallarmé. Thus the other source of Art Nouveau is the Beyond; never had spiritualism been so important as in this fin-de-siècle period, the style of which, rather than meriting the epithet 'flabby', should be called 'ectoplasmic'.

On the one hand Montesquiou's international culture made him more receptive to these foreign forms; on the other hand this son and grandson of excellent mediums felt more keenly than his rationalist compatriots the profound logic which lengthens forms to dissipate them in smoke. This inheritance was of great help to the critic; but unfortunately this man of essentially visual sensibilities wished also to be a thinker. In a vague sort of philosophy he compounded Jean Lahor's Wagnerian-Buddhist reveries with the spiritualism of Ernest Hello. Proust was quite right to write to his master that: 'Hello's thoughts are golden nails with which you build more nobly your noble constructions.' Such thoughts have given us poems on Christ, a Mystery play and a quantity of mediocre verse said to be dictated by spirits.

Huysmans, who attributed a tendency towards spiritualism to des Esseintes, followed up this taste, so widespread at that time, in *Là-bas*. But Montesquiou, who had avoided homosexual debauch, did not take the even deeper plunge into the filthy mysteries of the black mass. His was too proud and fastidious a nature to allow him to enter into situations in which the ludicrous gets the better of eroticism, squalor the better of trances. Also he had too sharp a sense of humour. Thus, when he hired for 50 francs a copy of *Justine*, it was to copy from it the most absurd passages. It is true that, following the dictates of fashion, he dedicated a long and bad poem to Gilles de Rais; but these pyres and massacred children were as much rhetorical devices as pastoral scenes had once been for the precious.

Marked by the supernatural atmosphere of Courtanvaux, Montesquiou would always have liked to speak with the dead. But his taste for objects led him only to memories; he was too much attached to appearances to go too far, too much attached to the world to become an initiate, as his temperament inclined him. He was also too acute to take part in the absurdities of the Rosicrucian brotherhood. This immense interest in the Beyond directly inspired only a handful of his poems. One can quote from *Les Paons* 'Those to whom the dead have spoken':

> They see what we cannot see,
> They hear what we cannot hear,

It is their special fate to be
Touched by strange hands we fear.

Like Hugo, Montesquiou heard 'what the Voice from the
Shades uttered'; like Balzac he did not scorn the Sybils of the
district. He had not merely a curiosity but an anxiety about the
subject. The poet wanted to leave the two-dimensional world in
which he lived and so to pass beyond aesthetic pleasures and
mundane distractions. This man who, owing to some disability
either of nature or of education, found that pleasure could not
induce oblivion and who preferred delightful appearances to the
realities behind them, required that the supernatural should bring
him some assurance of permanency and devoted his intelligence,
without considering for a moment that his pride itself might be
an obstacle, to experiences which demand, above all, an abandonment of self.

Mme Greffulhe also shared Robert's enthusiasm in this field.
They formed a connection with Dr Favre, more of a thinker
than a clairvoyant, whose tenets enchanted the poet in whom the
doctor had recognised this gift: 'the ruthless suppression of
inferior values'. Together they went to see someone called Ledos,
'who claimed to see the soul-sheath or envelope of the soul'.
Later, thanks to d'Annunzio, the cousins brought from Italy the
greatest clairvoyant of modern times, Eusapia Paladino. One day
the Countess's son-in-law was present at a séance; perhaps the
presence of this future member of the Academy of Sciences, the
Duke of Gramont, embarrassed the Italian pythoness, who did not
say much; but as the sceptic was leaving, a heavy ivory paper-
knife rose from a table and slowly began to circle the room.
Montesquiou had also made numerous experiments with Lady
Archibald Campbell, whom he had met at St Moritz. During a
storm a music-box vaulted from one piece of furniture to the next
and those present were surrounded by those little flames 'that
Tissot called "grated moonlight"'.

Montesquiou, however, always remained hovering on the edge
of the supernatural; and on that score one can apply to him the
apt judgment of Redon on Moreau. He remained attached to the
earth as much by reason of his passion for material things as of his
pride; but he 'saw', that is certain. Sometimes, he confused the
supernatural with the fantastic in articles the ideas of which were,

twenty years later, to become those of the Surrealists. Having discovered, by the light of spiritualism, both William Blake, whose sinuous lines pointed forward to 1900 and another English visionary, John Martin, the imaginary museum of Montesquiou was already partly that of André Breton. The poet emphasised the limitations of nineteenth-century scientific materialism: 'Materialism is a thick lid, which does not let in any light from above. It refuses all outside illumination, which it abandons to others. Those who have passed on themselves the sombre edict to remain under this vault, dig cells for themselves or excavate palaces, pacing back and forth in their cellars, which are often spacious and sometimes magnificently lit with artificial lights. They do not know and do not recognise any other form of habitation. If, however, one day there should filter down into the vault the feeblest ray of the dispersed and vibrating blue light from above, then in contrast with that, the illumination of the underground passage, however incandescent it might be, would seem lurid and smoky.'

In such a light and aided by his bewitching vocabulary Montesquiou considered the curious drawings of Victorien Sardou, who in his youth had indulged in spiritualist experiments. These fantastic dwellings, 'the seven castles of the Beyond', were described by the poet as follows:

> Doors, staircases in ornate iron-work, with sinuous carpets spread along them, lead to colonnades of palm-tree trunks, to apartments, to balconies of a variety of shapes. The windows open to glittering stars of sky and sea. . . . The whole wall is decorated symmetrically with the flower of the lilac; the ridge-piece is adorned with a confusion of ornamental foliage, which joins at one corner to form a bloom that is even more abundant and more complicated, opening out into tendrils hung with the little bells of oats.

This extravagant vegetation has its equivalent in Montesquiou's very handwriting, which in paragraph after paragraph seems to project on to paper the spirals of Art Nouveau.

> The iron-work presents, in filigree and Hungarian point, rose-windows in the form of plants, leaves and petals crushed together; pods opening into lattice-work; striped sea-wrack,

crinkling as it dries. . . . The floor speckled, enamelled, knotted like the heart of a pomegranate. . . .

This is surely more the description of a Gaudi or a Horta palace. Far more effectively than the digressions of a Péladan or the theories of a Jean Lahor, this text discovers the profound source of Art Nouveau: spiritualism.

How much better it would have been if the man who drew from this source had remained among his books and his flowers; if he had torn up at least half of the poems that ran so easily off his pen, and all his invitations. Alas! the vanity of a narcissist, the frivolity of an aristocrat and the ambition of a man who felt himself to be unappreciated, ceaselessly drove him into society. For a dinner, for a tea-party or for a first-night the magician Klingsor left his garden in order to shine in salons lit by lamps that were even more artificial than those of materialism. And God alone knew if he would be welcome at the outset of the new century.

The Golden Calf

Until 1914 the combination of an extraordinary prosperity and of perpetual improvements in the means of communication brought about an acceleration in the social life of a great many people with a great deal of leisure at their disposal. Robert was forty-five and the Paris of 1900 was the third Paris that he had known. The first, the rather provincial Paris of the Faubourg Saint-Germain, had either at last fallen asleep or enjoyed a rejuvenation by crossing to the Right Bank; the second Paris, which he had celebrated in the 'eighties, that of the Plaine Monceaux and the scholarly wives of bankers, now gave way to the new capital, its centre shifted to the 16th Arrondissement that was to fête the Russian Ballet. The superb international society of de luxe trains and transatlantic liners, caricatured by Sem, provided Montesquiou with a public, with victims and above all with clients for the artists he patronised.

Never had there been so much entertaining. From the duchess to the prefect's wife, every lady had her day, published in a directory with both district and date provided. Thus—and this kind of complication always made Montesquiou laugh—'Mme

Ganderax entertains on the first Thursday of each month and on every Friday except the first'. The press announced children's tea-parties, concerts, theatricals, garden-parties, coming-out balls for débutantes, dances for young couples, masked balls, fancy-dress balls. Each evening there was a vast number of dinners; 'intimate' luncheons were given to honour some highness who was passing through. Tout-Paris met at hundreds of suppers; actresses began to entertain, if not to be entertained, giving midnight suppers at the conclusion of their performances. There were also, of course, official receptions and those held at embassies.

Robert de Montesquiou was to succeed in giving parties which did not belong to any of these categories and the accounts of which overflowed the columns assigned to society journalists. These journalists were well-known people. Baroness Double signed herself 'Etincelle' (Spark); Mme Estradère was to the readers of *Le Figaro* 'The Princess de Mesagne'; Mme Legrand, now ruined, sent to the *New York Herald* accounts of 'the dinner from which one dies, the ball where one is crushed'. Tout-Paris society now included the 'grands bourgeois', who had decided to spend at least half their income—the Godillots had a little court of their own; the upper crust—Lucinge or Polignac—who had decided to have an amusing time; actresses who had decided to be correct—among them, Cécile Sorel was the most brilliant; and the boulevard writers who had decided to become academicians—Robert de Flers succeeded in that ambition, Francis de Croisset did not.

This life was open to many more foreigners than even at the time of Offenbach. Russians and Americans rivalled one another in ostentation, Italians and Rumanians in the number of their princelings; grand-dukes crammed Maxim's, infantas plundered Paquin, and William II dreamed of a state visit to France.

Regilded aristocrats gave to capitalism a splendour worthy of the 'grand siècle'. Polignac-Singer and Gramont-Rothschild erected palaces in the Avenue Henri-Martin to follow the example of the Castellane-Goulds in the Avenue du Bois. Never had such prodigal expenditure and such an accumulation of parties been seen as in this Belle Époque. The French should, like the English, call the period Edwardian; for the first decade of the century is so well represented by the corpulent German gentleman who was accustomed to moving in the wings of Parisian life and who surrounded himself with pretty women and great Jews as he reigned over his Empire. Never had the divorce been so absolute between, on the one side, power, money and society and, on the other, all that was new in literature and the arts. Architects copied the Trianon; Sargent and Laszlo imitated Gainsborough; Bourget caused hearts to beat and Rostand hands to clap. Montesquiou was alone in having both the commanding presence and the energy to stand up before this barricade of money and praise the true poets and the true painters; descanting, almost to a note of falsity, on merits far more rare than success, in order to engrave them on the soft wax of snobbery. Lectures and lampoons, poems and perfidies—all were used by the Professor of Beauty as means to impose his taste. The attempt would lead to his own ruin.

CHAPTER 16

The Pavilion of the Muses

Climb up towards this palace built of smoke,
Studded with irony and plumed with pride.

Louis XIV at Neuilly

THE GREAT fête of 1894 at Versailles seemed to Montesquiou the best of his lessons in Beauty; its success proved to him that he had a genius for parties. But Versailles was a theatre that was too distant, the pavilion a stage too small for the productions of which he was dreaming. He returned to Paris, first occupying a vast apartment in a building in the Rue de l'Université that came to him from his mother. Then he tried another apartment in the Avenue Bosquet. Finally, Yturri found at Neuilly a dwelling worthy of the master; a setting worthy of the parties of his dreams. Montesquiou had always liked houses more than people; this one, christened 'The Pavilion of the Muses', was the great love of his life—his superb Montespan greedy for jewels from her aesthetic Louis XIV. On the edge of the Bois de Boulogne, during the Second Empire, a man of taste had built, rather in the style of the Grand Trianon, this inconvenient house, situated a little too far from the centre of the city; it had been to let for a long time. The poet was charmed with it.

Let us follow the Count as he guided his visitors from room to room; but we need not linger as long as they were obliged to do to hear an anecdote before this curio or a poem before that piece of furniture. Montesquiou began by planting the courtyard with sycamores and placing in it oleanders in tubs. This courtyard 'lay in front of the vaulted protuberances of an ample rotunda, supporting a semi-circular terrace'. In the marble hall were two groups of statuary by Pajou and a naked Venus drawn by dolphins by the Austrian sculptor von Pfaffenhoven, known in France

merely as Pfaff, who had given to his model the features of Marie-
Antoinette. The reception-room was decorated in light oak,
picked out with fillets of gold. The furniture was more imposing
than welcoming: twelve crimson plush chairs with silver ornaments and a large sofa called 'de Julie',* since its upholstery
showed a garland on which birds were perched. From there one
passed on into the dining-room, the mantelpiece of which was
supported by four statues of Hercules ascribed by the Count in
lyrical moments to Puget. The portrait by Whistler dominated this
room, which had been painted in colours chosen to harmonise
with the grey chinchilla of the pelisse depicted in it. On the walls
were 'The Interior of the Studio' by Stevens; some views of
Versailles by Lobre; and a large portrait of a woman by Helleu.

The library was more a gallery. To brighten the shelves, the
bibliophile displayed, lying flat, bindings by Lortic and Meunier
and works which the Goncourts had had covered in Louis XV or
Japanese silks. On all sides the shelves were invaded by ornaments: aesthetic and literary relics from which Montesquiou, like
the devotee who collects the bones of saints, expected some kind
of special grace or, perhaps, no more than glory. There was the
bird-cage that had belonged to Michelet; the sketch in terra
cotta of Lamartine by Count d'Orsay; Desbordes-Valmore's
guitar; a lock of Byron's hair; Henri Becque's spy-glass; the eyes
of Jeanne drawn by Baudelaire; Sickert's portrait of Beardsley;
the medallion of Jules de Goncourt that had ornamented the
balcony of an artist's home; plaster casts of Castiglione's feet and
Mme Greffulhe's chin, on either side of Yturri's legs, clad in
cyclist's breeches, as drawn by Boldini. Everywhere there were
netsukes, Tanagra figurines and lacquer boxes. There were also
photographs of Amiel, Hello and Vigny; and, most beautiful of
all, of Victor Hugo 'listening to God'.

These reception rooms were on the ground floor looking on to
the Bois; on the first floor the rooms looked towards Neuilly. A
staircase, very much in the Goncourt style, its sides hung with
heavy cretonnes and Japanese embroideries, led to the private
rooms. The first salon, 'scarcely tinted with delicate mauves and
creamy ivory', was called 'the salon of roses', since in it was a

* An allusion to *La Guirlande de Julie,* a collection of madrigals composed
in honour of Julie d'Angennes, wife of the Duke de Montausier, early in the
seventeenth century. Trans.

piece of tapestry embroidered with an immense rose-tree. In this room Montesquiou had attempted to evoke the roses of Hildesheim, St Elizabeth of Hungary and the invention of the rosary by St Dominic. There was also a picture by Besnard, better than many a bad Renoir and painted with the same kind of palette, the title of which was 'The Rapture of Roses'. Then came the Empire salon, where Montesquiou leant against the piano near the Ingres drawing of Liszt when young—so like poor Delafosse—to recite one of his poems, 'Empirisme':

> I like the Empire style:
> The worst examples daze
> And dazzle me far more
> Than works of Louis Treize.

This poem was dedicated to Boldini, whose portrait of Montesquiou with a cane was the principal decoration of the room. As for the bedroom, it retained the stamp of an earlier taste. The bed was set in the coils of a dragon; the walls were covered with *kakemonos* and the pieces of furniture with ornaments in the shape of bats. But it was in a study, as high as the foliage of the trees, that Inspiration came best to the poet as he sat between drawings by La Gandara and Helleu. There too there were many objects : Venetian glass and mounted pieces of porcelain.

The paintings of Alfred Stevens give us a much better idea of Montesquiou's apartments than photographs do. They were not really decorated as one understands the word today, but arranged either by caprice or by affinities more subtle than those merely of colour or style. A lyre-backed chair went well in front of a Coromandel screen; a cashmere covered the upholstery; there were bunches of flowers on the console-tables; cloisonné was next to *Vernis Martin,* Gallé next to Japan. These private rooms gave on to a half-moon gallery which was used as a winter-garden; its furniture constructed of bamboo, it contained vast ornamental vases from which burst hydrangeas and azaleas. There an illusion of summer could be felt, and sometimes an actress would lean out of its windows to scatter the verses of a poem on to the guests assembled below.

'The archangel Gabriel' brought to the house its most beautiful ornament. Rummaging about Versailles, he learned that some nuns had in their garden a marble fountain basin, which might possibly have come from the baths on the ground-floor of the palace, altered in the reign of Louis XV. The king was said to have given it to Mme de Pompadour to decorate her hermitage at Versailles. After long negotiations and the payment of a quite considerable sum (which did not include, as jealous people maintained, the offer of a slipper belonging to the Pope by the artful Yturri to the innocent nuns) the ten tons of 'this nightmare in pink marble' had to be transported from Versailles to Neuilly. Montesquiou had the whole operation photographed in detail, like Louis XIV commissioning Van der Meulen to paint all the episodes of a siege. When the basin had been installed, poems were addressed to it, and now for the first time we see two rivals confronting each other for the esteem of the Count. Anna de Noailles sent a sonnet which began:

> Basin, of joyful rose unfurled in air
> Tender . . .

and Lucie Delarue-Mardrus a poem:

> Basin of bygone days, no cameo is rarer;
> There Montespan once bathed . . .

Montesquiou himself affirmed: 'The tears of things are in this block of marble from the Rance.' Lorrain of course evoked some horror—'The frightful mass at which a flux of entrails bleeds' (an allusion to the black masses by means of which Mme de Montespan tried to retain the favours of the king).

It was Yturri who had brought about a reconciliation between the journalist and Montesquiou; for, without the master knowing it, they would 'cruise' in each other's company. 'I should be delighted to exhume Eros and his loves for you', wrote the journalist, while at the same time sending to the Count a blue-grey silk cravat with yellow patterns and a spray of lilies: 'May these few heraldic and tardy stalks remind you of the fervent respect in which I hold you.' The atrocious behaviour was forgotten; Lorrain once more became a guest.

Neuilly was delightful; the construction of buildings between the Château de Madrid and the Porte Maillot had only just begun, the latter point being the rendezvous for cyclists (always dear to Yturri). The long straight streets were bordered by gardens, with here and there a pavilion like the one in which Gautier lived. The paths of the former park of Louis-Philippe became the avenues; the Ile de Puteaux, with its elegant tennis-club, concealed the horrors of the suburbs. Montesquiou and Yturri went to the tennis-club to have tea in the midst of women in white lace and to watch young Anglo-maniacs play lawn-tennis. A polo-field was very near, and the horsemen on the grass brought Persian miniatures to mind. Neuilly had something of the atmosphere of a watering-place. One visited neighbours more easily than in Paris, and there were a number of neighbours to choose from. Out of season, people went to the country to economise.

Barrès and France

Barrès was a temptation to which Montesquiou resorted with prudence; it was important that too assiduous an attendance should not fatigue this impatient man. In the study that looked on the Bois, the writer's profile, so like that of Le Grand Condé, would stand out from a background of bookbindings and heroic mouldings. With a tired hand he went through the letters from constituents piled high on a table supported by eagles, and eventually chose to open an envelope closed with a golden seal engraved with a maxim. How agreeable it would be to accompany Montesquiou on a walk in the Bois; the Count had an alert step and a quick mind. They would talk about Stanislas de Guaïta, his mysterious death and the Beyond; of Carpaccio and El Greco; of the Empress of Austria, whose sister, the Queen of Naples,* living nearby in a suburban villa, was often visited by the Count. But Mme Barrès, armed with her lorgnette, called her great man to order. There was the banquet of the League of Patriots to attend; there were academic visits to make. She did not care for this neighbour, detecting irony beneath his affability. Count Robert was a link with the aesthetic past, with Baroness Deslandes and perhaps also with Anna de Noailles. Sometimes Barrès made a hop as far as the Pavilion: he needed advice about a painter, he was in search of some abstruse quotation. He also needed to laugh. For all these services the great writer thanked Montesquiou royally in the dedication of his book on El Greco:

* It will be recollected that this 'heroine of Gaeta' saved M. de Charlus from the vulgar fury of Mme Verdurin. Trans.

To Count Robert de Montesquiou
To the Poet
To the inventor of many rare objects and forms,
To one of the first apologists of El Greco who himself
Will find one day his inventor and his apologist,
Friendly respects from his admirer and neighbour.

Montesquiou cried with joy when he read this tribute.

Another female dragon kept guard over another illustrious neighbour: a more amiable dragon but a more ephemeral neighbour and one who was also a little more distant. If one took the short-cut through the park the Villa Saïd was a quarter of an hour from the pavilion. There, too, was a collector of bric-à-brac and a bibliophile. Anatole France preferred idling to the duties imposed on him by fame or, rather, by Mme Arman de Caillavet. 'Monsieur, you must write a preface for this dear little Marcel. . . . Monsieur, you must receive this delegation of Portuguese intellectuals, of Greek freethinkers, of Belgian poetesses. . . . Monsieur, you must make up your mind to visit Montesquiou.' 'He bores me with his endless talk about his ancestors,' came the great man's reply. 'Monsieur, three years have passed since I promised him that you'd visit him. Your poems will be recited.' France plunged his tapir's nose into a box of engravings; he would escape once more with an affectionate dedication. But Madame returned to the attack: 'There will be a grand-duke there.' 'In that case, nothing in the world will make me go,' cried the left-wing writer, delighted to have this moral pretext to escape an unpleasant duty. When eventually he decided to pay this long-deferred call, he arrived and left so promptly that the other guests saw little more than his back vanishing towards some other more learned or more licentious distraction. But the old fox had been so lavish with his compliments to Montesquiou that he left him in raptures. Next day an amiable visit would be made to thank Mme Arman de Caillavet for her kind attentions; perhaps the Count would be accompanied by a woman friend of the upper crust or a young man with a future. The good lady feared Montesquiou like the plague; someone had told her that he was in the habit of reciting with relish a sonnet about her beginning:

Tiny Madame Arnaud de Collauxfesses*

* Colle = glue; fesses = buttocks. Trans.

There was another neighbour, Henri Bataille,* who was in all the glory of his dramas and in all the glitter of a dramatic love-affair. Montesquiou detected in him a resemblance to Baudelaire and greatly admired *Le Phalène*; by praising Berthe Bady and arranging recitals for her he gained for her a fame which attracted the affection of Bataille. In his relationships with his celebrated contemporaries, Montesquiou, who had venerated Moreau and Whistler, maintained no more than the forms of ordinary social intercourse. He believed that fame was earned by frequenting great men, as it were by contagion, exactly as a snob thinks (but in his case with more justification) that he becomes elegant by dint of frequenting duchesses.

It was again with a neighbour that Montesquiou himself made fun of snobs and duchesses. In the Boulevard Bineau lived 'Gyp', in fact the Comtesse de Martel, a novelist whose best works recall those of Ada Leverson and whose worst are little more than political and anti-semitic caricatures. An eternal *enfant terrible*, she imagined that she had caused a sensation each time that she had managed to say boo to some goose of an Academician.

In a large violet scrawl, this friend kept Montesquiou informed about the gossip of the day. Perhaps she suspected him of being responsible when, at a moment of crisis between Anna de Noailles and Maurice Barrès, the following announcement appeared in the personal columns of *Le Temps*: 'Very ill woman, desperate, begs M.B. to come back, give sign of life. Situation grave. A. Noailles.'

Gyp entertained every Sunday from midday till midnight. Montesquiou stayed on when he met Barrès or Doctor Pozzi at her house, but fled when he saw Boni de Castellane jawing away in a *bergère* which had belonged to Talleyrand, his ancestor through an illegal union. Both of them members of the upper crust, they had each lost class in proportion to the extent they shone in Tout-Paris; and each of them measured exactly the decline or the rise of the other. 'Robert pushes his gift of imitation to the extreme of imitating himself,' remarked Castellane, not without wit. Montesquiou would murmur:

> Boni de Castellane can pass
> For banker, daughter and ass.

* It is now becoming apparent that this out-of-date dramatist was also an excellent poet.

Each of them, however, willingly recognised that the other knew how to give a party. If their lists of guests were almost identical, the object and the manner of the diversions each offered to Tout-Paris were very different.

Charlus in his glory

'Do I entertain well?' Montesquiou wondered in his memoirs. 'Without doubt a little despotically. The truth of the matter is that I prefer the parties themselves to the people I invite to them—and perhaps my guests realise that. I have always regarded them as an inseparable—shall I say unavoidable?—detail of any reception, but a detail that is, alas! all too often recalcitrant. Guests are a flock of sheep, not easily guided and eager to nestle in the remote corners of an apartment or the recesses of pieces of furniture, rather than stand in the position suggested to them in a well-ordered gathering; their timidity dissuading them from showing themselves, as their garrulity urges them to speak and their disdain to leave.

One thing that made me laugh was the surly manner of those who had invited themselves. Their desire had got the better of them; but they reproached themselves for the lapse, did not forgive me for it and made everyone else pay for it by putting on a sullen look, which I in turn was not afraid to combat by the simple expedient of asking them if they were happy. . . .

I never entertained after dinner. I have often observed at evening parties that if one examines the guests, especially the women, the spectacle is usually agreeable, or at least tolerable provided that one begins with the lower extremities. Women nearly always wear well-made shoes and shod feet have no age. It is as one's gaze travels upwards to reach the region of the face and the uncovered parts of the body, that the picture not merely does not improve but, much more commonly, is actually ruined. During the day, there is less likelihood of this disaster taking place; since trimmings, hats, violets and other adornments all either prevent it or weaken its impact. Do not forget that I entertained for egotistical reasons, less to satisfy my guests than to please myself.'

In spite of the existence of blacklists, the possibility of subsequent quarrels and the obligation to buy *de luxe* editions of
works by the host or his protégés, everyone hastened to Neuilly
at a summons from the Count and intrigued to be among the
invited as soon as a party was announced. A week before the
great day, Montesquiou began to harass the servants and summon
the upholsterers and the gardeners, whom he proceeded to remind
of the principles of their art. Hoentschell, whose decorations
were admired both at Bing's establishment and at the Exhibition,
came himself to supervise the laying of the carpets that would
make the terrace into a salon and the pinning of the roses on to
trellises which would make the salons into the garden. Blue
hydrangeas foamed on either side of the flight of steps up from
the gate.

On the morning of the party telegraph boys, loaded with
express letters and telegrams, hastened to the house. Those
unable to come apologised at length for fear of penalties. Anna
de Noailles, for example, sent the message: 'I want to be there,
and if I am not there by three o'clock it will be because I have not
been able to move, not been able to will what I desire. But I
cannot imagine that.' Paul Valéry apologised: 'Your delightful
reception to celebrate the arts of poetry and music unfortunately
coincides for me with quite another kind of occupation, both
unavoidable and practical.'

Many reiterated their thanks; others requested the favour of
being allowed to bring 'a Russian lady, who is madly artistic',
or a young cousin whose 'whole life has been transformed by
reading *The Commander of Delicate Odours*'. With an imperious
Malacca cane, the producer indicated where the buffet was to be
set: at the bottom of the staircase as at the Marriage at Cana.
'Above all, masses of flowers to hide the orchestra. Only Litvine*
must be visible—and as little of her as possible—in a cloud of
grey irises with a poinsettia here and there to remind us of the
fire-theme . . . Gabriel, did you remember not to invite the
Bonnières? Are you sure that Mme Bulteau will know about
the party and suffer agonies of vexation? Lucien Daudet is to be
invited at the last moment—he was altogether too late in sending
his thanks after the last party.'

Yturri became breathless, but watched over everything; his

* A Wagnerian singer noted for the size both of her voice and her bust.

cranium began to resemble ivory, his colour grew leaden, but his heart remained golden. He did not want to lose a minute of these glorious hours. To enliven his spirits, Montesquiou began to imagine what kind of edifice Mme de Janzé would have on her head or imitated Flament not appearing to have arrived with his friend M. Bailby, the latter pretending to suffer at the feet of the beautiful Mme Hochon, and Boldini circling a beautiful foreign woman whom he wanted to take away from Helleu, like a toad circling a rose. . . . Both laughed uproariously until it was time to go and change. An hour later the two of them were at the entrance, each in a grey morning-coat, a rose in the button-hole. Menservants who had come from Belloir's with the gilt chairs mounted guard in the courtyard; headwaiters from Potel's were busy behind the buffet. 'Heavens!' cried the Count, who had had the cloth strewn with Maréchal Ney roses. 'We should have had Malmaison roses. This looks like a wedding or—or like an altar of repose at the Madeleine.' 'Oh, Robert, it's simply divine.'

'But here is the incomparable one—the most faithful of them all . . .'; and the two friends rushed forward to greet Countess Potocka, now grown stout and with a dark colouring that gave her a malignant expression. The chorus of ladies followed her shortly afterwards: the kinswomen with whom he had not quarrelled; Mme de Brantès or the Marquise d'Eyragues; the Marquise de Casa-Fuerte, always ravishing in the tulle which swathed her and accompanied by her son Illan, to whom the Count exclaimed, 'I forbid you to be so handsome!' The Lemaire ladies and Mme Alphonse Daudet arrived in the midst of a prattling crowd of young men, who, in order to prostrate themselves before Sarah herself, thrust aside veils and attendants. 'Divine, divine!' Rodin, his beard flying, came with what appeared to be a very proper Swiss gentleman: Louise Breslau, an excellent painter of children in pastel. Soaring above fashion with all the arrogance of her intelligence and her millions, Princess Edmond de Polignac gave the appearance of having presented to her for the first time a beautiful American girl, Miss Natalie Barney, whom in fact she knew very well. 'She could have married Lord Alfred Douglas, but she prefers Liane de Pougy,' shouted the master of the house in apparent confidence to Mme Barrès, who was less deaf than prudish. Proust arrived in the wake of the Princesse de

Caraman-Chimay: abashed, blinking, as if dazzled by the brilliance of the gathering. But he stored up in his implacable memory this picture of the master of the house:

> He meanwhile was posted between the house and the garden, by the side of the German Ambassador, leaning upon the balustrade of the great staircase which led from the garden to the house, so that the other guests, in spite of the three or four feminine admirers who were grouped round the Baron and almost concealed him, were obliged to greet him as they passed. He responded by naming each of them in turn. And one heard an incessant: 'Good evening, Monsieur du Hazay, good evening, Madame de la Tour du Pin-Verclause, good evening, Madame de la Tour du Pin-Gouvernet, good evening, Philibert, good evening, my dear Ambassadress,' and so on. This created a continuous barking sound, interspersed with benevolent suggestions or inquiries (to the answers to which he paid no attention), which M. de Charlus addressed to them in a tone softened, artificial to show his indifference, and benign: 'Take care the child doesn't catch cold, it is always rather damp in the gardens. Good evening, Madame de Mecklebourg. Have you brought your daughter? Is she wearing that delicious pink frock? Good evening, Saint-Géran.' Certainly there was an element of pride in his attitude, for M. de Charlus was aware that he was a Guermantes, and that he occupied a supreme place at this party. But there was more in it than pride, and the very word *fête* suggested, to the man with aesthetic gifts, the luxurious, curious sense that it might bear if this party were being given not by people in contemporary society but in a painting by Carpaccio or Veronese.

The rival muses

'The Countess Mathieu de Noailles!' announced the usher. 'I have kept a surprise for you,' Montesquiou announced to everyone. 'You are going to hear some divine verses. . . .' The young woman straightened her little head in its helmet of black, certain of being blessed yet again by the tutelary deities of the house; but an air of malice disturbed the faithful. 'Her Imperial

Highness, the Grand-Duchess Vladimir!'* 'Will Madame allow me to recite a poem inspired by the jewels which Fabergé set for her?' Leaning on a parasol, the handle of which had been made by this master, the Highness prepared herself to relish a very Parisian entertainment.

During the five stanzas that followed, the new arrivals, herded together on the steps, strained their ears to hear while those already present held their breath. In the uproar of flattery and relief that followed, a blunderer was heard to quote Rostand, 'Oh, oh, it is an Empress!' With a wide gesture the Count now welcomed the last comers. 'We can begin,' he declared. 'But Mme Greffulhe is not here!' groaned Yturri. 'She will come at her usual time,' Montesquiou retorted. Wagnerian chords rose up from behind the flowers; the Walkyrie, barely contained in a tailor-made coat-and-skirt and wearing a hat by the celebrated Caroline Reboux, swept Montesquiou far away from his guests with the splendour of her singing. Overcome by such a degree of admiration that for once he lost his voice, the host hurried forward at the conclusion of the performance to place at her feet a mass of flowers to which he had added the manuscript of a poem. 'In the ecstasy of complete and prolonged enjoyment'—as a society chronicler put it—the guests then advanced on the refreshments.

Some of them begged to be allowed to see the rest of the house and Yturri led them to the first floor, where they looked down on to a parterre of mingled aigrettes and roses. The Count went from one group to another: 'We are going to have the privilege of hearing a delightful, incomparable and very young poetess. She has gilded her genius with the splendours of the orient. . . .' All eyes turned to the Countess de Noailles; but the Count went on, 'Madame Lucie Delarue-Mardrus† wanted very much to read us this poem . . .'

An ephebe in a close-fitting dress, with the gaze of a sultana and the voice of a child, murmured enchanting phrases between two banks of roses. Wise people recalled a saying of their host: 'Every party should be given against someone.'

* The most Parisian of the grand-duchesses and grandmother of Princess Marina.

† An excellent but inexhaustible and therefore exhausting poet, wife of Dr Mardrus, translator of *The Thousand and One Nights*.

Suddenly the tide of admiration flowed from the stage to the hall—Countess Greffulhe had appeared at last, in a dress embroidered with golden lilies; a string of pearls, twisted in her hair, fell to her waist. She was going on to dine with the Queen of England. Without effort she reached the front row, where, as always, an armchair awaited her. 'She is Tiepolo's Armide,' Count Robert proclaimed. It was the worthy coronation of a party which the superb Mme Segond-Weber now concluded with a poem by the Count.

At that the people began to take their leave. 'What a lesson in beauty!' 'You have given us everything!' 'Magician!' Montesquiou watched the women go down into the courtyard. Footmen scurried to fetch a carriage or a motor-car. The evening was thickening the chestnut-trees in the Bois. The party was over: now was the time to make the autopsy and to comment on its moments both of sublimity and of farce. The host kept the young Clermont-Tonnerres for dinner. The Marquise, née Gramont, was the only woman of this circle that he judged worthy of understanding him. He was right; no one has better evoked memories of those parties:

The affecting traces of what was over-endured with a more exquisite charm, perhaps, than the thing itself. The piano is open, the figure of the musician still appears distinct between the keyboard and the stool. . . . The flesh-coloured azaleas have lost their azure butterflies. The tapestry-chairs are in disorder; the satin-cushions keep their dents. . . .

Dinner is served on a little table in the majestic courtyard, to the sound of the fountain in the darkness that is falling, while the house, its interior deserted but still filled with lights and memories, stands alone behind its gilded windows and its opulent peristyle, thrusting out to meet the visitors.

Montesquiou's voice rises above the roar of the motor-cars along the Bois. The flowers of the chestnut trees dare not fall. One sees the arm of a Venus resting on its elbow, which lightly sinks into the cushion of the stone.

Enraptured by the success of his party, Montesquiou speaks, orates, chats, giggles, guffaws. He is a one-man orchestra. He is exalted at having for four hours ordered the music and the poems, laid out the flowers, shaken all those illustrious hands and dominated the guests.

For six years the Pavilion of the Muses was to open for recitals of Fauré and Debussy, for performances by the stars of the Russian Ballet and for the declamation of the works of Mallarmé and Verlaine by the great actors and actresses of the Comédie Française.

CHAPTER 17

The Peacock and His Sorrows

At sunset a pavane is danced
Majestic in its solemness:
He, too, becomes a sun which fades
As fades his dress.

The beauty merchant

'It is already annoying enough not to have any money, without having to deprive oneself of other things!' retorted Montesquiou to his agent, who was worried that his master's reckless expenditure would seriously impair the capital inherited from his mother. 'Ah, well, a building can be sold . . .' Montesquiou needed money for parties, to repair his château at Artagnan and, above all, to buy things. At Edmond de Goncourt's sale the Watteau drawings were far too expensive; but Yturri none the less spent hours in the Salle Drouot, from which he returned loaded with *kakemonos* and pieces of lacquer—'exhausted from this conflict with emotions and microbes'. The poor boy had no time to rest; quickly, Montesquiou despatched him to visit Marcel Schwob's cat, which was ill, to choose some particularly hideous flowers for the engagement party of an ugly cousin, and above all to make preparations for their journey to America. The situation between the two friends grew tense, as each spoke of his 'poor overworked nerves', for an immense amount of energy was expended on this expedition across the Atlantic.

The idea for it originated in Versailles, where, in a charming pavilion in the Boulevard de la Reine, there lived three American ladies united by the most affectionate ties. These sisters of Henry James's Bostonians were: Anne, the daughter of Pierpont Morgan; Miss Elisabeth Marbury; and Miss Elsie de Wolfe, better

known as Lady Mendl, who continued to occupy the house until
1950. Henceforth, lesbians were to play a big part in Montesquiou's life. Often more intelligent and certainly less futile than
most society women, and at the same time less likely to be
condemned than their masculine counterparts, they formed little
groups torn apart by jealousies and terrible vengeances. The
three ladies of Versailles pushed Montesquiou into giving lessons
in beauty to New York, and he embarked, attended by his guardian angel. There was perhaps some matrimonial scheme behind
this expedition.

How much bustling about there was before the departure!
How many letters of introduction! Marcel Schwob wrote to
Marion Crawford, the novelist; Helleu to his lovely millionaire
models—the Duchess of Marlborough, Mrs Lydyg, Mrs Goëlet,
Gladys Deacon. A Missionary of Literature, Montesquiou left
in January 1903, loaded with curios. A Boston newspaper
announced his arrival as follows:

> The beautiful Count is coming to Boston.
> This gentleman of France is now a reigning divinity in
> New York due to his good looks and good clothes. He does not
> lecture but gives 'conferences' at $5 per ticket. Naturally the
> smart set rallies to his support. . . .

The Philadelphia *Enquirer* declared, 'Society will worship from
the Count's Breviary of Beauty.' Another journalist described
Montesquiou's manner of speech as 'a low pink voice studded
with emeralds'. Thus began a series of lectures by the Professor of
Beauty in drawing-rooms and large hotels. He also gave readings
of his poems, among which was 'La Prière du Nègre':

> Lord, though you laid the night upon my limbs,
> The lily's candour may still dwell in them.

He went as far as Chicago, where he was received by Mrs
Potter Palmer, collector and wife of a famous manufacturer of
biscuits:

> Pamela bears the palm as champion biscuit-baker,
>   On only one small point does she defy persuasion—
> To eat one of her biscuits you can never make her,
>   Even the finest meet with obstinate evasion.

Sem represented the aesthete before an audience glittering with Astors and Vanderbilts, whom Yturri is silencing with: 'Listen to the marvellous words . . .'; meanwhile, a Negro doorman, stupefied by the attitudes struck by the orator, asks 'Is that the cake-walk?' There was only one man in the whole audience of women: Boni de Castellane, who did not look very pleased. Montesquiou made a point of condemning the gentlemen who spent immense sums in antique shops, rather than on the works of contemporary artists.

In actual fact, when Boni was subsequently ruined, it was Montesquiou who guided his first steps as a dealer in antiques.

When Montesquiou was in need of ready money, he would employ his friends to sell some work of art on his behalf, harnessing people as ill-matched as Cécile Sorel and Bernard Berenson to dispose of Pfaffenhofen's Venus. The first of these wrote: 'My wild millionaires have arrived . . . but in the last resort the Americans declared for . . . a woman by Pajou which is no more than an ill-formed paving-stone.' The second wrote: 'I should love to visit your enchanting house, where I count on seeing your groups. Though I am only too willing to guide the staggering rich to recognition and possession of real works of art, I have no possible client at present.'

Montesquiou now began to yield up some of his finds to rich collectors. The poet might, like the Marquis de Biron, have been an antiquary of the first order, boasting about his things with incomparable erudition and spirit, if he had had a head for business and had been able to restrain himself from indulging in an insolence that often put to flight a prospective buyer. Thus he replied to a woman whose purchases he was guiding and who asked him, 'Don't you know of some old ruined couple from the aristocracy to rent my porter's lodge?' 'Oh, come! If you let it to people like that, not one of your guests would go any further.' To another, who insisted on being taken to see Countess Greffulhe, he explained gently: 'But don't you understand that your mere presence would rob the *salon* of the glitter which now attracts you to it?' The beautiful Mme Porgès, who accentuated her likeness to Marie-Antoinette by powdering her hair, was one of his pet aversions. To a cousin who apologised for being late with the words 'I have been hunting at Mme Porgès'' he retorted, 'You would have done better to have hunted Mme Porgès herself.' One day, when he had to go dressed as a sultan to a party at Mme Lemaire's, Montesquiou asked Maurice de Rothschild to lend him some jewels. He received only one very modest piece, with a message begging him to take the greatest care of it. 'It is a family heirloom.' Montesquiou replied: 'I did think that you had some jewels, but I had never suspected that you might have a family.' (Finally, Baroness Deslandes lent her opals and Bernhardt lent Theodora's belt for a costume that presaged the designs of Bakst.)

We know that Montesquiou was not in the very least anti-semitic, though this last remark might lead one to think that he was; it was merely that he required rich people to live up to his ideal with a certain magnificence. He was on terms of the closest intimacy with such collectors as the Ochse brothers and Mme Klotz, the proprietress of the Pinaud perfumery, who commis-sioned from him at the time of the 1900 Exhibition a sumptuous booklet entitled *Au Pays des Aromates*. Montesquiou flattered the greatest collector of his time, Camille Groult, who had assembled in his mansion in the Avenue du Bois, besides some of the best Fragonards, a pastel by Péronneau, entitled 'L'homme à la Rose', which sent the Count into raptures, and cases full of Watteaus and Hubert Roberts. This bookish collector also had many Turners: 'Sunsets which had not always risen at the home of their painter.'

Imposing and impertinent visits

During the first decade of the twentieth century, Montesquiou extended his social circle as much with the purpose of seeking out a life of luxury as of directing that life itself. M. Bardac, the son of a financier, has left an amusing sketch of a visit Montesquiou paid to the family house near Versailles. Not without complications, a dinner was arranged and a victoria was then despatched to fetch the Count and his secretary from Neuilly. From this vehicle emerged two gesticulating people, stained with blacking, each wearing white trousers and white shoes to show that they were visiting the country, but also the dinner-jacket and starched shirt usual at a dinner-party. Brandishing panama-hats and canes, they climbed the steps, at the top of which stood M. Bardac. Montes-quiou at once greeted him: 'Persons who are generally well-informed about such matters have told me that you have only fourteen millions. But now that I see the modest proportions of this dwelling—which is, of course, very pleasant, but certainly no Chenonceaux or Le Marais—I am convinced that you have ten times that sum.' He went on in this strain, to the amazement of the servants, until he reached the mistress of the house,* to whom he excused himself for having chosen a Sunday for his visit: 'I know that h-h-housekeepers like to spend their Sundays in the country. . . .' On the children being presented to him, he stared for a long time at the little girl: 'Charming . . . A most attractive sight. But we should have loved to see her this evening in the white frock of the Chartran portrait.' Turning towards the little boy, he launched into a tirade on the subject of the hate engendered among families from earliest antiquity: having taken in the House of Atreus, the Plantagenets, and a number of other instances, he concluded by yelling at M. Bardac: 'To this kind of relationship we prefer friendship—which knows how to open both the heart and the hand. . . .' 'Marvellous, marvellous,' murmured Yturri ecstatically. After dinner, to show that he was pleased, the Count took away M. Bardac's visitors' book, which he returned with these verses inscribed in it:

> One's right extends only to things
> Which one has bought with sufferings.

The poet crossed swords with another financier. He had ridiculed the enormous Madame Stern, who wrote under the name Maria Star, with the result that in 1904 her son, Jean, challenged Montesquiou to a duel in which the older man was wounded three times. Only Marcel Schwob was rational about the matter: 'You know how much both of us (he and Moreno) love you and admire you. I beg you, no more of these duels. Two are enough—in fact, two too many. You are too rare a man and too exquisite a poet to put your life in jeopardy for a banal distinction that should be reserved for journalists.'

Montesquiou was in the full bloom of his glory during the first few years of the century, but he had many bitternesses: decidedly he would never be for the world of letters anything but an amateur, a society figure. If he had friends on the *Mercure de France* such as Gourmont or Schwob, *La Revue Blanche* ignored him. Of course young poets sent him their works: Pierre Louÿs,

* On the death of her husband, Mme Bardac was to marry Debussy.

with the inscription 'Ab auctore reverenti'; Paul Valéry dedicating his *Introduction to the Method of Leonardo da Vinci*, 'To Robert de Montesquiou these Sleeping Papers;* Francis Jammes with the words: 'Thus, lost in the country, swarms of heather-wasps sometimes alight on the complicated flowers of exquisite gardens.' But the abundance of Montesquiou's work wearied the critics and his collection *Les Paons,* in spite of the Lalique cover, went unnoticed by the public. It seems that the sojourn at Versailles and the palace at Neuilly had turned the head of the poet a little. Whether assuming the role of Louis XIV or that of Ludwig II, he awaited tributes which, in fact, only came from society women. The velvet games of hide-and-seek played by his Bats brought him more success than the later strutting parade of his Peacock; so that eventually the Alexandrines were to resound in his poems like the halberd of a Swiss guard in a deserted gallery.

Of course when Montesquiou in person brought an article to his friend Calmette at *Le Figaro*, all the editorial staff rushed about and followed him down the stairs, while he posed on step after step to emphasise the effect of his amazing anecdotes. He had the same success at Charvet's when he went there to choose a waistcoat. Sem shows us the assistant bent in two to receive the edicts 'of our national Petronius'.

The Noailles comet and the Rostand sun

Decidedly these elegances were not taken seriously, and so far as even society was concerned, Montesquiou's literary success began to be eclipsed by two new luminaries. First, there was the young Anna de Noailles. Montesquiou did not like her; her mother had monopolised Delafosse and Gallé and she herself tended to detain Proust and Reynaldo Hahn for too long with her charm and wild laughter. But the most irritating thing of all was that the Count had to acknowledge that the prolix muse of his rival had astonishing success. Proust very much wanted his two friends to understand each other, and he therefore conveyed to the poetess the comments of the Count on *Les Pas Eblouis,* which he had just received: 'It is not merely sublime, marvellous, delightful. I can truthfully say, from the height of the competence of my taste, that

* 'Sleeping papers' in English in original. Trans.

it is, quite precisely, the most beautiful thing that she has ever written. . . .' At that Montesquiou had begun to recite with enthusiasm '"The sky this evening was a colour one cannot express".' Electrified by the violence of the shock that this phrase had given him, he stamped on the ground hard enough to break his heels, as though he were about to tumble backwards. '"That is the most beautiful thing that has been written since *Antigone*. What sublimity!"' This fervour, however, did not prevent a subsequent reserve, and after a morose article about another of her collections, Anna de Noailles wrote to Montesquiou: 'I find you very modest in your claims for me.' Always he tried to raise up rivals against her: first Lucie Delarue-Mardrus, then Marthe Bibesco. The following couplet began to circulate:

> To Mathieu each Noailles had said,
> 'On all accounts you must not wed'

The loquacious poetess, sublime and inexhaustible, kept an entire dinner-party hanging on her lips—by turns elegiac or political, tender or vehement. Besides this song-like effortlessness, the deliberate and imperious remarks of Montesquiou seemed to impart a chill. All of a sudden it came about that his lyricism sounded old-fashioned. One evening, when he dwelled too long on the emotions of an aesthete in a balloon—'And I felt the earth draw away from me'—Forain muttered in a corner, 'The earth too!'

The Rostands were also very irritating. Montesquiou had first met this extremely amiable little couple at Bernhardt's, when Rostand himself was aping Musset and Mme Rostand was a ravishing woman, greedy for society and success. They cooed at each other in Alexandrines. In 1898, Montesquiou readily applauded *Cyrano,* so many lines of which he could have written. Could it be that Rostand had read too deeply in *Les Chauves-Souris*?

In 1900, *L'Aiglon* received less wholehearted praise from Montesquiou, for he had given to Bernhardt a slipper that had once belonged to the King of Rome (an inheritance from Maman Quiou) and this relic had quickly passed on to the Rostands. What provoked Montesquiou was the atmosphere the Rostands created around themselves. The man was charming, certainly, and his work was too close to Montesquiou's own for the Count to ridicule it; but the family now monopolised the front pages of the newspapers. In fact, the Rostands had become the Royal Family of France, and such tit-bits of gossip as Jean's first tooth, Maurice's curl or Madame's hat were relayed with avidity. Montesquiou started to make a collection of 'pearls' about the man to whom he had given the nickname 'The Meteor'—like this one: 'M. Rostand is so simple that he must make an effort to forget that he is Edmond Rostand.' Around the Rostands, as around Anna de Noailles (though in her case they were of a superior quality) thronged a crowd of flatterers to burn incense at their shrine. This was typical of a period in which so many people had nothing to do. Like comets, the stars of the Parisian firmament moved only on an orbit composed of elderly ladies, time-serving young men, society women excited about letters and literary women excited about society. In addition there were always some Russian noblewomen. Bernhardt and de Max had their little courts. Each Academician had two or three female followers, whose salons he would adorn from time to time. Montesquiou had, of course, his chorus of ladies; but he was too hard on his admirers; disgrace and age had thinned them out, and after twenty years of witnessing him exclaim and be enraptured, they were in any case less likely to be convinced. A cruel ordeal was soon to revive Montesquiou's old fervour and bring him new friendships.

Goodbye, dear Gabriel

At the beginning of 1905, Gabriel Yturri was exhausted. His doctors advised him to rest and to diet; but he had so much to do that he did not listen to them. Soon nothing could check the progress of his diabetes. He would now lie out on the terrace which overlooked the Bois. Sometimes he would summon up enough energy to take the borzois out for a walk, but he would soon return, passing Montesquiou in the gallery as he was getting into his fur-lined coat. The Count went to tea-parties, to concerts and to private views, 'with death in the soul' (as he confided to his intimate friends) in an attempt to conceal from Gabriel the seriousness of his condition. But the unfortunate man realised it only too well. He thought that he had become repulsive and said to his friends in turn: 'If I can still serve, I beg God to let me live. But if it is for an existence of coughing and revoltingly shrunken cheeks, then I do not wish it.' There were scenes between the two men. Gabriel became attached to a little dog that would not leave his bedside; but Montesquiou only tolerated cats (the borzois were merely part of the decoration). Many ladies crowded around the invalid: Miss Bertha Cappel, later Lady Mitchelham, whom Helleu painted; the beautiful and intelligent Miss Barney and her friend Lucie Delarue-Mardrus; Baroness Deslandes and Jean Lorrain, reconciled for the tenth time. The bedroom was full of flowers; with gloved hands Montesquiou served tea in Japanese cups. When the situation became too strained between the two friends, they summoned Father Mugnier, who had restored harmony, or at least advised a mutual blindness, among so many couples of the upper crust who 'could only flap one wing'. His village-priest manner belied a style of conversation that was both erudite and mundane. The good priest reassured Yturri, who in moments of desperation saw himself as damned: 'The most important thing is not to have caused suffering around one.'

Proust was alerted: 'I was very sad to learn that M. Yturri was very ill, I had not suspected it, but none the less I must confess to you that I have the impression that he is one of those condemned men who are never executed, and that it will not be long before he receives his reprieve. I remember how several years ago my poor father found him dangerously ill, and see how he recovered his strength.'

Proust also paid visits, each time with some little presents. He conjured up social activities, which now seemed very remote to the invalid—that party at Madeleine Lemaire's, when he appeared as the faithful Jaffar to Montesquiou's Haroun-al-Raschid; or the day when Montesquiou, who was to appear as Anacreon, clothed in roses, failed to appear at the rose-painter's ball.

Today, again, perhaps Robert would not come. 'The Count is leaving me to die like a dog,' the invalid complained to the Marquise de Clermont-Tonnerre. But no—there was his light, jerky step on the flagstones; Yturri raised himself on his pillows and waved a fan in front of his face as though that would help to restore its colour. Robert entered, seething with indignation: 'Madame Bulteau is going to Sicily with Anna de Noailles and is using Barrès's nephew to conceal the journey!' At that he launched into an imitation of this virile blue-stocking, authoress of *La*

Lueur sur la Cime (*The Gleam on the Summit*), which was nicknamed *La Sueur sur la Lime* (*The Sweat on the File*). He succeeded in making his friend laugh by quickly improvising:

Oh, poor Yturri, Oh, poor Gabriel
Always ill, yet always getting well.

Then, with a pirouette, the Count ran off to get dressed: the Jean de Castellanes were giving a dinner for an arch-duchess. When Mme de Clermont-Tonnerre ventured to remonstrate with him for going, he retorted: 'If I go, he wishes it, and if I stay, he wishes it.'

Soon it was no longer possible to give adequate attention to Yturri at the Pavilion of the Muses, and Dr Pozzi had him transferred to a nearby clinic. His last words were addressed to Montesquiou: 'I thank you for having made known to me those beautiful things which—have so much charmed me.'

After years of a devotion that had seemed to him a little too artless, the poet now found himself far more alone than ever before in his life; and this man who had always maintained such a high degree of composure, let himself go completely in front of Mme de Clermont-Tonnerre. 'I saw him bursting into sobs and so absorbed in his grief that one could only respect it by keeping silent. "When I come home, I only find his little empty cap—his little empty cap"—and at that he twisted his hands together above his head.'

Happily masses of letters and telegrams, to which he decided to reply with the most correct politeness, saved him from despair. It is not only pink that suits frivolous natures. Black goes with them remarkably well. Frivolity lent to Montesquiou's grief forms that were as extravagant as the funeral obsequies with which Bérain surrounded the mortal remains of the Condé or the Duchesse d'Orléans. He kept and published both the letters and the replies to them produced by his bereavement. Proust wrote: 'When I learned that he had fallen ill again, I realised that this invalid had grown even dearer to me than he had been until that moment.' Cécile Sorel condoled: 'Heaven does not create two such men in a short space of time.' Miss Barney's letter was the most appreciative: 'You inspired a feeling the like of which I have never seen; and in appreciating its existence, I convey to you the most subtle homage.' The poet replied: 'You have drawn from me tears, which flow and flow.' In Chapter IX, entitled 'Libations and Dirges', of the work devoted to Gabriel, Montesquiou has preserved all his answers to these letters of condolence. For example, to Count Gabriel de la Rochefoucauld he writes: 'My grief exceeds, with so many tears, the ordinary limits set to last offices of this kind, that I must restrain myself.' There were letters for reticent neighbours, for people unknown, for someone who had been indifferent, and even one to thank an enemy. A kinswoman received this 'short note': 'Thank you for your sympathy. It represents on your part a beginning of fairness towards someone whom malice and blindness led you to misunderstand.' The longest reply was for Proust: 'His unsleeping devotion from beyond the grave undoubtedly looks for and finds a habitation in the hearts and spirits of those whom he has induced to understand me better and love me more.'

In the Gonards cemetery, at the gates of Versailles, Montesquiou had erected a lead statue, dating from the end of the eighteenth century, which represented the Angel of Silence, a dog at his feet. Yturri himself had discovered it at a demolisher's yard. The Angel now stands above a flagstone, beneath which the two friends have joined each other in rest. On the first anniversary of Gabriel's death, Montesquiou opened the Pavilion of the Muses again, for a meeting in honour of his friend. All Paris was there: the grand-dukes and grand-duchesses; Rodin and Gyp; France and Barrès; in short, everyone from actresses to antique-dealers, from clubmen to poets. Never had the Count's grandeur been so exalted as at this sort of Pavane for a Dead Infanta, with its performance of Gluck's *Orphée* and its declamation of poems. Of course, a sentiment so magnificently exalted could only express itself in such grandeur. . . . Forty chosen people left the Pavilion pressing to their hearts a stout volume, *Le Chancelier des Fleurs*, in which Montesquiou had told the story of this unique friendship. This exaggerated show of grief did, in fact, express a genuinely profound sorrow and celebrated a sentiment that one must believe to be unique. The wicked pun, attributed by Lorrain to Lajeunesse, was disseminated by Willy and repeated by those who had never been invited to the Pavilion of the Muses: 'Mort Yturri, te salue tante.'*

Whatever had been the relationship between Montesquiou and

* See p. 115 for this scurrilous pun. Trans.

Yturri—and it is quite possible to believe that it was innocent—
the poet never tried to find a replacement. In future he sought for
disciples, not a friend.

Montesquiou's faithfulness to the dead man's memory must
have astonished the wife of Gabriel de la Rochefoucauld several
years later, when she paid him her first visit. Montesquiou led the
young wife alone into a little room, which was dominated by a
portrait of Yturri, surrounded by flowers: 'My child, I hope that
you will be for your Gabriel what this Gabriel was for me.' One
can imagine first the astonishment and then the questions of this
new cousin who had scarcely crossed the threshold.

Chanticleer

After the death of his companion, Montesquiou stayed for longer
periods in the château of his childhood, d'Artagnan, which he had
made a little more comfortable. He put some cloisters in the park,
busts of poets and some obelisks: all these additions, rather ugly
and in bad taste, betrayed a nervous craving to build, no matter
what. Always the shadow of Ludwig II was upon him. . . . Perhaps
also a spirit of emulation impelled him to set up as a rival to the
Rostands, who were erecting above Cambo an enormous Basque
villa, surrounded by flower-beds, fountains and poetic altars for
which they spared neither marble nor geraniums. L'Illustration
and Lectures pour Tous quarrelled over the privilege of photo-
graphing the master, a panama-hat tilted over the right eye while
with the left one he observed the animals of the neighbouring farm
through a monocle. There was endless talk about this Chanticleer,
who after years of silence was about to deliver the definitive
message of the youngest of the Academicians. There was indeed
too much talk, for when the piece, Chantecler, was presented in
1910, it enjoyed only 'a great success' (i.e. was almost a failure),
with Lucien Guitry having 'an unequalled triumph' (i.e. his
habitual reception) and the house according an 'overwhelming
ovation' (i.e. applauding discreetly).

On the evening of the dress-rehearsal of Chantecler Montesquiou
was in the theatre. He began by pitying the actors who were
sweating under their plumage. He noted a number of echoes of
Hugo: Rostand's 'You make a standard by dyeing a rag', for

example, recalled the line from Hugo's *Choses écrites à Creteil*: 'To wash the radiant dish-cloths.' Decidedly, 'Rostand had cut himself a suit out of Hugo's royal cloak.' The Guinea-hen was amusing; one knew that she was going to send a communiqué about her reception to the Princesse de Mesagne of *Le Figaro,* and her repeated 'Good morning to you' was reminiscent of the Baroness Deslandes. Suddenly the Magpie Usher announced, 'The Peacock!' In onomatopoeia the Blackbird squeaked, 'Le chevalier d'E—on', while the Guinea-hen clucked:

> Master adored, approach the sunflowers yellow:
> Peacock, sunflowers—I think it so Burne-Jones.

When the peacock crowned himself 'the prince of the unexpected adjective', after a series of peremptory judgments, all eyes turned to Montesquiou in expectation. And with what wild laughter the stupefying pastiches of his own verses were now being applauded!

> Petronius-priest and Maecenas-Messiah,
> Words I volatilise, being volatile:
> Words which, o gemmate judge, midst my enamels,
> This Taste betokens of which I am guardian.

Let us leave to Montesquiou the task of commenting on the Guinea-hen's reception: 'The peacock appears in the midst of all this bustle of swindling and unsuccessful cocks and cockerels, the wise black swans, learned ducks and voluble ganders. All this world revolves at the dictates of the aesthetic Peacock, whose character, at one and the same time sumptuous and grimacing, offers us the disagreeable experience of hearing stupid things come from the lips of someone beautiful. The actor who played this part performed well; he had the right sharp and affected tone for the absolute ineptitudes he had to deliver, with an arrogance that was not without elegance and a vanity that was not without beauty.' But the impassiveness of the dandy was being put to a harsh test. How he must have regretted having so much promoted Marcel Proust, Lucien Daudet, Reynaldo Hahn and Léon Delafosse:

> I wished to show you some young gentlemen,
> Slightly superlative and truly precious.

Luckily the tirade of Chanticleer against the Peacock contained absurd lines, so little applicable to Montesquiou that the laughter turned against Rostand himself. But all the same, for one to hear it said that one would finish at the taxidermist's! To suspect the idiotic laughter of those whom one despised and to imagine the exultation of forgotten women, humiliated clubmen and evicted journalists was for the aesthete an ordeal far worse than that of recognising oneself as a des Esseintes, a character monstrous no doubt, but also highly original.

Perhaps Yturri would have slapped Rostand across the face; but the Count, in a voice like a peacock's, contented himself with asking his terrified friends questions about this character in the play. Montesquiou was not, in fact, a peacock but a phoenix: des Esseintes, Monsieur de Phocas, the Peacock are so many incarnations awaiting the last, the most original and the most tragic. Each portrait for which he had served as model brought fresh ridicule, which he first brilliantly took to himself and then belied with some new examples of his insolence. His passion for Beauty lifted him above unhappiness in a red-hot fire of enthusiasm. In that same year, he had no longer any need of Yturri; he found an object worthy of his fervour—an eagle, beside whose poetry the verses of Rostand were only farmyard tittle-tattle: d'Annunzio.

CHAPTER 18

The Hero and the Dancing Girl

While dancing for Herod, Salomé sometimes wonders —
What will my wages be for this new step?

D'Annunzio

No period had ever had so strong a sense of theatre as the beginning of this century. Like footlights, Glory held the poet in
its blaze, now presenting him as a splendid and extravagant being
to the fervour of the public and now as a curiosity to the journalists. Sarah Bernhardt unmistakably left her mark on a whole era;
and in the same way as the tragedienne, the geniuses who were her
contemporaries needed around them a half-real, half-fantastic environment of scandalous elegance and mad love-affairs. Even the
more perspicacious observers were dazzled by the brilliance of
these prima donnas; but in about 1910 Tout-Paris turned aside
from established glories, so that the great men of the time all at
once found themselves obliged to fall back on the provinces or on
foreign countries for their tribute of acclaim. Those who survived
the 1914–1918 war saw the theatre of their exploits boarded up,
while a new generation laughed at their moth-eaten robes and
jewel-less crowns. Loti and Anna de Noailles, Rostand and
Montesquiou, like the wax-figures of a bankrupt Madame
Tussaud's, were swept pell-mell into a corner of the anthologies
by such writers as Gide and Morand who had begun to discover
speed or swimming, America or China. If Glory still keeps its
search-light off these sacred monsters, they at least deserve a little
light to make here a jewel shine and there a gesture stand out.

Paris was the only setting worthy of these stars, who showed
the eagerness of prima donnas in snatching from each other
curtain-calls and bouquets and then, naturally, suffocating each
other under kisses. This sort of comedy amused Montesquiou

greatly; and thus it was that he arranged for Bernhardt to meet La Duse, accompanying the latter to a performance of *La Samaritaine*: 'The Italian woman affected a standing position throughout the evening, I suppose to show her respect to the rival who probably was looking forward to appearing before her guest in a role that became her. By bad luck, however, the odds were against her; the audience was small and not very warm.' Shortly after this La Duse made her first appearance: 'So as to make a great show of the support with which she honoured the newcomer, Bernhardt, crowned with roses like Iphigenia awaiting sacrifice, chose to applaud, herself also standing, at moments when no one else dreamed of doing so.' At this time, when everyone around Montesquiou was exclaiming about the genius of Bernhardt, he replied with his mot: 'She is sublime! Divine! Really there is only one Sarah—and that is La Duse.'

This fervour for the actress whose simplicity underlined all the extravagance of Bernhardt was a link with another genius sent from Italy—an ostentatious, irresistible condottiere or, rather, an operatic tenor playing a condottiere. In a single season d'Annunzio succeeded both in conquering the *salons* of Paris and in throwing its matrimonial beds into a state of confusion. The great poems which he had the courtesy to recite in French eclipsed the romanticism of Pierre Loti and the roundelays of Anna de Noailles. Montesquiou's was the honour of having both cleared the stage and prepared the public for the Italian's arrival. Certainly d'Annunzio was an aesthete totally impregnated with the decadent movement; but a remarkable lyricism forced itself through the absurdities. He also had a primitive strength which turned all conventions upside down. Mario Praz has rightly remarked that under the layers of Florentine and Venetian varnish, d'Annunzio remained a peasant from the Abruzzi, without fear, without scruple and—he might have added—without the least sense of the ridiculous.

The meeting with d'Annunzio dissipated the Count's anxieties (though it was also to bring him some sorrows), giving a new impetus to a fervour that before had had no object and vivifying for him the routine of social events. Montesquiou fell in love immediately: passing beyond the stage of mere friendship to a sentiment which seemed to him the replica of that which Ludwig II had for Wagner. After an encounter which miscarried at Sarah

Bernhardt's house, to be followed by a long absence on the part of the novelist, d'Annunzio came back to Paris in 1910. He at once wished to see Montesquiou again; and Don Juan could include another victim on his list: 'I experienced the heady intoxication of believing myself to be tenderly loved by a man of genius,' Robert was to write. 'I did what I had not, I believe, until then allowed myself to do with regard to any human being of either sex: I entered, *motu proprio*, into a contract of sentimental and even religious attachment for a period of one year, binding myself to one who accepted this homage, submitted affectionately to my respectful fantasy and who, exactly as if he had knighted me, gave me his accolade. I, in turn, resolved to do all that was in my power not merely to win such a friendship for myself, but to retain it and never forfeit it. . . .'

His very successes in love, even more than the marvellous voice of this little, bald seducer with a nose like Punch, swept along in his train a whole procession of enamoured women, both opulent and tormented. D'Annunzio had successfully revived the Byronic legend: as he passed by full-breasted women, standing in his way as Boldini would paint them, strings of pearls anchoring them to life—princesses and actresses, great Russian ladies and even middle-class Bordeaux housewives—they would offer themselves up to him. These admirers Montesquiou would jostle aside to assume the first place; and d'Annunzio accepted this enthusiasm with that coquetry so common among the Italians, for whom all homage is good. Besides, the Italian needed an impresario: scandals and debts had made his position in Italy difficult and Paris was the only theatre worthy of him. The luxury surrounding Montesquiou enchanted him quite as much as the Frenchman's conversation. At last he was living in the kind of house that he had described so often: the bearskins and Chinese vases, the marble stairs and the tapestried galleries—all the things that had been accumulated by the model for Huysmans' hero might equally well have been arranged there by the decorator of *Il Piacere*. Both men were very sensitive to the magic that ancient dwellings possess; the writer who had evoked the sorcery of the palace of Mantua in *Forse che si, forse che non,* let himself be guided by the poet of Versailles.

Of course d'Annunzio used Montesquiou, but he also admired him. As for Montesquiou himself, he seemed to have lost his head.

'His face,' he was to write, 'which not even a blind man would consider to be handsome, sometimes assumed appearances of beauty all the more striking because that beauty was in fact imperfect and made up of contrasts. The most moving of these expressive instants were those when his mask dropped its practical combativeness and sham cheerfulness. Then the sadness of the gaze, hesitating at the corner of his eyelids, seemed to dredge up from the depths of his soul something faded which denied all revival; the nostrils, like those on the face embossed on a battle-dented shield, would dilate out of shape and the corners of the mouth would turn down so despairingly that they expressed the unspeakable horror of witnessing a punishment for which no pity could be felt.' Is not this the portrait of a sadist by his masochistic adorer?

Ardent women

Montesquiou had to compete for this genius with a host of possessive and luxurious rivals: Cécile Sorel, magnificently established in the Quai Voltaire; Mme de Goloubeff (Donatella Cross) who offered him Persian miniatures and greyhounds; and the Duchess Cesarini Sforza, who owed a great many millions to the favours of the Baronne de Zuylen. Robert therefore decided to offer d'Annunzio the friendship on which he set the greatest value, precisely because it was the most fragile: that of Maurice Barrès. Accordingly, on 23 June 1910 at the Pré-Catalan restaurant, Montesquiou organised one of those dinners that blazed with all the glories of Parisian society. Barrès was very reluctant: 'As always equally divided—affable and disdainful: at first sight I did not like this Italian. . . .' The dinner was as brilliant as one could wish; the exquisite menu was illuminated with a pomegranate, the poet's emblem—the pomegranate found in a passage of *Il Fuoco,* that was now to be declaimed by Mme Bartet.* The poets were full of mutual congratulations. 'Your vision multiplies the beauty and the grandeur of every spectacle. I have admired you', bawled Montesquiou, 'ever since I read and quoted fifteen years ago this phrase, which is sublime for an artist: "There is nothing

* Jeanne-Julia Bartet (1854–1941), actress, probably the best interpreter of Racine of her time. Trans.

more intoxicating than hate." And I owe my vocation to you, after reading twenty years ago your meditation on Leonardo.'

Barrès looked on, turning up his nose when d'Annunzio explained to his neighbour how one made love to a lioness; but by the time the coffee was served, he seemed to be charmed—but only half so, or a quarter so. That evening he wrote in his diary: 'He is a portrait by Clouet, a little Italian with a hard expression. . . . He said that eighteenth-century Venetian art is interesting because it is impure. I caught a glimpse of the faded tradition of Jean Lorrain and Wilde, but this is something else as well. What? A business man who is looking for sleeping partners to lend him money. In my opinion—I am really only guessing—he is like the hard beak of a bird pecking at seeds: now he gathers words from books or conversation, now images from life, now the benefits of either women or money. Occasionally he becomes attached to the truth and so loses his artificiality. Then he interests me.'

Thus a friendship sprang up between the two romantics: a friendship that, in part at least, was created for the gallery or for posterity, and to that extent resembled Barrès's passion for Anna de Noailles. Montesquiou did not suffer because of it, since he recognised its basic artificiality. Willingly he acted as an intermediary. Barrès wrote to Montesquiou: 'May the year 1911 add to his glory, may he have many successes—their flowering is limitless. But when it comes to women, let him restrict himself, for after all their number is not infinite even in Paris. Already protective measures have been initiated against him in the interests of the sentimental French consumer.' It was, in fact, the women followers who exasperated Montesquiou.

Each time d'Annunzio took a new mistress, jealousy pierced Montesquiou's heart and at parties he would then wander about with the sorrowful grace of Mme de Beauséant on the evening of the departure of Ajuda-Pinto.* Often the friends would plan some ambitious project together. D'Annunzio wanted to go to India. 'I too have always wanted to go there,' declared Montesquiou. 'As a start, I will take a box at the Indian ballet.' Montesquiou was thrilled by the idea of an evening party at the theatre, to be followed by a voyage in the company of his hero. But there was d'Annunzio stepping into the foyer with a woman on his arm,

* Cf. Balzac, *Père Goriot*.

her eyes black-ringed from a recent experience of happiness; and such was her pride at her achievement that Montesquiou's spiteful remark failed to bring home to her that her presence was not desired. In the event, d'Annunzio went no further than to d'Artagnan for a visit, where Robert put up a plaque to commemorate the event.

So as not to lose the Italian, Montesquiou aimed to make his own selection of beautiful and intelligent women who would eventually conduct d'Annunzio to his salon by way of their bedrooms. His first choice was admirable: glitter, talent, name, fortune, youth—Princess Bibesco had all these. Montesquiou had first met her at the Japanese embassy, and had been enraptured by her beauty, which, in the manner of the old king of Bavaria, he added to his gallery. 'I hope that you are not married to one of the two terrible Bibescos,' said Montesquiou, who was suspicious of Rumania. 'No, to a third, and a charming one, whom you will not know!' The Princess went to Persia and brought back a book called *Les Huit Paradis,* to which Montesquiou devoted a whole article in *Le Figaro.* In it was that sentence which so much enchanted Proust: 'You were wearing, on an old-rose-coloured satin dress, emeralds like those of which Shakespeare described the charm'.

A little later Montesquiou asked the Bibescos to bring d'Annunzio to tea, and the three of them went off in the long white Mercedes towards Le Vésinet, where the poet was then living. Without great success d'Annunzio undertook the conquest of the husband, to whom he praised the beauty of *velivoles*—the name he had invented for aeroplanes. It was a magnificent tea, at which no one else was present. Montesquiou got out his talismans, put Castiglione's ring on the Princess's finger, entrusted d'Annunzio with Beau Brummell's cane. His conversation turned to the subject of nuptial songs, after which a string quartet was intended to lure the couple into the shrubbery, but the young woman looked at the Italian coldly. In the corridor of the Hotel Continental where they both lived, she had already discouraged rapid and indelicate advances. Klingsor had to choose another flower from his garden to offer to his friend.

Ballets Russes

Here Montesquiou's sentiments became complicated, since he was really himself in love with the person he now proposed to his hero; he had known her for two years and impatiently awaited her brief visits to Paris. This love at first sight dated from the first season of the Ballets Russes.

Robert de Montesquiou and Serge de Diaghilev had met in 1898, when the latter asked permission to show the portrait by Whistler at an exhibition in St. Petersburg. These two aesthetes of aristocratic birth had much in common: the same passion for perfection, the same taste for parties and the same toughness when something interfered with their craving to dazzle. Alexandre Benois had warned Montesquiou: 'Diaghilev the Impossibilist is like a Napoleon mobilising the world', and Montesquiou in turn alerted Countess Greffulhe, who set about organising parties and galas. The Russians cooed their gratitude: 'That incomparable lady, your cousin . . .' The aesthete in Montesquiou was both thrilled by the drawings of Bakst, who became a friend and to whom he gave some superb Chinese vases, and charmed by Sommof's delightful pastiches in porcelain. But his fastidiousness was perhaps a little repelled by the loud sounds of the new music and the violence of the dancing.

Montesquiou particularly liked the fantastic Versailles created by Benois for 'Le Pavillon d'Armide'. But too many people shared his admiration for this art, so that he had to be satisfied with applauding with the crowd and there was no need for him to fight to assure the triumph of the Ballets. He sulked a little in consequence. It was a woman who reconciled him to the new art-form; Ida Rubinstein. He saw her for the first time in *Scheherazade* as the sultana stretched out under the many-coloured tent, 'the tragedienne of silence'. With no more than a gesture, an expression, she seemed to organise all the incredible whirlwind of movement around her couch. Of course he found that Nijinsky* could effortlessly achieve 'the high C of elevation'; but confronted by this oriental Péri as dreamed by Moreau or Beardsley, comparisons jostled in his mind, and for the first time he had to admit: 'What I saw struck me as so surprising that I tried to

* Montesquiou went to see him at Rodin's studio, where the faun often spent the afternoon basking in the sculptor's adoration.

speak but could not.' A little later Diaghilev invited Montesquiou to attend *Une Nuit de Cléopâtre,* a ballet based on an idea of Théophile Gautier's. Dressed by Bakst, Rubinstein appeared, like the Queen of Sheba in Flaubert's *Tentation,* on very high clogs, with her hair powdered blue. 'But who is she?' Montesquiou enquired of a neighbour. 'An immensely rich Russian Jewess, who asked for nothing but to come to Paris for the pleasure of showing herself completely naked here.' In fact, Ida Rubinstein was the niece of Marie Kann and Loulia Cahen d'Anvers. Enveloped in her seven veils, she stamped rather than danced: 'Like Indian princesses, like Nubian women from the Cataracts, like Bacchantes from Lydia.' This Balkis, this Salomé hurled at the society of Tout-Paris, decapitated 'good taste' as though it were the head of John the Baptist, and the blood from it spattered Poiret's dresses and lacquered Dunand's furniture. Naked under clusters of real jewels given to her by millionaire lovers, Rubinstein went further than Bernhardt; indeed, went too far, so that her success was more a kind of induced stupor.

Montesquiou was infatuated with her. Was she not the flat and cruel hermaphrodite of whom he had dreamed when he was twenty? Since the Ballets Russes did not need his championship, it was for her that he would fight. Thus it came about that this fifty-year-old man was suddenly impelled into an international demi-monde, the women of which, with their multi-coloured aigrettes, seemed to have escaped from a harem kept by pashas who speculated on the Stock Exchange. Impossible to guess from where they had come. It was a kind of spontaneous generation, which in Tout-Paris made the upper-crust women, stiff under their finery, seem all at once old-fashioned. Very soon the former were to begin to imitate the latter, sweeping Montesquiou along with them in a whirlwind of quarrels and reconciliations, disorder and gallantry. Rubinstein had an elderly lover, Mavrocordato, whom Montesquiou christened 'Cold jellied crow'. She replaced him with an Englishman who was a little younger and much richer: Guinness, the brewer, later Lord Moyne. Palaces resounded with these dramas; cars were piled high with ladies' maids and jewels. Here, indeed, were all the ingredients of such novels of the twenties as *The Man with the Hispano, The Madonna of the Sleeping Cars* or *The Green Hat.*

Montesquiou had Ida Rubinstein painted by La Gandara: she

appears as the Queen of Sheba dressed, in the Empire style, by Worth, in a blue veil and with a crown of green feathers on her head; the profile is hard, the stance angular. Mirrors covered the walls of the mansion in the Place des États Unis, and heavy golden tassels kept back the hangings like curtains in a theatre. Rubinstein lived on nothing but champagne and biscuits; she ordered dresses made of rare silks which she wore only once. She had 'a knack of being super-eminent', so that even before the great fountains of Versailles she wore aigrettes that rivalled the soaring jets of water. The Peacock liked to arrive at Maxim's, to attend a first night or to visit a private view, supporting on an arm the most conspicuous woman in Paris. Rubinstein invented the modern conception of elegance; her silhouette suggested all the subsequent exaggerations of fashion-design. Among the beauties of 1900, who imitated orchids, she soared up like an arum lily. She had the wisdom not to enter into rivalry with the stars like Toumanova and Pavlova; Greece she left to Isadora Duncan; it was of the Orient that she wished to have the monopoly. After a long tour, Rubinstein came back to Paris to create a Salomé with de Max as Herod, for five evenings each of which cost half a million. Bakst's costumes seem faded and flattened by the photograph. It had been a costly carnival. In spite of Montesquiou's publicity, both by word of mouth and by numerous articles, the public did not appear. Guinness had to pay.

Thereupon d'Annunzio returned to Paris; febrile, he had been wasting his time on facile adventures. A woman admirer said to him, 'You are a god!'; to which he replied, 'There is no need for the "a".' Montesquiou placed his god in the presence of his Queen of Sheba. He sent d'Annunzio to the theatre, and d'Annunzio wrote the same evening: 'I have just seen Cleopatra. I cannot govern my confusion. What am I to do?' He also was stupefied; but he advanced more quickly and further than Montesquiou in his conquest. As in myth, these immortals must know a super-human joy; from their flashing pairings, thought Montesquiou, a masterpiece would be born. The extraordinary thing is that, in fact, a masterpiece did come out of this union: *The Martyrdom of St Sebastian*. Montesquiou, the instrument of the meeting, watched to see that its fruit might be worthy of the heroes and of himself.

The Martyrdom of St Sebastian

All the themes of decadent literature were reunited in this work:
its hero, a hermaphrodite and martyr, played by Rubinstein; its
décor, antiquity in a state of decomposition in Byzantium; its
equivocal Christianity, reminiscent of *La Tentation de Saint
Antoine*. As for the despot in love with St Sebastian, his is a figure
worthy of Jean Lorrain. But the superb richness of the language
turned what would have otherwise been no more than an echo of
the fin-de-siècle into a kind of masterpiece, which certainly had its
influence on Claudel. Montesquiou persuaded d'Annunzio to
write in French (as Wilde had composed *Salomé*), lending him
finery from his vast wardrobe of words. When the work was
finished, he carefully pruned away all Italianisms and too facile
archaisms. In executing this task he always remained subservient
to a lyric strength far superior to his own. Naturally Bakst was to
execute the décor. Montesquiou accompanied him to the Louvre
to inspect Sassanid fabrics, Byzantine enamels and bas-reliefs
from the Eastern Roman Empire unearthed in Egypt or Syria. He
examined art-books for the various forms in which printers have
depicted St Sebastian, from gaunt Memlings to soft Guido
Renis.

Rubinstein—straight, thin, half-naked under her armour, and
pathetically vulnerable among all the purple and gold—was
the sort of Sebastian that might have been drawn by Beardsley.
The drama would take place in front of colonnades heavy with
false gods and a black and red sky pierced by cypresses. But stage
music was necessary and Montesquiou decided on Debussy. He
had met the composer at the Princesse de Polignac's and at the
Saussines'. He had even dedicated some lines to him:

> Who seemed within a cage of gold to bear
> A fabled bird to answer to the wave
> Which danced a step, the fruit which sang an air.

Montesquiou put the musician in touch with d'Annunzio, who
nicknamed him 'Claude of France' and with Ida Rubinstein,
an ideal actress, since she demanded no aria, no brilliant step.
The incidental music and the chorus would be sumptuous as in
certain Russian operas. In short, the score would be far more
modern than the text.

To make doubly sure that fortune would be on their side, Montesquiou persuaded d'Annunzio to dedicate *The Martyrdom* to Barrès, a flattering but embarrassing tribute. In fact, the Vatican had just put the Italian's work on the index. What would the conformist Right, the League of Patriots, have to say when they read the great man's name inscribed on an equivocal work that was played by a scandalous actress to revolutionary music? Barrès pondered the most suitable reply: '. . . You have given me a superb present. You whom I don't really know, whom so many things separate from me. . . . A poem heavy with gilt, and you have given it to me in a public letter to which I do not think that my going to embrace you was an answer. . . . I would have been like you if I were not from a country which has duties.'

This reserve shown by Barrès seemed to Montesquiou to be frightful treason. To console his friend and to ensure a triumph for *The Martyrdom* he organised a tribute to d'Annunzio in a hall belonging to Manzi, director of the review *Le Théâtre*. He defied an interdict emanating from the archepiscopal palace and dazzled all Paris with one of his best lectures. D'Annunzio, who was genuinely moved, gave him an extremely rare copy of Petrarch in an Aldine binding. He had returned from Le Moulleau to superintend the rehearsals. Montesquiou did not miss one of these, giving advice about the lighting in the first act, which was intended to convey the impression of a stained-glass window on which was presented the Mystery:

> Of this Florentine in exile
> Who stutters in the Langue d'Oil.*

He jumped on the stage to show the choreographer, Fokine, the gesture of St Sebastian as he throws towards the sky arrows which miraculously do not fall to earth again. He was enraptured when Ida Rubinstein walked on the embers:

> I dance on the intense heat of the lilies,
> I trample on the whiteness of the lilies,
> I crush the softness of the lilies.

Each day, with the same emotion, he saw 'the saint stretched out, ecstatic, on the lyre of which he has stifled the voice, while he himself feels stifled under jewels and roses'. 'Bakst never did

---

* The old French language spoken north of the Loire, while the Langue d'Oc was spoken south of the Loire. Trans.

anything more beautiful,' he exclaimed at the dress-rehearsal, confronted with the scenery for the fourth act, which was all red. In the interval he commented, for those who could not understand, on 'the chaste youth tied to the trunk of a laurel, as it were clothed in the ropes which encompass him, so that only an emaciated shoulder emerges. These attitudes [of Ida Rubinstein] have at last conveyed to us what our fathers told us about Rachel.' The last act sent him into transports: 'Within the violet twilight, the blue archers—obedient and desperate, the artisans of the celestial will—sob on their slackened bows. . . .'

Melancholy after the party

The Martyrdom was a great success on its first night, but not at subsequent performances. Like Ludwig II, Montesquiou was alone in his stage-box. His contempt abolished a reticent audience; each performance took place for him alone. 'I have seen many things, many beautiful things, but I have seen nothing comparable to this, offered to our eyes by this creative spirit. I call her the Archangel of Gold, Michael unmasked, with, under the little helmet, that ivory face with gem-like eyes capable of looking into our hearts, and locks of hair which seem to be the expression of the poet's phrase "clusters of pain".'

It did not matter, after such happiness, to be alone. 'I do not like victors. They are separated from us by all the people who neglect them at those times when we stay by them to console them for being deserted.' Montesquiou had served d'Annunzio for a year in accordance with his vow. 'But nothing altered the fact that, after the expiry of my sentimental engagement, no scruple of the heart, of the mind or even of gratitude gave me the desire to renew it; for all the sentiments which this man inspires have no more effect on him than what he himself has termed the shadow of wings on pure hands. He has no reason to be embarrassed; these are for him the means of combustion for an existence in progress; he sees higher, he is going further.'

Thus a coolness sprang up. But on the following New Year's day Montesquiou went to place flowers on the grave of the other Gabriel. On his way back he called in at an antique-dealer's where he found a medallion enclosing a relic of St Sebastian.

At home a long telegram awaited him from d'Annunzio: 'To forget, in the presence of your nobleness, low things which have made me suffer.'

Ludwig II had received Wagner's kiss, Mme de Beauséant forgot her grief. Montesquiou relented; but thenceforward the paths of the two friends were to cross but rarely. Without consulting Montesquiou, Ida Rubinstein asked d'Annunzio for another theme, and on this occasion it was the absurd story of *La Pisannelle* or *La Mort Parfumée*. Ida Rubinstein, nun and court-esan, recited a text reminiscent of Maeterlinck with a Russian accent to music by an obscure imitator of Monteverdi. In spite of Bakst's costumes, taken from Carpaccio, and some glaring publicity, *La Pisannelle* was a total failure. The Italian returned to his country. As a farewell bouquet, however, he wrote a flam-boyant preface for *La Divine Comtesse*: 'A preface' said Montes-quiou, 'so full of beautiful things that I thought he must be speaking of himself.' This work, as thick and luxurious as it was useless, was devoted to the Comtesse de Castiglione and dwelled with the extreme care of a fetichist on details of the dresses and even of the chemises worn by the mistress of Napoleon III. Cer-tainly the author was still thinking about Ida Rubinstein when he wrote: 'She had a strange way of taking silence for her beauty, much as a modeller takes water to knead his clay.' Among the interminable descriptions and the macabre inventories of the Castiglione possessions (all those stuffed and moth-eaten pugs) Montesquiou found these beautiful sentences which would apply to the last ten years of his own life: 'One discards the vulgar, and the vulgar take it for granted that one has been discarded. The proudest natures understand immortal sorrows.' After La Castiglione—he had seen her only on her deathbed—the poet evoked all the beauties he had known: Mme Greffulhe remained his goddess, but he remembered the Comtesse de Beaumont, née Castries, the Duchesse de Chaulnes, née Galitzine, and of course the Marquise de Casa-Fuerte. To these he had added some new beauties, among whom were Marquise Casati, who rivalled Ida Rubinstein in extravagance ('Medusa or tigress, she smiles as though she would bite'), Princess Bibesco and Natalie Barney, a whole dazzling new generation: Scheherazades dressed by Poiret, for whom the ageing aesthete wished to give parties even more beautiful than those held at the Pavilion of the Muses.

CHAPTER 19

The Palace of Quarrels

The building now is finished: beautiful and solemn,
 Reared on the days and nights, it challenges the wave,
Then, mute and suddenly, dissolves, column by column,
 Since its great corner-stone was destined for the grave.

The art of making enemies

THE THEATRE in which Montesquiou presented his last performances was a pink-marble palace discovered by his secretary
Pinard, when the Count was obliged to leave the Pavilion of the
Muses. 'Imagine a lover distraught with grief at having to
abandon a blonde he adores, to whom suddenly there appears a
red-head as a compensation. Such was my architectural, horti-
cultural, sentimental adventure of that period.' This house, still
standing today in the midst of the villas of the Richmond-like
suburb of Le Vésinet, is a Trianon with pink pilasters, to be
approached up a vast flight of steps, before which lies a triangular
flower-bed. The other side of the house is shaded by a little park.
Resembling a wing of the Castellane Palace on the Avenue du
Bois, it was built for a Parsee millionaire, Mr Tata (Montesquiou
promoted him to Maharajah, since he could not bring himself to
pronounce his name*). At the time when his secretary found it,
the Count was in the Engadine. A presentiment came to him to
rush to view the house as soon as his factotum submitted his
report. Having viewed it, he declared to Pinard: 'If this house—
which is not for sale and which, in any case, would seem to be
far beyond my modest means to purchase—if this improbable,
impossible and yet miraculously real house is not mine tomorrow,
I shall die!'

* The equivalent in English would be 'Mr Pansy'. Trans.

Two days later, the house had changed hands and the Count was bustling about adorning his marble deity. He installed the fountain-basin from Versailles under a little octagonal temple, erected vases, laid out paths. Yturri was no longer with him; and these exertions made him both tired and melancholy. Once the first enthusiasm had spent itself, there he was alone in his palace. Le Vésinet was a little too far to attract daily visitors and, in consequence, he was forced to go to Paris for parties which amused him less and less. These social events, endured whatever the cost, engendered a bitterness; at them he himself reaped a wearisome harvest of often-repeated compliments, while he watched ridiculous women and pretentious writers welcomed into the front rank. 'An elegant gathering', he commented, 'has given place to a brilliant barrack-room.' His malice was exacerbated by the spectacle of the buffoonery all around him: the firework of St Sebastian having now burnt itself out and the house now having been set in order, the whirlwind of enthusiasm in which he had been carried away was quickly followed by quarrels. Now that the bourgeoisie lived in the Louis XVI white-and-grey of the eighteenth century, the world of Helleu had over-reached itself. Bakst and Poiret had splashed both drawing-rooms and the women who inhabited them with tomato and gold; the purists reacted, and suddenly wanted nothing but black and white. It was in these sober tones that a young American girl painted portraits of Montesquiou's women friends; adopting the Whistlerian manner, she anticipated the sobriety of the 'thirties. 'Black and white on the canvases, white walls, floor covered with black tiles, white peonies in black stone-ware vases, white pieces of porcelain on black lacquer tables. . . .' Miss Romaine Brooks was of the Spartan school, while her friend Renée Vivien* was dying in the fin-de-siècle rainbow. Miss Brooks, slender as a figure in a Beardsley drawing, fascinated Rubinstein and d'Annunzio. They commissioned her to paint their portraits, and for this purpose she followed the poet to Arcachon, only to run away with the dancer, whom she was painting to look not unlike Holbein's Christ.

What dramas, what a hullabaloo! Montesquiou missed not a single detail. Miss Brooks was madly in fashion and Princess Edmond de Polignac came to sit for her. Montesquiou no longer

---

* An Englishwoman, whose real name was Pauline Torn, she had a tumultuous friendship with Colette.

cared for this imposing woman, who ruled both the musical
world and a court of young and elegant girls. She had not been
sufficiently grateful to him for having presented her with a
husband who was at once so well-born, so musical and so discreet.
In consequence he wrote in *Le Figaro* that in the Brooks portrait
the princess looked like 'a Nero, a thousand times more cruel than
the original, who dreams of seeing his victim pricked to death by
sewing-machines'. (It was known that the Princess's fortune came
from Singer sewing-machines; and already, after one of her
concerts, Montesquiou had exclaimed, 'Now we are going to
have supper prepared by little sewing-machines!') Mme de
Polignac had appointed herself the protectress of his old enemy
Cloton (Mme Legrand, née Fournès) and Miss Brooks now
painted the latter returning from the races. Montesquiou succeeded in having presented to him the portrait of 'the hard-up
Gioconda', and this aggravated his quarrel with Mme de Polignac.
Miss Barney attempted to put things right, but she was too
intimate with Mme Delarue-Mardrus, now judged to be 'wild,
perverse, disconsolate, obsolete'. Rémy de Gourmont's intelligent
Amazon received this curious explanation from Montesquiou: 'I
do not continue to believe in a friendship merely because I once
believed in it. If I have stopped seeing you it is because I have
made it my custom and even my LAW that, when I see two people
whom I have introduced to each other forming a connection
with each other, I sacrifice one of them in order not to lose them
both.' Miss Brooks's other models were two of the famous women
decorators who invented Café Society just as Mme Straus and
Madeleine Lemaire had once invented the society of Tout-Paris:
Elsie de Wolfe (later Lady Mendl) and Baroness d'Erlanger.
There was also Mme Errazuriz, who discovered Picasso.

An intelligent young woman, who could have equalled the
Duchesse de Clermont-Tonnerre in her friendship to Robert, was
the Princess Lucien Murat (née Marie de Rohan-Chabot); but
he ridiculed the good duchess, her mother, too much. On the day
of the wedding which united the Faubourg Saint-Germain and the
Napoleonic dynasty, the Count gave Marie Murat a present
calculated to annoy his old enemy Princess Mathilde: 'a disgusting
object, a fan painted by her Highness, the design of which baffled
one as to whether it represented calves' kidneys or orchids. I had
it framed with a magnificence which only threw its poverty into

sharper relief. When the painter found herself face to face with this old sin against art—this mixture of botany and butcher's meat—such was her rage that she nearly gave up her old Corsican soul to the devil who was waiting for it.' There was also a meeting to hear Montesquiou declaim the Duchesse de Rohan's poems:

> If he is God, why did he make the Negroes?
> Can an entire race be blackened thus?

Then parodying the proud motto of the Rohans, he found the following for the Duchesse: 'Hugo I cannot, Musset I deign not, Mirliton I am.'* To crown so many acts of perfidy Montesquiou offered to this woman who had been such a devoted friend to him a place among *Les Quarante Bergères,* in a poem which concludes:

> Her lyre scents itself and from afar resounds,
> And her desire to write is held in narrow bounds.

Montesquiou was for once caught in his own trap when, at a party at Madame Lemaire's, he attempted to tease the daughter-in-law of Mme Arman de Caillavet, a young girl naïve enough to imagine that the poet was in love with her. He began to recite a portrait of the mistress of the house; then he proceeded to attack his old friend:

> Her speech is like a pea's, Madame de Collauxfesses;
> With burs and tares her hair is always in a mess.
> She is the roundest thing of which I have heard tell;
> Her silliness is also round—she means quite well.
> So like a package made of little soft balloons. . . .

Indignation prompted the young girl to take an amusing revenge: 'Now I know who wrote the abominable portrait of you which has lately been going the rounds. The perfection of the lines, the sharpness of the wit—everything proclaims that you could only have written it yourself!' 'What! A poem about me is going the rounds!' the Count screamed in fury. 'I heard it under the strict seal of secrecy,' the young woman went on. 'But you will easily find some indiscreet woman to recall the little masterpiece for you.' At that, beside himself, the Count raced off in search of the imaginary poem.

---

* The actual motto runs: 'Roi ne puis, prince ne daigne, Rohan suis.'

The world of Sem

These portraits in verse which Montesquiou was in the habit of reciting to set the seal on his quarrels constituted in his mind either a heroic-comic satire in the manner of Pope or 'a senate of women such as Heliogabalus imagined'. Trembling and with their ranks decimated, the chorus of ladies would none the less beg the Count to recite these poems which, according to himself, had 'the suppleness of malice and not the shrivelling of hatred'. In them much ingratitude and a number of facile jokes and vulgarities are to be found; but it must be said in favour of the author that these ladies of 1900 were monuments of absurdity. A certain physical charm, a certain taste, a certain verbal facility— things of which no residue now remained—had acted as the cement holding together a mass of pretensions. Not one of these hostesses could hold a candle to a Geoffrin or a Deffand; their letters are worthless; not one of their sayings remains. It can be easily understood how the stars of this so-called Belle Époque exacerbated the spirit of a sensitive man to the extent of making him indelicate. The disciples of Sappho, among whom he counted so many friends, were not spared; but today it is difficult to know whether he is lampooning that Dutch baroness nicknamed 'the Brioche', protectress of Renée Vivien, or the Marquise de Belboeuf, who was the lover of a great woman novelist.

Old Parisians can still identify some of the shepherdesses, however. Thus Limone is an actress, very much alive today, who has become a writer of memoirs:

Tall as a boot, a gallows or a length of twine.

Aglaure is the Countess Adéhaume de Chevigné:*

An intimate of grand-dukes, almost chamber-maid.

This collection, published posthumously, is as difficult to find today as the unexpurgated memoirs of Viel-Castel.

Most of these women appear again in Sem's albums, and it must be admitted that they have very ugly faces: hard or lascivious, distorted by snobbery or crumbling under jewels. The prettiest, like Mme Letellier, look like idiots—'They will be sent

---

* Born Laure de Sade, she is said to have been one of the models for the Duchesse de Guermantes.

to the devil by ridicule,' exclaimed Montesquiou, enchanted. 'Worldliness is the broth which nourishes the culture of caricature', he wrote in an article devoted to Sem, in which he congratulated the artist on expressing 'over-excitement in immobility, loquacity in silence'. Montesquiou reviewed the victims of the 'Hokusai of Périgord', among whom was Maurice de Rothschild, 'for whom all *poules* have teeth'. The chronicler did not spare himself: 'Count Robert de Montesquiou in the process of ratiocinating, bent in a semi-circle under his chestnut-coloured Tyrolean hat, in the company of his Russian greyhounds in turquoise collars'. At this exhibition of Sem's panorama, 'Tout-Paris in the Bois', Montesquiou improvised couplets that did not increase the number of his friends.

> To speak of women always will
> Seem impolite to Radziwill

made an enemy of a powerful clan.

> Nothing can explain the vogue
> Of this Monsieur Paleologue*

must have caused pain to Mme Bertet, of whom the diplomat was the most faithful admirer.

One can imagine Proust's laughter on hearing:

> If there is no light, you must take care
> Not to leave your son near Humières.†

The world of Sem was no longer the bold, impeccable one of Caran d'Ache; it had grown relaxed in the back of motor-cars or dancing the tango. New faces had begun to appear: like the suave Pringué and that indefatigable organiser of cotillons, André de Fouquières.‡

In the years after 1910 such a sublime contempt was not justified by any really remarkable works. Montesquiou's genius seemed concentrated on malice, while his critical writings became as anodyne and mildly scented as rose-water (significantly he was

* French Ambassador to Russia.

† Robert d'Humières, paederast and a great friend of Proust and translator of Kipling.

‡ Both have written some amusing recollections of the period, in a style reminiscent of Daisy of Pless.

now giving lectures at the celebrated garden of Hay-les-Roses). The poet had succumbed to fashion. These writings are only 'iridescent shot-silks and glistening Chinese damasks'. On the subject of the Bakst exhibition he noted 'Mme Delarue-Mardrus with a coral bracelet round her ankle, Mme Godebska with her pear-shaped emeralds. . . .' But for the décor of *Scheherazade* he found some attractive phrases, among them: 'A combat between cactus and amaranth, a carnage of geraniums'. Among the crowds at fancy-dress balls and at afternoon dancing parties, the poet pursued his friendship with Princess Bibesco. He was proud to see that this young woman preferred his company to that of the most brilliant young men; but he had an ulterior motive in making the most of the Princess. After a party at the Countess Greffulhe's, he wrote to his hostess and friend: 'I saw the raven's eye of Mme de Noailles gleam when I asked the whereabouts of Princess Bibesco.'

Tout-Paris repeated Montesquiou's compliment before the portrait of the Princess by Boldini: 'Her beauty changes when she changes her dress.' But to a famous bore, Fournier-Sarlovèze, who boasted that he was 'painter in ordinary' to the Princess, Montesquiou retorted, 'Yes, very ordinary.' At Princess Bibesco's, Montesquiou became more friendly with the affable Father Mugnier. 'I would not confess to you before I died; my sins would not astonish you enough.' 'Monsieur, you astonish me!'

Yes, the world had changed. Who was this Missia Godebska Edwards, who knew all the painters, and this Mme Mulhfeld, to whose house everyone was beginning to rush? The former married in turn a man called Nathanson, a newspaper proprietor, Edwards, and finally the Spanish painter, Sert; the favourite model of Vuillard, she was a great friend of both Diaghilev and Picasso. The latter was a delightful invalid, whom one was always sure of finding at home. The sister-in-law of the caricaturist Cappiello and of the novelist Paul Adam, she used her literary relations as bait to attract the upper crust to her house. Her conversion hastened the evolution of her salon and won for the arriviste this witticism of Forain: 'She has only known the Holy Virgin for three months and she already calls her Mary.'

Baroness Deslandes was odder. Poor Elsie—she had grown fat and she no longer saw the dust that dimmed her crystal ornaments. To be even more conspicuous, she agreed to appear in a cage with some lions during a Castellan fête, her short sight saving her from panicking. She wanted to add d'Annunzio to a list of lovers which had included Barrès and, so she maintained, Oscar Wilde. 'Yes, I swear, I shall take you,' proclaimed the Italian as though he were going to bite her, 'in your coffin.' Decidedly men were not what they were, and the Baroness became a lesbian.

Happily, like a meteor leaving behind it a trail of aigrettes and strings of pearls, the Marchioness Casati arrived from Italy, with this beautiful commendation from d'Annunzio: 'A unicorn, the only woman that astonishes me.' She was also the only woman who frightened the Princesse de Polignac, the only one who spent more than Rubinstein on lamé and sable. Excess and waste were the daily habits of this Medusa, who combined the macabre side of Princess Belgiojoso with the beauty of La Castiglione. Her costumes were modelled on Bakst and Aubrey Beardsley; she started the fashion for jerseys in gold, and panther-skin trousers; she wore furs at the Lido, tweeds with Lalique pendants on top of them at the opera; she pinned emeralds into her red wig and daubed her dead white face with black. It was she who invented the style of the most extravagant stars of the silent screen—women like Musidora, Theda Bara and Napierkowska. She is to be found in the perverse and jagged drawings of Alastair, and there is a brilliant Cecil Beaton photograph of her in old age. La Casati was the last incarnation of Moreau's Salomé; but she only passed momentarily through the life of Montesquiou.

The Count did not always become accustomed to the stupidity of the world

Women were at first flattered to be treated like works of art, but the moment always came when they expected Montesquiou to assume a more active role in their lives. Disappointed in this expectation, they would quarrel with him and go on their way. Only the Countess Greffulhe remained always faithful. She was entering that age when women are called 'ever-beautiful'; but she was more so than anyone else of her generation if one is to believe Laszlo's flamboyant portrait. (In contrast this Hungarian portrait-painter shows us a very disillusioned Montesquiou.) Only this one friendship withstood the vagaries of Montesquiou's character. 'You seem', the Countess wrote to him, 'in the mood to try having a quarrel with me. I advise you against such a course, for you will not succeed, and that would make you waste time which you could, to the same end, employ more profitably with others.' At the same time Montesquiou wrote this very wise maxim: 'We should forgive those who speak ill of us, but never those who report it to us.'

Mme Greffulhe and her sisters would each year rent a châlet at St Moritz with their cousin Robert. There they were joined by the Italian novelist Matilda Serao: a fat woman with a slight moustache, who was extremely talkative. The authoress of *Pays de Cocagne* rivalled Montesquiou in vivacity, so that despite her ugliness she was adored by her lover, a rich and aged Greek, and by her husband, the owner of the biggest newspaper in Naples. From Italy also, on his way to London or Boston, came Bernard Berenson, who spoke at length about pictures to Montesquiou. No doubt it was about Montesquiou as much as about Wilde that he was thinking when he recalled the art of the great conversationalists in his memoirs:

> There is no better example of intuitive spontaneity than the brilliant talker, the wit, who is stimulated and inspired by his listeners. Almost unconscious and even surprised to hear what comes out of his own mouth, he utters the winged word, the unforgettable phrase that amuses many, stings others, and deeply offends a few. The wit, the verbal clown, is suspected of a deliberate desire to poke fun, or to offend. That is seldom his intention. Nor, as is often imagined, does he act primarily through vanity, to show off, to solicit admiration. Like every other artist, he welcomes and enjoys applause, but the most determining reason for his action is this: that under certain circumstances he cannot resist the impulse to talk brilliantly, even when vaguely aware that he may give offence, and draw upon himself the vindictive displeasure of his listeners.*

All those who entered into conversation with Montesquiou could not be equally philosophical; and even Berenson quarrelled with the Count, after he had refused to pay 30 francs for a copy of *La Divine Comtesse*. Montesquiou levied this tax on every one of his admirers who crowded the Palace at St Moritz: rich Egyptians,

* Bernard Berenson: *Aesthetics and History*, pp. 18–19.

Rumanian princesses, Russian balletomanes, Viennese bankers' wives and some American women whose names could be found in the Almanach de Gotha—all enraptured at the prospect of meeting the arbiter of elegance. A Levantine asked: 'Master, what is distinction?' 'The first thing is never to think about it.' Occasionally the Count invited the habitués of the Palace to a reading in his villa. When the poems had received all the praise that the Orient could offer, the Count offered a general salutation and retired. Then the secretary, having uncovered a table on which *de luxe* editions of the Count's works lay displayed, proceeded to pocket the louis which, on occasions, were slow to be proffered.

No doubt it was in reference to this not entirely attractive custom that Bernard Berenson was to declare many years later: 'He and Yturri formed a "société d'exploitation", which was utterly devoid of scruples. . . . They milked money wherever they could.'

Another holiday place, and a far more quiet one, was d'Artagnan. Under the pictures of his ancestors, Montesquiou undertook the editing of his Memoirs, *Les Pas Effacés*. This collection of acid portraits and delightful reflections is spoiled by his acrimony at feeling his poetic gifts to be insufficiently appreciated. For by now there was little doubt that Montesquiou had been relegated to a humble place in the literary world, in contrast with that which he held in the society of Tout-Paris. Thus he had to harass Loti to get an article from him on the reissue of the *Hortensias Bleus*. Only for a moment did Proust and Mme Straus think of using him as the candidate of a literary cabal for the seat the boring Schlumberger was seeking. He was alone at Béarn, for his neighbours could not stand him: first because he had an unsavoury reputation; and secondly because he had bought their family furniture for very little and later sold it at a handsome profit in Paris. Hearing that the son of a local squire, M. Bouvet de Thèze, was a good pianist, he invited him to come and play Debussy and Chopin. The young man found the Count by the fireside, his legs in a fur rug as in the statue of him by Troubetzkoy. 'The old wolf will not eat you,' he said. The recitations of the poet amazed this young neighbour, who in his turn lulled the Count's melancholy. One day Montesquiou asked: 'Why does your father never invite me?' 'Well, it's because——' 'I understand.' This charming companion never crossed the threshold of d'Artagnan again.

To occupy the hours of his solitude, the poet became a novelist. *La Petite Mademoiselle* is one of the most laughably odd books ever written. Among characters who could have been the creation of his friend Abel Hermant,* Montesquiou portrays himself in the guise of an English governess to whom he attributes the hoaxes of his youth at tedious Charnizay. Miss Winterbottom wants to found a museum for the blind, has *Ave Maria* sung to an accompaniment of the *Prélude à l'Après-midi d'un Faune* and draws up the same kind of absurd questionnaires as those devised by Montesquiou at Courtanvaux. A literal travesty, Mademoiselle speaks like Montesquiou and dresses like the Marquise Casati; she wears 'a baroque pearl of a scandalous shape', and instructs her pupils in the most bizarre games. Unfortunately the extraordinary verve of this tale is slightly diminished by the ardour with which the governess avenges Montesquiou. All his female enemies have a place, even including the old Queen of Rumania, Carmen Sylva— 'wild and boring sub-prefect's wife'; and Jaques-Émile Blanche, with whom Montesquiou had not ceased to be angry after a rupture of thirty years, is also there beside them. There are some happy phrases in the book, like this description of a female pianist who takes up painting: 'Not content to torment the cat-gut, she must now set the sables on edge.' People laughed but were afraid; and thus an emptiness formed around him.

Horrible vengeance

Le Vésinet was too far. It was necessary to badger friends and even enemies to drag them there, to promise them the most exquisite society, the most bewitching music. People were on their guard against the sly dig that might accompany the host's words of welcome and dreaded the interminable readings of some actress or poetess hunted out to annoy Sarah Bernhardt or Anna de Noailles (both of whom were not, in fact, annoyed at all). Of course young and intelligent men had replaced the dapper generation of Reynaldo Hahn and Lucien Daudet; but they were less amusing. The success of Daudet particularly annoyed Montesquiou, who also vigorously denounced the matrimonial conspiracy which had

* A fertile and witty novelist, somewhat in the style of E. F. Benson.

thrown the delicate and extremely rich André Germain* into the
arms of fat Edmée Daudet—'this will be a white and gold
marriage' predicted the Count. In fact it was out of admiration for
Lucien that the heir of the Crédit Lyonnais allied himself with this
literary family—'like a little Persian prince (yet another) whom
the Phoenicians are going to rob'. On the day of the marriage
Mme Alphonse Daudet received a telegram of condolence,
followed shortly after by a note which apologised for the blunder
of Montesquiou's secretary. When, in consequence, the triumphant mother-in-law became a little less amiable towards the
Count, he was astonished and began to write her ten-page letters
asking for the reasons for her coldness and affirming his affection.
By each post, now, like an anti-pope in exile, Montesquiou was
sending out ultimatums, restatements of fact, black lists. He was
more and more alone.

To redirect attention to the Palais Rose, Montesquiou decided
to pay tribute to Verlaine in a ceremony which, in its combination
of refinement, ancient costumes and light music, would not fail to
make the new pastimes seem crude. Marie Lecomte and Gabrielle
Dorziat would play *Les Uns et les Autres* in front of Montespan's
fountain-basin. Everyone was busy decorating the palace:
Verlaine's bust was put on the steps, surrounded with superb
candelabra; garlands of roses linked one pilaster to another;
trophies of greenery surrounded the gate; grass-plots concealed
the orchestra that would play Fauré's music. The Professor of
Beauty spent without counting the cost and kept an eye on everything; he wanted perfection. Upholsterers and gardeners sur-
passed themselves; a restaurant-manager prepared a buffet for
three hundred people; extra servants were fitted out in French-
style livery which had not been used since the parties at the
Pavilion of the Muses.

On the eve of the great day some clouds worried Montesquiou;
but on the morning of 12 July 1912 they had disappeared and the
sun shone fresh on the forests of full-grown trees, on the lilac-
bushes and on a frothing mass of roses of the kind that one sees in
Fragonard's pictures. However, the telephone never stopped
ringing, voices were anxious. Would the party be taking place?
Was the weather not threatening? 'Yes, of course,' screamed

* A sprightly chronicler of this period, he kept a brilliant *salon* in the period
between the two wars.

Montesquiou, 'the party will take place! You are all idiots.' Then it was the turn of the actresses, who were furious at the prospect of performing to an audience of chairs. 'But there will be more than three hundred people,' Montesquiou assured them, to receive the reply: '*Le Figaro* announced this morning that the party had been cancelled.'

Cancelled! It was now too late to contradict this news. The situation was made even more terrible by the fact that there was a margin of uncertainty. Who would come? Who had taken the trouble to make enquiries? At five o'clock a few motor-cars began to arrive. The actresses in their Trianon shepherdess costumes were on the brink of hysteria. The footmen mounted guard on the deserted staircase, while the orchestra played a serenade to the birds. The Count's self-control was perfect. He would not deprive his faithful friends of a delightful spectacle. 'Those who took part in this function, at once enchanting and spoiled, will retain the memory of a tied-up bird and a bruised bouquet.' Then, after the light applause had ended, he led his group of thirty people to the immense tables, laid as at Versailles with flowers and cakes alternately, crystal and silver. On the next day, Montesquiou hastened to *Le Figaro* to ask the writer of the social column for an explanation. She was Mme Estradère, who signed herself Princesse de Mesagne. She showed him an express letter. The Count's handwriting had been imitated with some skill, as had been his style in announcing that the party would not take place. But the letter began with the two words 'Chère princesse'. 'And in spite of that you believed the rest that it contained!'

The Count returned to Le Vésinet, having made up his mind to abandon all idea of seeking for the culprit, as being beneath his dignity: he had hurt so many people. Surrounded by the disorder of faded garlands, useless chairs and hampers of untouched food, he entered on old age as he penned these lines: 'When our destiny has decided to take us back to an out-of-date function, it performs whatever surgery is necessary and then cauterises; probably the hour had struck for me to give up receptions and parties.'

CHAPTER 20

The Plato of Le Vésinet

My stamp will last upon these youthful brains,
Deep in their hearts I sow desires and fears,
Talking of Homer, Dante and the gods:
The crop will spring as I decline in years.

In search of a disciple

THE UNSUCCESSFUL party saved Montesquiou from the ridiculous fate of the old man who chases after fashion when he can no longer set it. But, never having known the meaning of rest, he now dreamed of turning the Palais Rose into some kind of Platonic academy. Society would be banished from it; handsome and intelligent young men would hasten to it to receive the lesson of Beauty. From among them he would choose the disciple capable of continuing his struggle and glorifying his memory. But events did not turn out exactly as he had planned, since the invited never knew if they were meeting a friend or an admirer, a thinker or an antique-dealer, a magnificent nobleman or an impatient prima donna.

Montesquiou's spiritual and even temporal heir must be the son of Mme de Casa-Fuerte, the handsome Illan Alvarez de Toledo, Marquis de Casa-Fuerte. This young man had already had many admirers, among them Proust, and a meticulously scandalous draughtsman, Arthur Chaplin, for whom he had sat as model for an 'Ambiguous Missal'. This artist brought together in a beautiful apartment on the Ile Saint-Louis a group of intimates which was something of a branch establishment of the Montesquiou circle and which Lorrain described in the last of his novels *Les Pelléastres*.* Montesquiou, who wanted very much to possess the

* Because they admired Debussy's *Pelléas and Mélisande*.

'Ambiguous Missal', sent his photograph to Chaplin with some fine presents. Chaplin was: 'So pious and so perverse, so scandalous and so decent, with his holy-water sprinkler and his sable brush, his anklet and his rosary.' Illan's presence attracted Proust again to the tea-parties at the Pavilion of the Muses, but he did not go to Le Vésinet. It was at Neuilly that Pierre Loti met Proust and confused him with God knows whom: 'I live so much outside everything that I did not even know of the existence of this Marcel. I was so astonished at finding him so superior, that I thought that he must be the other Marcel' (1908). Yes, Illan could have been the long-sought heir, but he was too independent and not intellectual enough. He married very quickly, quarrelled with his mother and vanished from Montesquiou's life after an exchange of some rather harsh letters.

The following letter, addressed to someone unknown, clearly demonstrates the difficulty of having a relationship with the poet: 'Monsieur, you have beautiful handwriting, which seems to me to mean order and a taste for decoration—a graphologist could expatiate on it at greater length. Your subject matter speaks in the same way: it is balanced, rather *formal*. Your *vivacity* of the other day had more eloquence and consequently more range, but no doubt it was—as in nine cases out of ten—no more than curiosity. Beware of vanity that is wrongly taken for pride, or reserve that seems like dignity. These are the caricatures of arrogance, they destroy the endowments that would give the right to arrogance itself. But perhaps you only desire little happinesses and deserve no more. In that case, I hope you have them—for to get more than one wants is to get *less* than one would like when one is not *greatly* ambitious.' The severity of the Professor of Beauty could repel sincere admirers. So M. André David, who had had the bad luck to be praised by Anna de Noailles, received this short note:

Young man, is it modest of you to brandish about prefaces by sensational ladies, as you might wave in the air a feather-hat too big for one head or even for twelve? You would do better to prepare a beautiful book in silence. . . . I write to you because you came to me spontaneously and gracefully and because I like vivacity. But if you are afraid to hear the truth—which alone has any value—then address yourself to others. I accept your 'admiration'—it is you who mention it—because, if I deserve it, it is for having produced my works in the sole ambition of being worthy of the approval of those whom I admire and for having obtained that approval, and not for the idiocies of decorations, prizes and membership of academies. *Sic dixi Sursum corda et altior*. Montesquiou.

By visits and gifts of his poems, Maurice Rostand had managed to erase the memory of the *Chantecler* episode. He enjoyed being at Montesquiou's much more than at his parents' house. As for André Germain, he could find at the Count's—much better than at the house of his imposing mother—that mixture of esotericism and society life, the exact dosage of which he was to continue to seek out until our own day.

A madly brilliant young man, of whom Montesquiou's friends —the former 'young men', such as Proust, Lucien Daudet and Reynaldo Hahn—were inordinately fond, wished at all costs to shine at the Palais Rose. The day the Count left the Pavilion of the Muses, he received this poem from Jean Cocteau:

> White-gloved, grey-coiffeured, violet-clad, hydrangea-full
> And faithful to the number nine, you now exchange
> Your mansion for a refuge new; your voice's range
> Sword-like transfixes every dolt, from frog to bull.

The poem was followed by a charming letter: '13 August 1912. I arrive from Algiers—horrible captivating town, in which floats a faint odour of Marseilles absinthe and Arab camels.' After a thousand compliments on *Brelan de Dames* the young man concluded: 'I thank you with a respectful and faithful heart for having opened to me this unyielding and heavy door of enthusiasm.'

But at a rehearsal of *Le Martyre* the poet glimpsed Cocteau. Irritated already by some fault in the staging and now provoked by the ultra-poetic manner of this young man, he thundered at him. A touching letter did not succeed in lifting the excommunication: 'The empty hall seemed like a nave to me, the stage an ample chest uttering a cry towards heaven; and it was there and then—at a moment the beauty of which was increased by the sudden discovery of your presence—that you reproached me for my unworthy presence.'

Henceforth when Montesquiou met at the theatre, at Mme

Daudet's or at Romaine Brooks', a thin young man with sharp
features, beautiful eyes and very expressive hands, he pretended
always to confuse him with Anna Pavlova and affirmed 'I know
her well' as soon as anyone wanted to introduce Jean Cocteau to
him. It is, however, thanks to Cocteau that we have been able to
hear some echo of Montesquiou himself: the absurdities and the
exquisite quotations, the fabulous or grotesque anecdotes, the
wild laughter behind a raised hand. Unfortunately Cocteau
wished to please and spoke familiarly to anyone and everyone. His
superficial kindness, pierced with flashes of malice, was never
comparable to the insolence of Montesquiou. Alas, Cocteau did
not leave us a portrait of the older man in his marvellous *Portraits-
Souvenirs*.

Half a century later, it was surely of Montesquiou that Cocteau
was thinking when he wrote, 'Nothing is harder to sustain than a
bad reputation', on the subject of a young fool who wanted to act
the little Montesquiou.

Adelsward von Fersen* certainly followed bad examples (which
are said to be the easiest to follow) in dedicating his *Les Cortèges
qui sont Passés* to Countess Greffulhe and *Le Menuet des Caresses* to
the Marquis de Tanlay. He had his poems read by de Max at tea-
parties honoured by the presence of Rostand. The young
man regarded himself as the Heliogabalus of the Parc Mon-
ceau and the last chapter of all this was to unfold in a police-
court. Montesquiou, who was perspicacious, had always refused
to allow anyone to introduce Fersen to him. He was to express
himself on the imprudence of commentaries devoid of charity and
to scorn collaborating on *Akademos*, the review which Fersen
founded on his return to France.

Apophthegms

Montesquiou was not a prude, but he had a horror of scandal.
For his disciples, or rather for his guests, he would note down
reflections which betrayed a taste as extraordinary as the following: 'Coitus in the open air suits uncouth partners in touch with
the earth, rocks and all the roughness of the Great Glebe. They are
fauns, hamadryads.' He moved his guests by reading them the
account of a visit to Ludwig of Bavaria which he had got from an

* See *The Exile of Capri* by Roger Peyrefitte.

actor, and he made them laugh by commenting on the *Cantique des Caresses*, an equivocal parody of the *Thousand and One Nights* written by Chaplin for Illan de Casa-Fuerte, with quantities of pearls and incense, and of sentences like 'There they did love each other' and 'Thy belly appears to me like a cushion of rare down'. 'One sees', commented the Count after a particularly scabrous passage, 'that the author has his highs and lows. But the principal characteristic of these divagations is that thirst to become the other—a resuscitation of the hermaphrodite cut in two at Plato's banquet.' He had apophthegms for collectors: 'A collection of china is always an infirmary.' His great wish was to infect his friends with a disgust for the world: 'Society people have no wills, they only have whims.' Making fun of women who push themselves forward by doing social work, he commented: 'Charity has done much harm in the world.' For a notorious seducer the Master had a charming phrase: 'Agreeable women do not follow you as far as they lead you.' He covered the bore, who thought that he had pleased him, with confusion by remarking: 'I am not stupid as you seem to be.' When the bore had gone, the sage drew a lesson for his pupils: ' "If the cap fits, wear it" is much less true than "If the cap fits, let others wear it".'

To reward his well-beloved guests, Montesquiou would invite them again to meet some beautiful woman. These prizes were La Casati, the Duchesse de Gramont (née Ruspoli), and Princess Bibesco. The latter said simply on one occasion: 'I have an appointment with Princess Mary of Greece, who is beautiful and learned and who deserves to be known by you. An old friend brought us together again—Monsieur Bergson.' Actresses came to have lessons in the deportment of high society; Sorel and Dorziat organised dinners for the master. Montesquiou arranged for Rodin to do a bust of Lady Sackville, who arrived accompanied by a shy young girl, Vita, already a poet and later the model for Virginia Woolf's Orlando. Lady Sackville very much wanted the Count to visit her at Knole, which had furniture of silver and miles of tapestries. But at that time his journeys were only to take this or that cure.

Sometimes d'Annunzio paid a whirlwind call, Barrès telephoned, or a short letter from Anatole France was read out—all events very exciting for the apprentice writers. The master taught the young men to laugh at society and disillusioned them about the women whose photographs in *Femina* gave them a factitious glamour. He recited the unpublished *Bergères* to them.

Having learned that Edward VII, on his last visit to Paris, had invited his old enemy Mme Legrand to dinner, and thinking that perhaps it was she who had cancelled his party, Montesquiou worked himself up into an aesthetic fury. The King of England should have invited Rodin or Anatole France or even Sarah Bernhardt. He was delighted when Olivier, the headwaiter at Maxim's, uttered this remark, worthy of Proust, about the woman who was to become Mme Leroy: 'One begins to be disgusted with her.' And he improvised:

> Prudence in the world of wealth and fashion
> To be the maid-of-all-work takes delight:
> Lesbian or procuress or, if one wishes,
> A poker-player or a parasite.

Sometimes Baroness Deslandes, returned from Florence, was exhibited to the young men. In Italy, in the company of her friend Comtesse d'Orsay, she plunged herself into all the frivolities of Catholic Sapphism, which were to inspire a young Englishman, Ronald Firbank, with ideas for his extraordinary novels. Montesquiou would have loved this rich and languid aesthete whose stinging pen, in *Valmouth* and above all in *The Artificial Princess,* seems to be inspired both by the habitués and by the *décor* of the Palais Rose.

The discovery of Raymond Roussel

Montesquiou, irritated by young men too eager to please, ended by forming a connection with a writer who resembled Firbank in being handsome, rich, a great solitary and outside any literary fashion. With his very sure sense of quality, the Count had discovered among all the books presented to him one of singular merit. Many of these books carried flattering dedications: from Julian Benda for example, 'Where you write of Bergson, let me congratulate you on the passage in which you recognise in him the Rostand of philosophy'; and from Kayserling, 'You have admirably understood what a strange and sublime master was Gustave Moreau.' But the book which now interested him was by a neighbour in Neuilly.

The poet replied by writing a long article about the work sent to him by Raymond Roussel, whose eccentric meanderings enchanted him. Perhaps it also pleased him to find in the solitary dandy some flashes of his own youth. He praised in *Impressions d'Afrique* 'this composition which is at the same time spontaneous, madly repetitive and judiciously portioned out . . . this frenzy for the inessential'. He found in it 'the tone, at once dogmatic and airy, of *L'Eve Future*' and put his finger on the profound reason for the genesis of such a work: 'Roussel wants to read a book of this nature, and since no one else will write it for him, he has written it for himself.' In reply to this article a letter arrived at Le Vésinet.

Dear Sir,

How very much overwhelmed I was to read the beautiful article that you devoted to me in *Gil Blas*. I feel that I am so unworthy of such high appreciation that I would almost like to add a reproach to my thanks. How can I tell you the extent to which I relished—while forcing myself to forget what was its subject—the article itself, so admirable in the style of its lightest paragraph that each line of it was *signed*.

What disconcerting erudition you have! And how were you able to expend so much dazzling brilliance on material so pitiable? The Angel of the Strange, the hair of Balkis, 'the grey shoes of Spinoza', the drawings of Granville, the quotation from Baudelaire and so many other brightly coloured and unexpected finds, which amaze and delight me! For the first time I have the feeling of being justified in writing my books, since they have been the humus from which such beautiful blooms have sprung. Besides, is it not the case that the worse the cause, the more opportunity one has to admire the talent of the lawyer?

Roussel travelled, but postcards kept him in Montesquiou's mind. There were some from St Moritz, from Monte Rosa, from the banks of the Rhine and, the last, in 1920 from Tahiti. 'I am making a pilgrimage on this delightful island. I have seen the Fotocroa waterfall, which runs in the opposite direction to that of the Bois de Boulogne, and I have heard himénés (sic!) in the moonlight. The Queen has introduced me to several of Rarahu's descendants.' When the novelist was not travelling he sent postcards of stations. Montesquiou felt slightly piqued, and replied on the backs of the views of the Gare du Nord, which delighted Roussel with their incredible banality.

Could Colette Willy be classed among Montesquiou's disciples? She also sent many postcards and her admiration seemed to be sincere: 'I have an almost guilty passion for Beardsley—so many drawings of this slightly mad young man speak to what lies hidden in me.' But there was something indigent and even a little shady about her letters. 'I would like to know the name of the lady whom the faun pleased. I have so few friends, monsieur. . . .' 'I have invented a sort of slow dance. If it would please you some time to see an ex-faun with fine muscles dance in front of a little idol arched under night-coloured veils, I should be happy to place myself at your disposal.'

Another young friend whom Montesquiou guided through the medium of numerous letters was the designer Georges Barbier, who by imitating the Beardsley line and the whites and blacks of Romaine Brooks, entirely changed the fashion of design, and with Iribe prepared the style which was to flower at the Exhibition of Decorative Arts.

Barbier, Drian, Marty and Boutet de Monvel, created a new dandyism in the wings of the Ballets Russes. Poiret's women wanted men worthy of their elegance. These designers were encouraged by the writers of their age: Jean-Louis Vaudoyer, Edmond Jaloux, Marcel Boulanger. To these young men of twenty to twenty five Montesquiou seemed not merely a model but also a redoubtable guide on account both of his barbed shafts of wit and of the reputation to be gained by frequenting him. Moreover, his licentiousness was only verbal. He wanted to please, but when alone with a young man he seemed to grow uneasy. Was he afraid of losing his dignity, of revealing himself as less brilliant in actions than words? One day this man who always wore gloves noted in his private papers, with the comment 'Very important', these words of Gobineau: 'Presence is annoying.' In a tête-à-tête conversation this impression was exacerbated, so that for some trivial reason he would discard the most devoted friends—those who could have been most tender, since his good looks remained. He withdrew to the bottom of the garden, near the red marble fountain-basin, to re-read Gabriel's letters, the flowery postcards he had sent to him with little presents ('I hear join a thousand papagallic things from your Pipistrello') and the more solemn visiting-card of New Year's Day, 1901: 'Dear, Your dear telegram is the only gift which could affect me. The rest is the incomprehensibility and hatefulness of family life, the insufficiencies and inattentions of friendship, the unjustness and brutality of existence. You at least, with your serious defects, represent something which not only does not doubt but has confidence, which believes and hopes. It is for that that I love you and—I can well say it—love you alone.'

CHAPTER 21

Hour-glasses and Tear-bottles

To those who listened once, he offers now the silence
Of one who, used to please, has learned to hold his peace.

A new world

IT IS a little too convenient to set the date for the beginning of the
present age and the end of that so tiresomely reiterated 'Belle
Époque' as 2 August 1914. From 1905 onwards the motor-car
and the telephone had accelerated the rhythm of life; in about
1910 the Cubists had become known and the cinema had begun to
replace the theatre; 1912 saw the twin triumphs of Poiret and the
tango; the Ballets Russes had shaken up the conventional forms of
entertainment. Luxury and machines carried the old society along
a course that was to be interrupted by the 1914 War but then
resumed at a dizzier speed to the sounds of jazz. This vibrating
rhythm astonished those who were over forty, among them
Montesquiou who wrote a very post-war novel *La Trépidation*,
followed by the rather less successful *La Petite Mademoiselle*. The
title of the first of these works was inspired by a cascade of broken
porcelain in the glass cabinets of Baron de Rothschild, owing to the
vibration, even then, of the Rue de Rivoli; as inscription there
was this line from Gobineau: 'I care little of what will come of
your ravages—above all if it is new.'

Montesquiou understood that he had no place in this society.
He went out less, and again took up painting—executing flowers
in pastel or water-colour that were clever but a shade too poetic.
The poet wished to go one better than nature, as always—as the
English put it 'to gild the lily'.* He wrote many articles, fewer

* In English in text. Trans.

poems (though he was to make up for their reduction in quantity during the war) and an enormous number of letters.

From the pink hermitage flew out notes, telegrams and above all postcards of the house, its summer-houses, its picture-gallery, its steps. Some samples chosen from among the bundles of letters kept by the heirs of the recipients show us Montesquiou's anxieties in the year 1913, the most serious of which was the dread of solitude. To M. Léon Bailby: 'Dear friend, I entrust Flamant to transmit to you my invitation to lunch on Sunday week and to act in concert with you to ensure that the project succeeds. A word in reply, I beg you, so that I can tell my roses not to fade.'

The most beautiful letter of the ageing Montesquiou is certainly one to Countess Greffulhe. The truth was that the expenses of receptions in the Rue d'Astorg, hunting at Boisboudran, and the munificence of the Count to a young woman passionately fond of painting,* had begun to jeopardise the quasi-royal situation of the cousins:

'What a removal of all the past! And what a melancholy astonishment at seeing the columns, I do not say collapse, but change their bases! No doubt of it, we are wrong to despise the insect world—they gnaw the beams and the whole building moves. You have at least the good fortune to be one of those who have only to remain themselves to stay right; but you need thoughtful and positive advice from competent people. Mine—which is, alas, only theoretical—amounts to saying to you that the main point in these seeming disasters is to persuade yourself (an easy operation when it is the truth) that you represent the centre of the action: others *behave*, you *act*. Pride redeems, ordeals ennoble. But how much time and trouble are consumed in extricating oneself from these enormous and yet mediocre struggles of existence! It is of no use for the philosopher to talk: of course all this would have no effect if viewed from Sirius, but when one is oneself playing the leading role in the piece, one cares not a rap for Sirius. Tell me your news when you can and remember that I am closely bound to your fate.'

Every kind of news reached the solitary. Thus, he enjoyed the adventures of the always handsome La Gandara: first Colette

---

* Madame de la Beraudière, in whose house Proust was first to approach Comte de Greffulhe, the original of his Duc de Guermantes.

Willy was mad about him; then it was the abandoned wife of d'Annunzio who threw herself at him. Helleu, the fashion for whom was waning, had himself become something of an antique-dealer:

> Helleu has found a Watteau, it is charming,
> Now it is cold, now it is sad, now dark.
> Good-fortune flickers . . .

Montesquiou, who was now endeavouring to become good, discreetly followed the desertion of Mme Arman de Caillavet by Anatole France and regretted, when the fat lady of Avenue Hoche died of grief, that he had ever placed her among *Les Quarante Bergères*. However, presumption and success could reawaken old hatreds, and thus it was that he confronted Bourget with the ghost of Juvigny, a very intimate friend of the Academ-ician, who had died young and one of whose novels Bourget had plagiarised. Little wickednesses were the recompense he allowed himself after a week of kindness.

*Falling in love again**

Two new friendships replaced those that had been worn thread-bare by habit or destroyed by irony. After having read a long and intelligent study of his work, Montesquiou met the critic Pierre Lièvre. He also was a connoisseur, who had in his apartment in the Place des Vosges collections of drawings, bronzes and faience. Pierre Lièvre's chance finding of a bust of Montesquiou in a dealer's shop sealed this friendship. Montesquiou was pleased that his portrait had risen up 'in the path of the man who wished to clear away from in front of the proud and sorrowful countenance the undergrowth of the jungle of injustice'. Henceforth, Pierre Lièvre received invitations that were at once extremely flattering and extremely exacting. In another article he was not permitted the smallest reservation: 'Not that your work is faulty', Montesquiou wrote, 'but because nature is less implacable than logic, and because the mechanical nightingale that you have admired in my show-cases will never utter the sublime false note of which his model has the secret.'

* In English in the original. Trans.

The other friend of these last years was Dr Paul-Louis Couchoud, Hello's disciple, who was greatly attracted by eso-tericism and who had written some works in the same category as Schuré's *Grands Initiés*, with titles like *Sages et Poètes d'Asie* and *Le Mystère de Jésus*. Dr Couchaud encouraged Montesquiou to hasten the publication of his Memoirs, which could carry as their inscription his often-repeated words, threatening in the past, but now melancholy: 'I have to complain!' Between pages of ma-licious gusto and of delightful description, the poet slipped in disillusioned reflections, and remarks on eternity and kindness reminiscent of the methods of Coué. 'I am good and I have a beautiful soul,' Montesquiou repeated to himself; and in his case the cure all but succeeded. He often went to rest in the doctor's house at Saint-Cloud. Mme de Clermont-Tonnerre saw him there on the occasion of a luncheon that Couchaud gave for Anatole France and Mlle La Prévotte, who had supplanted the former mistress. Montesquiou said that he would not attend the luncheon, but that he would come afterwards to greet the guests; and he added prudently, 'Tell them that I love them all!' Alas! this feeling was not reciprocated, and when he entered the salon a sinister void formed around him. France firmly left the room, muttering, 'I cannot stand that man, who always speaks to me of his ancestors.'

'What is sad is not so much seeing people of merit withdraw their friendship from us as seeing them grant it to people of lesser worth and thus diminish retrospectively the value of what they gave to us.' Instead of Anatole France, Montesquiou fell back on Saint-Saëns. The composer seemed a little surprised: 'All is mystery, all, including the sympathy which unites two beings as dissimilar as ourselves.' But they were more dissimilar in appear-ance than in reality. Each of them had an interest in young people; but it was on to religious ground that Montesquiou wished to draw the old unbeliever. He called in the aid of Father Mugnier, but the amiable priest shirked his duty and offered conversation instead of conversion. It seems that towards 1916 Montesquiou was moved by a young writer at the front, who wrote him long letters. 'I would so much like to play in your life the mysterious and beautiful role that you seem to destine me for. . . .' One day Miss Barney paid a call on Montesquiou at Le Vésinet and found him very worried. He had had no news from the soldier for a long

time. Had he been killed? Or had he renounced his superhuman
role of disciple?

However, it was in Dr Couchoud's family that for the last
time, in the last year of his life, Montesquiou was to nurse the
hope of winning a disciple and experience a last fervour for
another's beauty. It was 'a love of the eyes', as one terms what is
in fact a love of the head: an aesthete's passion, which would
know happiness merely at seeing a delightful silhouette outline
itself at the head of a flight of steps or a perfect profile against the
false light of a Japanese screen. Alas, Montesquiou also exacted
from the loved object the same quasi-mystical devotion—and it
was harder to play such a role than merely to be corrupted. The
master was doomed to disappointment, the disciple to boredom.

One day the Count noticed on the Couchaud's piano the photograph of an adolescent with an Anglo-Saxon beauty. He paused,
put his hand on his heart—would he again have the strength to
suffer? He was informed that it was Jean, the son of Mme Couchaud's first marriage; his mother was a Sevastos, and so a descendant of the illustrious Byzantine family of Doucas. The youth was
at boarding-school, and it was there that Montesquiou sent him
a magnificent copy of *Hortensias Bleus*. With the consent of the
parents a correspondence began. 'You say—you even write—
charming things, which is hardly done any more. And you write
them in a hand which is already a little troubled by what life
seems to promise, by what it holds for you, by what also sometimes, I hope, it will do for you. Goodbye "dear young man". I
do not add again "O killer of gazelles", but I will add it.' The old
gentleman sent sweet-meats from Royat, where he was taking a
cure; his heart, however, remained alarmingly young. 'One
cannot, all the same, correspond indefinitely with chocolate
violets and preserved cantaloup melon; the hour of the calamus
has come, if that of the verb has not yet sounded. Your last floral
communication, however, made me want to have you sent a
crystallised lily of the valley—but I cannot find one. Be content,
then, with these unreal sweets. . . .'

At times melancholy made the old lover more lucid: 'I used
very much to like being seen, but I do not like it any more at all.
One only likes what one does well, and to show oneself off is not
for all ages. . . .' He signed himself in Japanese style: 'He who
is late in crying in the autumn.' This tenderness took Montesquiou

back to his own adolescence: 'Portrieux-Saint-Quay—so it is there that you are! I have some youthful memories of it; it was there that I had a red suit made, in which I leapt on to the swing with the arrogant wish to make the night purple with my flight. There was a missionary there, who wore a garment of black silk with amber buttons and said astonishingly ingenuous things.' This young correspondent was already going out into society and he and his sister gave a little party: 'I find it nice that she should have thought of me in decorating the flower-stands for your "hop" with hydrangeas; probably it would have been even nicer to think that she was going to "hop" on my last gasp. . . .' But there was something more serious: the descendant of the Doucas was introduced to Princess Bibesco and fell in love with this Byzantine beauty. 'I noticed with dismay that you were enamoured of the lady with the green stones, I warn you that she is a siren, even a Circe who will change you into a beast. I am convinced that you would be a very nice little beast, but I should prefer that you kept your fine intelligence and open receptivity.' This correspondence went on for more than a year: fervent, anxious or playful, without the master ever meeting the disciple, who went from college to stay in the country. At last a meeting took place; and of course it was a disappointment. '. . . You have come out of the mystery that shrouded you and have put me in the presence of a correct, reserved, circumspect and cold young man, whose harsh voice surprised me on the telephone and whom I was subsequently disconcerted to meet in a spiritless reality. That visit, which you offered to pay me when I did not know you, you no longer offered me when it seemed to be indicated, and thus the misunderstandings of proud souls have begun to weave their invisible but not unfeeling web.' After that the correspondence dragged, the misapprehensions multiplied, and the last letter, written four months before the death of the poet, as his final bouquet offered up to Beauty, has the bitter odour of the dust: 'From the time that I loved you without knowing you, I would have been moved to wander over places:

> Honoured by the steps and lit by the eyes
> Of the charming young shepherd.

Today I only see the graceless vista of a place both unattractive and dry.'

'Presence is annoying': Gobineau was right.

Patriotic doggerel

Nevertheless, more serious wounds were soon being expressed
in poems more numerous. War was declared. After Montesquiou
had played with the idea of being shot on the steps of his palace
by Uhlans before they proceeded to burn all his collections, he
prudently went to join Mme de Clermont-Tonnerre at Trouville.
There they met the Mardruses and the Guitrys and Isadora Duncan,
who expressed the desire to have a child by the Count. The front
became stabilised, Montesquiou reached d'Artagnan in an over-
crowded third-class coach, and followed the operations from his
château. The aesthete alternately made room for a bellicose
gentleman, who was always fretting about the war, and a woman of
charitable works, for whom the dead inspired some rather moving
poems. 'When you hear me groan', he instructed his servants,
'you will know that I am writing. Do not disturb me.' The
patriotic and Catholic upper crust and also perhaps his Protestant
heredity were now taking their revenge on the Commander of
Delicate Odours. If, until this moment, it has seemed deplorable
that the Count's frivolity so often enticed him to deal with ridiculous themes, during these last days of his—dignified as they were
—it is impossible not to regret that the same frivolity did not
enable him to skirt lightly round the tragic happenings for which
he was not made. Such was his chauvinism that, when this man of
society wrote of the Emperor of Germany, he referred to him as
'the frightful Kaiser. . . . This monster, this William.' Was it the
Duchesse de Rohan who was holding his pen when he wrote:

> The black Senegalese who are not at all weak
> And whom we used to admire in the public gardens.

These lines are from *Les Offrandes Blessées,* a collection which
brings together, each in three stanzas of four lines, 'offerings'
categorised by the author as political, fairy-tale, topsy-turvy,
antique, fertile, resigned, lachrymal, boreal, hereditary, sigillate,
initialled, sacrificial, flagellatory, derisory, peccant, atavistic. . . .
The best recall the *Prières Pour Tous,* and the others François
Coppée. In this period, when silliness seemed inseparable from

good morals, the author of these poems experienced a small return to fame. The war was prolonged, and quickly a new collection appeared, *Sabliers et Lacrymatoires,* from which Rubinstein, garbed as a nurse, recited some poems in the Sarah Bernhardt theatre. Malicious fate again avenged the good duchess by whispering these lines in the Count's ears:

> All burnt alive, the dreadful Zeppelin crew!
> And it is just, for they burned child and woman.

Mata Hari must have inspired the Alexandrine:

> See how the dancing-girls now set about their task.

Finally, in 1919, there appeared *Un Moment de Pleur Eternel,* in which between pieces on Rohan and Deroulède there is a complaint in which the neglected poet compares himself to Jesus.

'You see,' wrote Montesquiou to Pierre Lièvre, 'I am not modest, and the role of angel which you recognised me as playing against my old Jacob, barely suffices me. I need divinity, but, I hasten to add—the divinity of a recumbent god, like poor Robert d'Humières.'

Perhaps the Beyond brought some consolation to the great dramatist of Le Vésinet. But no! 'Lately,' he wrote to Mme Straus, 'I received a spiritual communication, the conclusion of which was this: "You are going to learn to know souls. . . ." I, who thought it was what I had always done! Not at all. From that day, the masks began to fall and I saw only rather villainous faces. . . .'

Some tributes

But there, it must be admitted, Montesquiou was being unjust. He forgot that everyone was extremely occupied during the war, that Le Vésinet was far, and that his friends' chauffeurs were at the front. The American ladies were busy with ambulances, the chorus of ladies was occupied in hospitals; as for Mme Greffulhe, Berthelot had charged her with the task of negotiating a separate peace with the young Emperor of Austria. Montesquiou could live in the Palais Rose only in the summer, since there was no more coal to heat the salons, and the interminable dead seasons were taken up with cures. Nevertheless, on poetical natures the Professor of

Beauty still exerted his enchantment. Lise Deharme, the novelist and surrealist poet, recalls having seen, when quite a young girl, the arrival at a hotel at Capvern of enormous trunks with armorial bearings upon them, containing marvellous Chinese hangings embroidered with flowers and birds, destined to decorate the apartment which the old poet was going to occupy. One season she was to see him progress, stiff and extravagant like Barbey d'Aurevilly, towards the bathing establishment.

When he was at his lowest, he received in July this message sent from Italy by Ida Rubinstein: 'I will come in my new aeroplane, which has been baptised by the poet. I come, I climb, I have wings.' This champion of Living Dangerously* brought a poem from d'Annunzio:

> The messenger whom you had ushered from above
>   In my shut garden seemed both beautiful and bright:
> Then leaving, torch in hand and certain that my love
>   Remains for you, he opened wide his wings in flight.

When Montesquiou came to Paris, he waited for his train at the house of Coco Madrazo. Coco, who already knew all the old man's stories, asked Louis Gautier-Vignal† to keep him company, and for this charming young man Montesquiou proceeded to show off, fabricate and jeer with a verve that Cocteau alone was to rival in his best days. But there it was: those who had been in society since before the war were already familiar with the descriptions of Mme de Janzé's hat, of Mme Porgès' parties and of Mme de Béarn's Byzantine boudoir. 'I could end all Montesquiou's sentences myself, I anticipated the inflections of his voice, I waited for the place where the laugh came when his foot tapped the gravel. Montesquiou's effect on me was no more than that of an old photograph.' It was the Duchesse de Clermont-Tonnerre, the most intelligent of his friends, who wrote that; but none the less she kept for the poet during his last years a patient, if slightly ironic, affection.

The Duchess did not belong to the Red Cross and Montesquiou congratulated her on that; for the extravagance of his spleen knew no bounds on the subject of the devotion to duty of society

---

* In English in the original. Trans.

† A lecturer; uncle of the present Duchesse de Gramont.

women, to whom he attributed motives not so much patriotic as snobbish or fashionable.

It is she who remains our best witness on the subject of the strained friendship between the two writers after the appearance of the first volume of *Remembrance of Things Past*. Montesquiou was astonished to see fly with his own wings—and what wings!— the protégé of whom he had said to Barrès, 'He will always be our young man.' Proust did not set foot in Le Vésinet. He had so much to write, so many people to see and so little time in front of him. No longer did Montesquiou have anything to teach him. Proust retained for the Professor of Beauty an affection in which fear had ceased to be anything more than a polite formula; but none the less he often wrote to the Count in order to follow his reactions to a book which owed so much to him and each volume of which brought back, often scarcely transposed, the bouquets of the *Commander of Delicate Odours* and the trumpeting insolence of the Peacock. From the depths of his bed, Proust watched the reactions of his victim, who was also his hero, and whom he named Palamède de Guermantes, Baron de Charlus.

CHAPTER 22

St Charlus

Forgotten tombs, chipped marble,
Flagstones grown worn and used,
Names half-erased, grave-plots reclaimed,
And recollections bruised.

Robert pierced by Marcel's arrows

WHEN, IN 1913, Montesquiou received *Swann's Way*, he was extremely reticent: 'I don't know if this irretrievable young man will one day find his own voice in a work—to permit myself an expression that is often abused; I admit that I do not think so, because his "voice" consists, perhaps, precisely in having *no* voice that is truly his own. He is the author of a book at once luxuriant and inextricable, for which he has, it must first be stated, found a pretty title. . . . His writing (of which I have bundles) is illegible, confused . . . it leaves marks on the paper not like the feet of flies but rather like those of ants.'

Within a Budding Grove was published in 1918; in it Baron de Charlus put in his first appearance at Balbec. Montesquiou wondered perhaps about this Guermantes, who showed the same severity at the Jockey Club as in literature. He went through all the members of the upper crust that Proust could have met at his house. But here was this character speaking: 'In these days everyone is Prince Something-or-other; one really must have a title that will distinguish one: I shall call myself Prince when I wish to travel incognito.' Robert himself had made this remark when his cousin, Aimery de la Rochefoucauld, obtained the title of Prince in Bavaria. What style! But, alas, also what a voice!—'like certain contralto voices which have not been properly trained to the right pitch so that when they sing it sounds like a duet between a young man and a young woman. . . . One could hear their laughter, shrill, fresh laughter of school-girls or coquettes quizzing their partners with all the archness of clever tongues and pretty wits.' Is this not the peacock of *Chantecler* who cried out on a beach in Normandy, 'My cousin, Clara de Chimay!'? Really, it was too bad! Malicious tongues would link the Count with this absurd baron—who also, in his youth, must have been a famous dandy: 'One wet summer, he ordered an ulster of a loose but warm vicuna wool, which is used only for travelling rugs, and kept the blue and orange stripes showing. . . .' 'A dark green thread harmonised, in the stuff of his trousers, with the clock on his socks, with a refinement which betrayed the vivacity of taste that was everywhere else conquered.' Using a Persian dagger with a jade handle, Montesquiou continued nervously to cut the pages of the novel. He followed the baron into the narrator's bedroom; the sad remarks on the subject of youth touched him; and certainly he too would have mocked this young man who had anchors embroidered on his bathing-costume. But would he have pinched the back of his neck while calling him 'a little rascal'? Did Proust imagine for an instant that the Count had nursed for him feelings more turbid than a sympathy for his intelligence? It was the young friend of Madeleine Lemaire who used to present to the Professor of Beauty copies of works in sentimental bindings.

In October 1920 the first volume of the *Guermantes Way* appeared; to be followed, six months later, by its conclusion and the beginning of *Cities of the Plain,* bound together. Montesquiou was amused to find in Mme de Villeparisis's *salon* ladies who were already old in his youth and about whose clothes and rivalries he had so often reminisced to Marcel: Mme de Beaulaincourt, Mme de Bloqueville, Mme de Janzé. He smiled at the portrait of Count Greffulhe as the Duc de Guermantes. But when Baron de Charlus reappeared at the end of the first volume, uneasiness returned: 'At every social gathering at which he appeared and, contemptuous towards the men, courted by the women, promptly attached himself to the smartest of the latter, whose garments he seemed almost to put on as an ornament to his own. . . .' Montesquiou then heard his own voice address the Marcel-like narrator: ' "That sort of politeness means nothing," he rebuked me coldly. "There is nothing so pleasant as to give oneself trouble for a person who is worth one's while. For the best of us, the study of the ants, a

taste for old things, collections, gardens are all mere ersatz,
succedanea, alibis. In the heart of our tub, like Diogenes, we cry
out for a man. We cultivate begonias, we trim yews, as a last
resort, because yews and begonias submit to treatment. But we
should like to give our time to a plant of human growth, if we
were sure that he was worth the trouble. That is the whole
question: you must know something about yourself. Are you
worth my trouble or not?" '

Really! There was the epitome of a whole sublime life, emerging
from the mouth of a person already ridiculous and soon to become
odious, although admittedly the baron was not denied a certain
nobleness of feeling and an immense intelligence. Proust empha-
sises once again the need for a disciple, which obsessed Montesquiou's old age: 'I have young relatives who are not—I do not
say worthy, but who are not capable of accepting the moral
heritage of which I have been speaking. For all I know, you may
be he into whose hands it is to pass, he whose life I shall be able
to direct and to raise it to so lofty a plane.' This long tirade of the
baron touched Montesquiou all the more because, at the very
moment he was reading it, he was expecting a letter from that
young man whose photograph had bowled him over in the house
of his parents; he was hoping for a visit from this person who
would perhaps be worthy of receiving the treasure which Delafosse did not deserve and which Yturri had not had the strength
to carry. This treasure Marcel had now pilfered.

The scene which the baron makes to the narrator was the echo
of Montesquiou's lecture in 1894, when Marcel believed, after
producing Delafosse, that he had a foot in the household. A little
further on, there was the story of his cousin Aimery refusing to
hear of the death of a relation in order not to miss a party. The
exuberant health and the noisy grandeur, approaching vulgarity,
of Count Greffulhe, which had so often irritated Montesquiou,
must now have caused him to laugh when they were transferred to
the Duc de Guermantes.

At this point Proust received the Prix Goncourt and became a
great man; Montesquiou in *Elus et Appelés* devoted to him a page
on the subject of lesbians: 'He hunts people out, he flagellates
them, he takes aim, he finds his mark; and through all this progress
he never leaves his bed, to demonstrate that the Procrustean bed
is not his but that of others.' The correspondence between the two

friends again became frequent; but to what page of the novel do the following beautiful lines of Montesquiou allude? 'The hearts that I touch are rare, and they are ones that I have chosen. I am proud that you have so quickly recognised me in the beautiful sentence which I allowed you not to guess, and I would feel very honoured to be named in the future edition.' Of course, Montesquiou was excited by the clues. Proust assured him that Charlus was Mme Aubernon's scandalous cousin, Baron Doazan. But Montesquiou was suspicious: 'I have only glimpsed this baron and his waxen hair and waxed moustache. He had none of the breeding which you confer on him and which lends, in spite of everything, some style to his vice. . . . The clues in themselves have no more interest than the slice of bread in the salt-mines of Stendhal. . . . And to choose rather glittering types, is La Duse the heroine of *Il Fuoco* and Robert de Montesquiou a character in Huysmans?' Doazan was the screen which saved the Count's self-respect at the moment when all Paris was exclaiming, 'Charlus is Count Robert'. Anna de Noailles, who could imitate marvellously well the voice of the poet she had eclipsed, dammed the stream of her own eloquence after dinner in order to declaim Charlus's tirades. Thus those who were climbing the stairs as after-dinner guests thought for a moment that Montesquiou had emerged from his hermitage.

Montesquiou, whom the war had made so conventional, was astonished firstly that a novel by Dorgelès (*Les Croix de Bois*) had not been awarded the prize, and secondly that Marcel should spend so much of his time at the British Embassy and at the Ritz. There was a tiff over a letter of thanks for which Proust had failed in turn to thank him, but dear Mme Straus restored peace between them. Montesquiou continued to note the anecdotes, the portraits, the bouquets and the reproductions of pictures that Marcel had gathered in the course of ten years of friendship. In reality the so eagerly awaited disciple, the one responsible for his future glory, was to be the cruel novelist. Certainly master and pupil had different points of view on the subject of aestheticism. Proust's world was that of the Impressionists. He described Renoir's young girls and Pissaro's orchards; Françoise was a Degas* figure. Montesquiou's mystic world was that of Moreau and Redon. The Beyond cannot have any place in a work in which

---

* The Preface to the book *De David à Degas* by J. E. Blanche underlines this preference and must certainly have irritated Montesquiou.

Time is the principal motive force; for those who communicate with another world, whether through spiritualism or through their art, deny all reality to the continuance of time. We are told that Charlus is pious; but his chivalrous Christianity has nothing to do with the esotericism that was so dear to Montesquiou from his childhood and became the source of his hope when he renounced all his vanities. What differences, too, between the original and the literary character in their social viewpoints! Certainly Montesquiou thought that Abel Hermant had represented good society more precisely; but in the works of Proust he relished the paraded foolishness and pretentious hardness, the whole monstrous side of an idle aristocracy from which he had himself suffered and which he had derided.

When the second volume of *Cities of the Plain* appeared, Montesquiou filled a whole notebook with remarks: 'The character of the great but perverse nobleman, already revealed as a distinguished invert, opens up a perspective full of gamy promise in the 3rd volume, which is entitled *Sodome et Gomorrhe*. When the time comes, the necessary will be said, be sure of that, to ensure that the names of the two Biblical towns are accepted as easily as if they were Chatou and Nanterre and that the Lake of Salt takes on the false appearance of Lake Enghien.' But he congratulated Marcel: 'For the first time someone dares, you dare to take as a straight subject—in the way that an idyll by Longus or a novel by Benjamin Constant treats of love—the vice of Tiberius or of the shepherd Corydon. That was your intention, now we shall see the consequences of it; and I do not doubt that you have already tasted some of the effects. . . . Will you be enrolled in the battalion of the Flauberts and the Baudelaires, who passed through infamy to reach glory?' Montesquiou seemed reassured by the very horror of the opening scene of *Cities of the Plain*. What was there in common between himself and the old grizzled and obese homosexual, who did dirty things with a waistcoat maker in the back-room of his shop? But the picture of paederastic society promised to be amusing. On the whole the Count had nothing to fear from Marcel's indiscretions; and he always enjoyed the ludicrousness engendered by a vice from which he escaped by a hair's breadth—the sordid situations in which his pride prevented him from being involved. '*Suave est mari magno . . .*' But truth in literature is truer than truth in life—Montesquiou knew that

better than anyone. He was Charlus and would die being thought
to be him. He confided to a friend: 'I am in bed, ill from the publication of three volumes which have bowled me over.'

Hope from the Beyond

Thinking of Proust became an obsession. The poet suffered more
from friendship betrayed than from the odiousness of the portrait
itself. He questioned a clairvoyant, and this is what he reported of
the interview:

> Spirit communication 1918   Concerning P.
>   his estrangement
> not because of infatuation but incomprehension
> *There is dimness.* I did not dare to think that this could be a thing
> desired and prepared. There will be return.

It was through this medium, Mlle. Suzanne Meyer-Zendel, that
he communicated with the other world. This noble-hearted
Pythia with an indefatigable pen had been Judith Gautier's friend
and took care of her house, Le Pré aux Oiseaux, in Brittany.
Montesquiou kept bundles of papers, covered with her pointed,
overlapping writing, and this haughty misogynist allowed her—
admittedly in verse—to address him as 'thou'.

This woman, whose astral name was Defdea, was sometimes
involuntarily comic:

> You, who as far as mystery is concerned, have a needle-
>   sharp mind,
> You have succeeded in perceiving under my woman's
>   clothes
> A falsely boyish air. Of the ravelled skein
> You hold the right end.

When one reads this doggerel, one sees the influence which
produced Montesquiou's last poems:

> In advance I have plunged into the Styx of your faith
> And we shall conquer time and its morose roses.

But Defdea had a warm heart and the master impatiently
waited for her letters: 'And I write, I write, without knowing

from where it all comes to me. This superabundance could have only been sent to me from the Beyond.'

Shattered health, which obliged him to undergo cures, to stay in rest-homes and to seek for a change of air, kept him away from Paris, in the company of his faithful and dull secretary, Pinard. The Palais Rose was too big and too costly to keep up; Montesquiou had much less money than before the war. Feeling the approach of death, he busied himself with composing a record for posterity. One of his most beautiful claims to be remembered is this letter to Pierre Lièvre, dated 1 May 1921. Every other word underlined, it is really a kind of barrister's speech:

Dear Monsieur Lièvre,

I thought, *during my hours in the clinic,* of *the affectionate dedication of your beautiful book,* in which you tell me *to learn to appreciate myself.* As I do not like *promises that are ineffectually followed* up, I dreamed of the *beautiful obituary articles that you* would write *about my career, which is voluntarily closed and sterilised,* from the *human and worldly* point of view under the obligation to *fertilise it with platitudes* and to *irrigate it with the begging that has* become *so universal.* One must receive *only that to which one has the right without saying so,* while one *pursues that which flees.* During the time that you were thinking about the return of spring to my *double* lilacs (*for double they are*) there was *I in the act of inhaling them* with a feeble breath, *yet none the less convinced that I was not unworthy of them.* I think that life is *ugly* because of what one puts into it. That *which is put into it by itself* is pure *beauty and kindness.*

Your . . .

At the same time the poet wrote the last pages of his memoirs: 'An impression which is even more extraordinary than painful is that which consists of suddenly observing, without any warning, that one's life is over. One is still there, more or less physically dilapidated or still putting up one's resistance, and with one's faculties apparently intact but ill-adapted to the taste of the day; one feels disaffected, a stranger to contemporary civilisation, which at one time one had anticipated, but whose present manifestations wound and shock less than they seem vain. In a word, a water-tight partition separates one from Picasso's artistic conceptions, from Czechoslovakian aestheticism or Negro art; and this is not a good way to feel oneself in fashion.' Montesquiou derived

this resignation from spiritualism, and also from the novels of
H. G. Wells, who, even more than Maeterlinck, seemed to him to
satisfy his idea of the Beyond. But the sentiment which sums up
these meditations is this reply made by Mme de Casa-Fuerte, when
one day he asked her what she felt about 'the great mystery':
'An immense curiosity.' He himself was no longer in the least
curious about the world, since the war had either plunged so many
of his intimates into oblivion or dulled the brilliance of friends or
enemies whose adventures he had followed for forty years.
Countess Potocka, for example, now ruined and fat, lived alone
with her dogs in a pavilion near Neuilly; Baroness Deslandes, her
sight almost gone, attempted with her last remaining pieces of
jewellery to dazzle the first Surrealists; Sarah dragged herself
along on one leg to recite the *Marseillaise* in the provinces; Helleu
had been supplanted by Van Dongen; Cloton Legrand, née
Fournès, made up bridge-fours at the house of Princesse de
Polignac. The chorus of ladies had been dispersed by death or old
age; friends like the Marchesa Casati, Miss Barney and Ida
Rubinstein had been gripped by a frenzy for travel: to Venice, to
New York, to the East. The Count was not always resigned, and
sometimes he grumbled like an old gentleman who reads *Le
Gaulois* in the depths of the country. 'What a jazz-band baptism!'
he cried at the reception in honour of his god-daughter Corisande
de Gramont, Mme Greffulhe's grand-daughter, for no attention
had been paid to his elaborate remarks. The young men who had
not known the society of the period before the war regarded him
as a duck-billed platypus. And everywhere Proust was being
talked about—his telephone and his late visits were eagerly
awaited. The Count asked Mme de Clermont-Tonnerre: 'Will
I be reduced to calling myself Montesproust?' He resolutely
turned his back on Count Étienne de Beaumont, even though he
was now giving the same kind of parties for which the older man
had once been famed. At these Countess Greffulhe presided,
organised, and received such august guests as the Queen of the
Belgians, Paderewski, Painlevé and Rodin.

She found time, none the less, to attend to her cousin, writing
beautiful letters to him:

Dear brother and friend,
    We none of us take proper care of ourselves, for we ignore the

chemical laboratories which are our bodies. . . . One can thus prepare oneself, quite gently and without bitterness, for the transfiguration of the chrysalis, eventually to fall naturally from the terrestrial tree like a ripe fruit whose pleasure consists in being enjoyed by a god.

The great lords of letters—Barrès, France—kept their attentions for brilliant young men, who would one day be very willing to regard them as their masters. At this time, the beginning of the Years of Folly, no one had time for quarrels and reconciliations, for arranging flowers or for recitations.

You can't take it with you

Robert de Montesquiou had no illusions. In the world in which he had shone, 'one must not go beyond the limits of worldly indisposition, and a relation is never permitted to die at the beginning of the season'. A faithful male friend noted the Count's disillusioned remarks. 'You must reassure me', wrote a female friend, to which Montesquiou replied: 'I am certain that I am going to die.' The lady did not show herself again. Another woman friend, after hearing the news, 'pretended to be dead', thus eliciting from Montesquiou the comment 'That is my role, not hers.' To Proust, whom he persisted in looking upon as a *malade imaginaire,* he wrote:'I hope that you are quite cured and that your complete resurrection will come at the same time as my death—that is to say, soon.'

'There is only one thing which can be as difficult as finding someone to leave you his property, and that is to find someone to whom to leave your own.' On the eve of his death, the Count sold d'Artagnan to strangers; the Montesquiou family were informed too late and, already encumbered with other châteaux, gave up the idea of purchasing it. To whom should he leave the family furniture and the furniture that was for sale: the Chinese vases; the lacquer boxes crammed with silks and masks; the gilded writing-desks; the ebony chests overflowing with the shawls so dear to Alfred Stevens and with William Morris tapestries; the collection of canes; the Coromandel screens and the cloisonné flower-pot holders; the rather frayed embroidery pictures from

Japan; the *kakemonos* which had not been unrolled since the Goncourt sale; portfolios of engravings by Helleu and Whistler; the enormous modern-style sofa-bookcases; the vases by Gallé, Venetian glass and Turkish beads? At the beginning of the autumn of 1921, under the grey light filtering through stained glass, Montesquiou wandered through the picture-gallery and salons brightened only by clusters of chrysanthemums. All at once he felt detached from these things to which he had been more faithful than to his friends; they no longer had the slightest interest for him; and out of pity for the man he had tyrannised for fifteen years as much as from the desire to irritate the Montesquiou family, he left everything to his secretary, with the exception of certain legacies, of which there were some to the Library at Versailles, in memory of Yturri.

He was now ready to abandon everything; and he therefore decided to spend the winter at Menton, in memory of the times when he had consoled the anguish of Passiflora. At the end of November the trunks were packed: the last servant closed the high shutters of the Palais Rose; the furniture was put under dust-sheets; the books were locked up; the last dahlias grew black in the lead vases; dead leaves blocked up the fountain-basin of Mme de Montespan. It was time to go.

Erect and thin in his iron-grey check suit, Count Robert stood with his sharp profile outlined against a pilaster as he readjusted the long Scotch cashmere scarf round his bowed shoulders and then, with a golden-handled Malacca-cane, scattered some leaves. Countess Greffulhe had sent her huge Panhard to take him to the station. The secretary, clutching a sheaf of manuscripts tightly to his chest, busied himself with the little tasks of departure.

He counted the trunks which the footman strapped on the roof and the suitcases piled on the luggage-rack behind; put a vicuna rug over the Count's knees; and then got in beside the driver. The motor-car made its way through the substantial but bare gardens of Le Vésinet. Robert de Montesquiou had only three more weeks to live by the palm-trees and orange-trees in boxes, at the Pavillon de l'Amirauté, dominating the old town of Menton. His last pleasure was to run through the proofs of his collection of articles, *Elus et Apelés*, that Pinard had gone to fetch from the printer at Orléans.

The sick man revived a little when the postman called: and

it must be admitted that his old friends remained faithful to him. Mme Straus wrote charming letters; Barrès sent him a warm letter from the Chamber of Deputies. Defdea continued to transmit messages, Lucie Delarue-Mardrus poems and Ida Rubinstein news of her voyage to Egypt. It was in reply to Ida Rubinstein that Robert de Montesquiou was to inscribe his last lines, on 3 December: 'This which will remain in your life, like the passing of sorrowful man, threatened with not being able to bring to a successful end the manifestations of his art or the justifications of his equity. As far as you yourself are concerned, what hurt me cruelly was not to have been able to play my part in the marvellous Shakespearean conspiracy, which has set you on such a high pinnacle. . . .'

The poet succumbed after an attack of uraemia on 11 December 1921.

Some flowers and many pieces of paper

The body was brought back to Versailles and a service was held at the Chapel of Sainte-Elisabeth before the interment in the Gonards cemetery. About twenty friends followed the coffin to the stone under which Yturri rested. The family were not represented; they left Montesquiou to the people he had chosen for himself. Ida Rubinstein, swathed in dark veils, stood as erect as a yew-tree among the graves. Also present were the Duchesse de Clermont-Tonnerre, Miss Barney and Madrazo, and Louise Breslau. Dr Couchoud said a few words and Lucie Delarue-Mardrus read a poem.

The first snow fell on the sheaf of orchids brought by Ida Rubinstein. Where were the ladies who used to beg Robert to visit them; the young men who would fight for an invitation to his parties; all the actresses and the musicians whom he patronised? Where, indeed, were d'Annunzio and France and Proust?

On the day after Montesquiou's death, the Duchesse de Gramont received this long letter* from Proust, charged with an ill-restrained melancholy:

* This letter was found among some kindling-paper at the house of the Duchesse de Gramont, on the same day that the author received the proofs of the French edition of this book.

19 December 1921 (date of postmark)

Madame la Duchesse,

I will not say to you, as Hugo said to Saint-Victor, 'One would write a book to have a page from you in return'; that would be flattery without basis, for you are almost unknown to me. But I will put it like this: if, in reply to your few lines, I let myself go to the infinity of my recollection and if illness did not prevent me, I would in fact write, in return for your page, volumes and volumes on M. de Montesquiou, so inexhaustible is the subject. I shall tell you one thing only, which will teach you nothing and which may seem not very nice on my part, though in fact it is infinitely the reverse. It is this: among all the people of whom he spoke to me, there was no one whose memory he took more delight in relying on than on yours, with a tenderness that I found natural and with an admiration that seemed to me biased, since I saw you so rarely that I could not well discern the reasons. This outburst of frankness must, nevertheless, not go so far as to make me lie in the opposite direction. Naturally I never expressed my slight surprise at this unique preference. I relished the sweetness with which he used to pronounce the name 'Elaine' and the tender smile with which his eyes would then express their wonderment. I thought that by saying this to you I would alleviate your grief more than if I were to speak to you of my own personal grief or tell you so many laudatory things about him. Without doubt you know many such things also; but since we were never together, they will be different. I got to know him at an age when I was still young enough for him always to remain for me what a 'great personage' is to a child. The miracle is that during a period of so many years in which I saw, one after another, so many 'stars of the social firmament' suddenly become 'old bores', viewing this transformation with the astonishment of someone who, not having been informed that summer-time started the day before, does not understand why his watch does not tally with others— the miracle is that, during all those years, there was never a cloud between us and that he would, with a smile, always allow me to reproach him with his conduct towards so many people. I say no clouds, or at least not ones that I noticed; but he was not a man to conceal them and his manner was more that of one who is about to hurl a thunderbolt. However, his memoirs will put me right about that. It is not, however, possible (and up to his last weeks, in spite of his assertions to the contrary) that he was not slightly angry about the disproportion, in effect radical, between the little success of my book and the frightful obscurity into which his own had fallen. It is one of the great injustices of our time, and from it he suffered terribly. He never knew all that I undertook to defeat a conspiracy of silence, for which in the beginning he had himself been perhaps in part responsible. But I nurse two hopes about him. The first: I do not believe, in the literal sense of the word (and in spite of all the telegrams that he sent me last year from a nursing-home) that he is dead. Was he even really ill? In any case, if he was indeed ill, that must have given him the idea of a sham death, at which he would be present like Charles V, to surprise us afterwards. He was a brilliant stage-manager. The departure for Menton is inexplicable if he was dying; and other things too.

If, alas, the death was not feigned but true (which is what I do not believe) he will come back all the same. Injustices have their day. And at least in spirit and in truth he will be reborn. It was to have some details about his illness and about his end, whether real or not, that I asked your husband to come and dine on Saturday last, the first day on which I had risen from my bed for seven months and on which the presence of Walter BERRY would have brought no hindrance to our conversation. Unfortunately when I telephoned the first time, he had gone hunting, and on the second had gone out to dinner in town (an 'in town' that was not at my house, to my sorrow, since you know how much I like your husband).

If you see Madame your Mother, the immortal Egeria of the vanished poet (who published about you poems that life did not continue) will you tell her with what respect and emotion I associate myself with her grief? I cannot write to her, for I am forbidden to write. I would have infringed the prohibition and drawn momentary strength from some injections, if I had thought that a letter from me would not have displeased her. But a consensus of evidence makes me believe the contrary— even if it does not take away my grateful devotion to her.

Be so kind, Madame, as to accept my very respectful compliments.

MARCEL PROUST.

The last part of *Cities of the Plain* (*Sodome et Gomorrhe*) appeared in the spring of 1922 and began with the party at the house of the Princesse de Guermantes. In the Princess there are certainly some of the characteristics of Mme Greffulhe: the Holy Roman Empire side, the elegance derived more from romance than from her dressmaker, the Wagnerism, the Dreyfusism. During the whole of this party, Charlus is an exact replica of the arbitrary Montesquiou, arrogant and already in decline: 'Monsieur de Charlus well knew that the thunderbolts which he hurled at those who did not comply with his orders or to whom he had taken a dislike, were beginning to be regarded by many people, however furiously he might brandish them, as mere pasteboard. . . .' He insulted Mme de Saint-Euverte, and the mistress of his brother, but deployed all his charms for the superb sons of the latter. Proust suppressed a long passage which would have put Charlus in an even more odious light than did his affair with Jupien. In this passage he is seen to prefer the company of a frightful bus-conductor to that of the Princesse de Guermantes, who adored him. One can believe that Proust suppressed this passage (restored only in the Appendix of the La Pléiade edition) to spare his old dying friend. In the chapters that follow, Charlus and Morel at Mme Verdurin's house were to recall, for the frequenters of the old *salons*, Montesquiou and Delafosse at Mme Ménard-Dorian's or at Mme Madeleine Lemaire's. Next we come to the fall of Charlus. The odious scene with Mme Verdurin, from which the Queen of Naples saves him, is the literary counterpart of the fiasco of the Verlaine party. But in the last volumes Charlus ceases to be Montesquiou—though the crapulous adventures and the dotage are artistically right for the literary caricature, Charlus's vice and his craving for abasement in one so proud conferring on him a dramatic relief which Montesquiou wholly lacked. Charlus had flesh that bled when blows were rained on it; Montesquiou had a starched shirt which protected his vanity. The anguish of being forgotten which haunted the poet's last years is that of a man who, instead of living, has given a good performance. This scandalous yet chaste man remains a two-dimensional figure, like the heroes of Mme de Ségur, whom he loved as a child.

Proust's sadism always impelled him to humble those whom he admired: the Duchesse de Guermantes ceased to be in touch; the Duc de Guermantes crawled at Odette's feet; the Prince de

Guermantes married Mme Verdurin; Berma's children rushed to Rachel's house; and the daughter of Vinteuil flouted her father. One can measure the admiration that Montesquiou inspired in him by the degree of horror to which he reduced poor Charlus.

Montesquiou, more faithful to things than to people, lived again in the memories awakened in his friends, when Pinard dispersed his collections. At Miss Natalie Barney's a Persian tapestry strewn with roses was always the background for aesthetically social gatherings. The copy of *Hortensias Bleus* decorated by Whistler reposed in the shop full of Art Nouveau objects kept by La Gandara's daughter. Boldini's portrait triumphed when it was exhibited at the Jacquemart-André Museum and the Troubetzkoy statue seemed to preside over the Salon des Antiquaires at the Grand Palais in 1964. The poet's goddaughter collected in a library all the things he had particularly liked: his portraits by Helleu, Laszlo and La Gandara; watercolours of Venice in the style of Whistler; and a photograph of Mme Greffulhe. There too are the albums in which Montesquiou assembled the hundred decorative ideas he offered to the world when arranging this or that house as an expression of his taste and elegance.

Several of these houses still stand: the mansion in the Rue de Varennes, where he was born, and that of the Quai d'Orsay, home of des Esseintes. The pavilion at Neuilly has been destroyed and the Château d'Artagnan burned down, but the house at Versailles and the Palais Rose remain, surrounded by flowers. After Montesquiou's death this latter house came into the possession of the Marchesa Casati, whose extravagances he had encouraged. She walked about there dressed as the Queen of Sheba or La Castiglione, until that summer in 1930 when a terrible storm dispersed her guests, who were covered in satanic baubles like figures from Beardsley.

Left alone, Pinard, the secretary, realised what remained of the fortune he had inherited—enough for him to live on simply, without any occupation other than the gathering together of the mass of papers left by his master. . . . More or less following chronological order, he cut out, classified and collated letters, photographs and documents. He recopied, in his modest clerk's hand, the most scabrous anecdotes and the most touching stories. Apophthegms and catalectics, press-cuttings and invitations, visiting cards from Heredia, Mallarmé or André Germain, postcards from Whistler or from Cappiello, the useless jumbled up with the exciting: all this was amassed in some 500 files, on the first page of which he never failed to write:

> Continuation of the collections of very numerous
>   documents, autographs and other matter
>   concerning
> his ancestors, his family, his childhood, his adolescence,
>   his beginnings in literature and poetry
>   his houses and his fashionable receptions
> his works published in manuscript and unpublished
> his library, his books, his correspondence
>   with friends and admirers
>   his death followed by his obituary.

A last act of malice, prepared many years before, came to light shortly after the death of the Count. Madame Arman de Caillavet's daughter-in-law, who imagined that she could tell the poet everything since she lived with the delusion that he was in love with her, had been in the habit of writing to him constantly. In his will, Montesquiou bequeathed to her a casket, which his solicitor announced that he would bring to her. The unfortunate woman summoned all her friends. 'You see, he loved me—I am the only person to whom he has left a souvenir.' The casket arrived in due course and with beating heart she opened it, a circle of friends round her. It contained all the letters she had ever written to him; and none of them had ever been opened.

Céleste, Proust's maid, was a person who had been delighted to hear of the Count's death. She had regarded him as a sorcerer and had been in the habit of hiding the little presents which, from time to time, he would send to Proust, as though they brought bad luck.

But Montesquiou survived intermittently in still another manner than through the memories of those who had loved or hated him or through Proust's portrayal. His spirit returned from time to time to talk with his friends' mediums. M. de Beyle, in a most serious article, reported a spirit-message from the poet: 'You must write what you know—my great faith.' There was also a poem which is not worse than the worst of those written when he was alive:

I have stripped off my body, frail pretence
Of garment for my soul in all its feebleness.

The inscription on his grave 'Non est mortale quod opto' confirms this faith.

Berenson's verdict is characteristically shrewd: 'Montesquiou's taste was a genuine gift; not the best perhaps in certain particulars, but it was his manner of "loving" certain materials, of touching objects, which was like real gold, while in d'Annunzio it became pinchbeck.'

The catalogue of Montesquiou's library, sold a year after his death, was a roll of all the oddities and all the sciences, of all the poetry and of all the farces which had diverted his always quivering taste for curiosities. This catalogue carried a Preface by Barrès, which constitutes the finest tribute that this so difficult man could have wished for:

Proud and noble spirit, who set an exceptional mark on Parisian life by passionately devoting himself to rare things and who, incomprehensibly, was neglected by fashion, of which he should have been a great favourite.

He was neglected and that is good; for that neglect gives to his destiny a certain bitterness, which makes him seem more human in recollection than his first reputation had made him. I love him better in his solitude than at his parties. And that kind of defeat in which his days ended has still more style, to my way of thinking, than his successes in the Pavilion of the Muses. Between his two haunts—the one so popular, of his youth, the other, a little forgotten, of his old age—the curve of his life is moving and true.

Some day it will be realised that this expert in precious things prepared in a manner both systematic and pedantic (in the best sense of that word) the most trustworthy catalogue of the objects which a man of consummate sensibility singles out and prefers; and from this point of view he will be studied as far as the Sorbonne.

Index

Montesquiou—*cont.*

Jardin d'Algabal, 135; *Mal Aimé,* 135; *Un Moment de Pleur Eternel,* 258; *Les Offrandes Blessées,* 257; *Les Paons,* 134, 182; *Le Parcours du Rêve au Souvenir,* 134; *Les Pas Effacés,* 238, 254, 267; *Pays des Aromates,* 205; *Les Perles Rouges,* 135, 136, 139, 146; *La Petite Mademoiselle,* 251; *Prières de Tous,* 133-4, 257; *Les Quarante Bergères,* 136, 232, 247, 253; *Les Roseaux Pensants,* 124, 159; *Sabliers et Lacrimatoires,* 258; *Servante-Maîtresse,* 139-40; *La Trépidation,* 251; poems quoted, 15, 24, 26, 36, 49, 56, 68, 69, 70, 73, 74, 75, 76, 77, 80, 86, 87, 90-1, 98, 101, 108, 116, 119, 127-35, 137, 144, 148, 149, 163, 176, 180, 182-3, 188, 190, 191, 202, 203, 206, 217, 225, 229, 232, 233, 242, 247, 251, 253, 256, 257, 258, 261

Montesquiou, Count Thierry de (father), 19-20, 26, 33, 34, 113

—, Count and Countess Wlodimir, 19, 33

Montluc, Blaise de, 17, 49
Moore, Mrs, 144
Morand, Paul, 9, 11
Moréas, Jean, 136
Moreau, Gustave, 12, 13, 37, 38, 51, 55-6, 58, 61, 68, 78, 81, 90, 98, 102, 103, 116-17, 123, 125, 143, 152, 176, 177, 183, 194, 222, 247, 264
Moreno, Marguerite, 123, 133, 142, 206
Morgan, Anne, 202
Morgan, William de, *see* De Morgan
Morris, William, 75, 84, 87, 97, 181
Moufflard, Lorrain's secretary, 102
Moyne, Lord, *see* Guinness
Mucha, Alphonse-Maria, 178, 181
Mugnier, Father Arthur, 210, 235, 255
Mulhfeld, Mme, 235
Murat, Princess Marie, née de Rohan-Chabot, 231

Nadar, photographer, 60
Napoleon I, 18
—, II, King of Rome, 18, 208
Natanson, Thadée, 235
Nerval, Gérard de, 32, 81
Neuilly, 188-94, 243, 247, 268, 275
New York, 203
New York Herald, 186
Nijinsky, Vaslav, 222

Nittis, Giuseppe de, 41, 99
Noailles, Countess Anna de, 131, 132, 194, 196, 198, 207-9, 210, 216, 217, 220, 235, 239, 243-4, 264
—, Duchesse de, 35
Noë, Count de, 34
Nolhac, Pierre de, 137, 139, 140

Ochse brothers, 205
Olivier, headwaiter, *see* Dabescat
Opera, The, 36, 78
Orléans, Princess of, 146
Orsay, Count Alfred d', 189
—, Comtesse d', 247
Otto, photographer, 42, 149
Oxford, 83

Padua, Duke of, 34
—, Elise, Duchess of, née Montesquiou, 23, 35
Pajou, Augustin, 188, 204
Paladino, Eusebia, 183
Palais d'Industrie, 74
Paléologue, Maurice, 234
Palmer, Mrs Potter, 203
Pange, Countess François de, 9
Parizot, Dr, 121
Parnasse Contemporain, 34
'Passiflora', *see* Montesquiou, Countess Pauline de
Pater, Walter, 85, 86, 114, 123
Pavlova, Anna, 245
Péladan, Joséphin, 11, 37, 101
Perronneau, Jean-Baptiste, 205
Petronius, 51
Peyrefitte, Roger, 245
Pfaffenhofen, S. G. J. Pfaff, Baron von, 188, 204
Picasso, Pablo, 231, 235
Pierrebourg, Baroness Marguerite de, 71
Piganiol de La Force, Jean-Aymar, 139
Pinard, Henri, 229, 240, 267, 270, 275-6
Pisannelle, La, 228
Plato, 142
Poe, Edgar Allan, 47
Poilly, Baronne de, 39, 41, 52, 62, 122
Poiret, Paul, 230, 249, 251
Polignac, Duchesse de, 35
—, Prince Edmond de, 44, 59, 65, 87, 88, 186
—, Princesse Winaretta de, née Singer, 121, 197, 225, 230-1, 236, 268
Pompadour, Mme de, 191

Index prepared by Oliver Stallybrass